THE GREAT PLAINS WRITERS GROUP

Echoes

from the

Prairie

A COLLECTION OF SHORT MEMOIRS

EDITED BY NICOLE MUCHMORE

Cover photo and design:

Sunset in Jefferson County, Kansas, by Nicole S. Muchmore

Interior photos courtesy of the authors

ISBN-13: 978-0615808116

ISBN-10: 0615808115

Library of Congress Control Number: 2013938767

ACKNOWLEDGMENT

Without the encouragement and support of our great friend and classmate, Nicole Muchmore, this book would never have come to fruition. We are all deeply indebted to her for her hours of work, great patience, and faithful vision as this project unfolded.

The Great Plains Writers Group

TABLE OF CONTENTS

TABLE OF CONTENTS

TABLE OF CONTENTS

PART V

EDITOR'S PREFACE

This collection "echoes" *Voices of the Great Plains*, published by the Great Plains Writing Group of Lawrence, Kansas, in the summer of 2011. Rather than alpha order by author, as its predecessor, the stories in this volume have been arranged in four sequential parts. Interestingly, many of these stories, collected from both within and outside of the writing group proper, echo each other in pairs or clusters, often by subject, but also more subtly in voice and construction. "Coincidences" and "Night Train" represent one sort of pairing; "Letting Go," "Natural Strangers," and "Aunt Stella" comprise another such relative set.

The first part is a series of three very different retrospective works that answer this question *"Why write memoir?"* from the perspective of each author. The second, third, and fourth parts are, at first glance and most obviously, separated according to the temporal phases of life: childhood, transition to adulthood, and adulthood.

The second part also illustrates the dynamic variety of voice and experience in childhoods revisited as well as similarities in what constituted memorable drama. "Rooster's Demise," "Miss Mabie's Babies," and "The Other Shoe," impart lasting impressions of childhood events, whereas "Imagination at Play" and "Sidearm" record more mundane but equally significant recollections. The long-lived marks left by early religious experiences are documented in "Mixed Blessings" and "Three Ages of the Soul."

In parallel, tales of adolescence and coming of age that make up the third part provide a delightful study in growing up, ripe with contrast among the authors. Mary McCoy's "The Tomcat and the Tomboy" and "The Red Velvet Fish" beautifully convey this difficult period of life, while "Tales from a Teacher's Daughter," "Chrome Dome," and

"It Was Early" highlight more humorous memories of high school.

The selections in Part IV pair the poetically mundane and the poignantly intense moments that epitomize adult life: "Heirlooms" and Treasures," "Imaging Yourself as a Mother" and "Star Wars," and others. Although each story is a gem in itself, the pairing in this section provides particularly powerful contrasts.

The final section is made up of a series of pieces that regard the passage of time, further highlighting the importance of writing memoir in the uniquely personal growth that fulfills and defines the latter period of life. The final selections, "Letting Go," "Natural Strangers," and "November," poignantly articulate the process of coming to terms with losing a parent.

Relationships among the stories in this volume are intended to emerge as they do among works of art placed beside each other on the walls of a museum gallery. The comparisons created by juxtaposition and clustering highlight the context and style of each author and the possibilities awaiting each of us as writers of our own stories. Some of these authors featured here have attended the Great Plains Writers Group over several years; this collection also represents the effect of the group setting on our writing. We are challenged and supported as writers by our mutual individuality, experience, and perspective as we workshop our pieces.

In addition, the respective comparisons with the earlier works of authors appearing in *Voices* are worthwhile. In this volume, authors such as KL. Barron and Sheryl Williams have offered much more heartrending and closely held memories. The present works of Sue Suhler, Mary McCoy, and Tony Pierce also illustrate the fruits of much effort and care. In all cases, the value of courageous perseverance in both unearthing memories and in artfully advancing our personal writing craft is evident. Enjoy!

Nicole Muchmore
July 11, 2013

INTRODUCTION

Anyone who writes a memoir is trying to stop time, to recover something that's been lost to the furious passing of years, to set down in words what once took place so that it can be given permanent form. It all comes down to the same thing: we write about the past to defy the passage of time. And through our writing we both discover and define who we are, hoping that others will acknowledge us in all our complexity and idiosyncrasies. If those others are our children and grandchildren, our narrative can serve as a starting-point for the story that they might like to tell someday. Just as we shape an identity partly by combing through the past, they will see a part of themselves emerging out of the written record that we leave behind.

But the past as a recoverable object, a stable series of things and events that merely need to be discovered and described, does not exist. In the first place, the past that we think we know exists only in our minds as electro-chemical events, if we are to believe contemporary neuroscience. (The term "memory" is more congenial to us than the scientific description, but we all know that memories reside in the brain; they have no external dimensions.) Second, the past that memoirists scribble down in books is an assemblage, a reconstruction: it's not direct experience but recovered experience, filtered through the individual sensibility of each writer, sharpened (or distorted) by feeling, and shaped finally by the narrative devices of point of view, selection of telling details, and order of presentation. In other words, memoir is as much invention as fact, just as history is a narrative based on what we hope is reliable information that is given form by the historian. I'm not claiming that history is merely something "made up"—only that it doesn't stand still and await discovery, like eggs in a basket. An infinite amount of factual data can be found in libraries, court records, national archives, family documents, personal accounts, and the like. But this material has to be sifted and weighed, trimmed and tailored, formed to fit a narrative arc. It shifts with the passing of time, the circumstances of its chroniclers, their political leanings, the general increase of the world's store of knowledge, and the historians' ability to master the mountains of data at their disposal.

Similarly, the grasp of our own past changes as we assign greater or lesser importance to individual events, as we age and memory deteriorates, and as our reasons for writing about the past change. The memoir about childhood (for instance) that we write this year isn't going to be the memoir we would have written about the same subject ten years ago, let alone the memoir we might have written when we got married and started a family. All the intervening years have placed their burden on the emerging story of our lives. Or, to use a different metaphor, the intervening years have enlarged our perspective, forced new priorities on us, and enriched our understanding of our story. After a certain point—middle age, I suspect—we realize that any single thing we write about ourselves is connected to everything else we have ever known or felt. It is all so complicated that we have no choice but to simplify the narrative if we want to write about it: certain things must be omitted, others guessed at; events have to be shaped to make sense, like chairs in a living room that's being made ready for guests. Plausible scenes and dialogue must now be imagined. An audience also has to be imagined. We must decide what's important to include in our narrative and what has to be avoided when the feelings or fates of others could be involved. An inescapable conclusion presents itself: it's harder to write about ourselves than it is to write about things and people at a distance from our experience. The "I" that we use is in our memoirs is a handy fiction for kaleidoscopic consciousness itself, the flow and welter of awareness.

As memoirists, we have an implicit pact with our reader not to write about people and events that have never existed. But we must use our imagination to arrange the shards of memory into some sort of recognizable pattern. Pattern-making is the key. Once we recognize that the story we intend to tell has to be *made*, has to be *given imaginative form*, has to be *confected* like a cookie from the inert ingredients in our cupboard, then we have taken the first step toward being effective writers. In other words, we have to construct the truth from the raw materials of experience. We introduce necessary distortions and simplifications in the larger interest of telling the truth about ourselves, our families and friends, and the events that have greatest importance for us.

Memoirists work hard to capture the real thing, life in its mysterious and concrete specificity. In some cases, memoirists have such powerful recall that they seem to be transcribing—*filming* might be a better word—the past literally. They offer their experience to us in such a lifelike, convincing manner that we have no trouble accepting it as true. We accept their account as hard currency. But even in these instances it is the *art* of memoir writing that gives their narrative its validity and believability. The sequence of events, the narrator's tone of voice, the point of view from which the action is seen: these and other tricks of the writer's trade infuse a story with lifelikeness and durability. "Lifelikeness," not life itself: art lasts longer than life.

Memoirs—no matter how exalted or shocking or quirky— invite us into the lives of their writers and show us how those lives resemble our own. They reveal the universals of the human condition in the careful attention given to individual lives. In this excellent collection of brief personal narratives we find that practically the entire range of human experience has been represented. The authors give us stories of birth and death; accounts of parents, grandparents, aunts, uncles, and siblings; tales recalling the emotion-filled relationships between children and their parents; narratives dealing with interactions between the writer and the natural world; and, of course, memoirs of childhood—a great many of these, in fact. Childhood and growing up are, as we all know, staples of memoir writing. We all look back to our formative years, which seem to linger even when more recent times fade from our thoughts. We examine the days of our youth in the hope of discovering how the children we were became the people we are now. Memoirists mine these years like Forty-Niners digging for gold. When we read these vivid stories, we're all swept back into our own childhood. We identify with those youthful figures—boys or girls—as they struggle to understand the adult world because we too once made the same journey and faced many of the same dilemmas.

Some of the writers here revisit troubling or tragic events that altered the course of their lives. A great many of them, however, recover moments of unremarkable living, seemingly unimportant moments in themselves, that nevertheless proclaim the miracle of the everyday. Every piece of writing here enlarges our sympathies by offering a fresh interpretation of or a unique voice to report on the human dilemma. All of the stories in this impressive book—whether happy or sad—will impress the reader with their honesty, their passion, and their courage to reach back in time and rescue from its irresistible, withering force possessions of inestimable value.

Jerry Masinton
April 25, 2013

PART I

Tuning My Piano

When my daughters, Ann and Rebecca, were 8 and 4, and we were visiting the ruins at Machu Picchu, Peru, they heard us talk about the ancestors of the present-day Incas whom they had seen on the streets of Cusco and elsewhere. Of course, they wanted to see some people who fitted that large and portentous word, "ancestors," and they were disappointed when that proved to be impossible.

Well, now here am I with four grandchildren, already an ancestor, and getting ready to speak of his ancestors and himself. To some readers of the life account, story, autobiography to follow, this may seem quixotic. After all, neither I nor any of my ancestors has done anything particularly noteworthy. Our family life as a whole has been invisibly ordinary, like the lives of most other families. Yet people such as I write accounts such as this—and have done so for centuries though this autobiographical writing may seem hardly more than egotistical.

Who could blame anyone for thinking that? Not I; I can only hope that careful tuning will help me play a more acceptable song. Remaining silent might deprive me of an opportunity to make sense of things, and the result would only be ignorance down the line, wouldn't it? Some of my descendants might find their grandpa's or great-grandpa's account worth something to them personally, as I'm discovering by learning what my sister and I are finding as we investigate our own family history. Perhaps, like Mimi and me, they'll have questions about ancestry and identity. Besides, I've made a choice not to be blotted out.

My Grandma Lena, referring to some helpful action of hers, used to say to my Mom something like, "So you shouldn't forget you had a mother." It was a half-joke: you can see in her words no less than in

1

mine an attempt to leave a trace behind, a desire not to disappear into the nothing. Yet that hope to be remembered—how futile it is! Yes, children and even grandchildren will remember parts of you, parts that will grow dimmer and less real with time; but beyond a couple of generations you'll be gone. And why shouldn't you be? That's the "way of all flesh." I can't answer the "why" question, but complete erasure feels painful; most of us would like to leave at least a trace. This may be my main trace.

That reminds me, prof. that I am, that "trace" is a pun and a good metaphor for life. A trace is also a road, and traces—to put one more twist on them—are a harness. We follow a trace in our traces. And we leave some sort of trace, however dim. Or some of us, with startling life choices, break our traces. Well, I don't think I ever broke my traces and ran wild across the landscape, though I loosened them a few times and didn't always stay in my lane. I've asked myself whether that conformity during most of my time has been a good thing, or not. Narratively speaking, my story makes for less interesting reading than those told by Augustin Burroughs, David Sedaris, Keith Richards, Shirley MacLaine, or even Katie Couric, sorry to say. Here are some facts: Grandpa Haskell wasn't ever in jail; he wasn't an undercover agent; he wasn't famous; he didn't have another family in another town; he never made lots of money; he didn't steal or cheat; he didn't abuse his children, his students (or anyone else). So what of interest could be left to tell? That depends on who you are. You'll have to read on to see.

More tuning: mundane story or not, now is the time for me, the writer, to make some decisions; they're difficult ones: to write a chronological history of my life and what I know of my ancestors?— that's one way to go. To write a series of narratives and reflections about that life is another. Combining the two seems comfortable to me. In either case, I'll be limited by my faulty memory and by the first-person perspective that inescapably skews an account. From one point of view (with which I agree), all writing is first-person, presented in a variety of forms. In a legal document the first person is deeply buried;

in an academic article less so; in a novel it's still closer to the surface; and in an editorial, a letter, a memoir, it gets progressively closer to being manifest and literal.

Though I might, in some idealized universe, say everything, obviously I can't without spending the rest of my life at this keyboard, following a will-o-the-wisp, the ungraspable phantom of life. Then too, how should I identify significant matters over time: What should I focus on?—Accomplishments or feelings? Words or actions? The psychological, the economic, the intellectual, the sexual, the philosophical, the political, the religious? Love of wife, of children, of literature, of dogs, of nature? The history of my times? Being sort of Jewish? Answer: Yes. I anticipate at least a bit of everything and I wonder what my own life will look like once I put it into my own words?

Actually I might ask, "How would I like it to look to my audience?" That is, I can't ever forget my readers, who are most likely to be family. It's obvious, isn't it, that writing about family (if the writer cares what family thinks and feels) is always full of pitfalls. Many of those holes probably can't be avoided; but "beware," I tell myself: it's all too easy to create hurt feelings; it's virtually inevitable that actions and events will be remembered differently by different family members, who are likely to be strongly invested in their own versions of the past. And before long, I'm sure, I'll come up against the internal contradiction of the honest urge to reveal versus the conservative desire to conceal.

Today, it seems, nothing is omitted from personal narratives for the sake of privacy, or at least the narratives make it seem that way. (McKenzie Phillips is a prime example, with her account of incest.) Though shock value seems somewhat diminished these days, it still sells; prurient curiosity is all around us. These aren't the days of Frank Harris, Anaïs Nin, Henry Miller, or Colette, but today we're more than ever fascinated by sex. It was always a fascinating subject, of course, even in prehistory; the worldwide evidence is abounding. But in the late 20th century we made sex part of the public discourse, and commoditized it on a huge scale. No citations needed to support this obvious point.

So is it important to write, among other things, about sex—personal or familial? Well, that depends. It may be pertinent if others are to understand ancestors' lives. Let me tune this key and then play a chord:

My mother understood the importance of sexual happiness. When she was 80 years old and about to meet the woman who became my wife a year later, she asked me two questions as we were driving into Lawrence. The second was, "Do you have a good physical relationship?" When she heard my surprised but smiling affirmative she was happy. Wise woman, my mother!

That one was easy, but my chord is a complicated ancestral example. My paternal grandmother, taking her four small children, returned to her home town in Europe after six years in New York—according to my Dad's interpretation—to avoid becoming pregnant again. Extremely poor as they were, presumably ignorant and with no money for doctors, she had already lost four small children in New York, probably to dysentery. (My grandparents probably did not have legal access to contraception in the State of New York, even if they knew about it and how to use it.) So there was a hiatus of one and a half years in family life because of sexual fear. How did this break with their father affect his two young sons, one of them my father? What was the impact on his father, that lonely, sex- and love-starved young man pressing pants in Brooklyn?

When they returned, were the children able to resume their previous relationship with their father, whatever it had been? If not, how might that have affected my Dad in his fathering? Were both husband and wife happy to be together again when she returned, or was she also still fearful? What might her state of mind have done to their intimate life and to family life? In any case they had no more children. All this arises from my Dad's interpretation of that return to Europe. But he may, after all, have been wrong about the reason.

Nevertheless, I see his difficulty in creating closeness with me, and mine with him, ditto, as stemming from that history. Psychiatrists who use family systems analysis would no doubt agree. He was taken from his grandfather and other relatives when he came to this country as a small boy and had to learn new ways and a new language. Then, having returned to Europe from the United States after being in the States for a few years, and having re-started the old life in the old language, he re-immigrated to the U.S. at the age of 10. I think of his losses as accounting for much of his adult self-control and his emotional distance; and I think my own earlier problems with emotional distance stemmed from him.

As a younger man I did have such problems, and even more to the point, sex did have a huge and surprising impact on the middle of my adult life and on the young lives of my daughters. So, is there good reason to write about such intimate stuff in my life? Yes. Will I? I don't know.

And now, tuning my last strings, I want to say a few things about truth and memory. Supposedly, to tell everything is to tell the truth. But what is that? In courtroom testimony, "the truth, the whole truth, and nothing but the truth" is promised by witnesses. But truth is a convenient fiction: no matter how truthful the witness intends to be, there's no such thing in human experience as the whole truth and nothing but the truth in the courtroom or out.

Compounding the problem of ungraspable truth, memory is slippery. In fact, memory has such creative qualities that it is sometimes pure invention, though each of us might deny its pertaining to ourselves. In looking back at my memories I can see first of all great gaps. Where I don't see black holes, I know that I may have inadvertently filled in spaces with wish fulfillment, the words of others, and even realistic dreams. Certain gross things are so, we know. A child was born on a certain date; a house had a mortgage of a certain amount; a divorce occurred. But the context—the wide, deep, complicated context—probably has little in it that we can with certainty call truth.

Our brains have seized, believed, shaped, wiped out, and filled in what may or may not have been.

The more I have read about memory and the more I've thought about it and exercised it, the more I realize how untrustworthy it is. And yet we believe that despite our lapses, what we do remember is retained quite accurately. We know we have lost a great deal, but we usually consider the remainder to be true. As for me, I don't any longer consider my memories to be true: Despite my best efforts to remember and report truly, any account I write will be questionable, and even in part unintentionally fallacious. This is a tough principle to accept, but it's in the back of my mind as I write, and should be in the back of yours, my descendants, as you read.

And so to begin.

The Second Law

A t roughly the same time, quite independently from each other, Richard Feynman and I began to think about the Second Law of Thermodynamics. Feynman, at the time, was a physicist of world renown, and a recipient of the Nobel Prize. I was five years old and had not yet learned to count past ten.

Feynman and his contemporaries, like other great minds before them, framed the Second Law in terms of mathematics; I, on the other hand, only noticed that everything falls apart. Physicists have a word to describe the enigmatic property at the heart of the Second Law, the property that measures the extent to which a system is disordered: they call this entropy. I didn't know this word, but I noticed that paint peels, sidewalks crack, iron rusts, wood rots. I knew early on that every living thing dies: trees, grass, flowers, animals, my grandparents, my parents, my brothers—and even I—would die.

It would be nearly twenty years before I would hear about Richard Feynman and know the word entropy and learn that it applies not only to me and the part of the world I know, but to everything in a universe thought to be 100-billion light-years across. I would learn that entropy is irreversible, immutable, ineluctable. Everything, following as it does this irrefutable law of nature, is slowly and by degrees falling apart. Our sun will someday cease to shine. This word I didn't know bothered me during my young life—not all the time, and not every day. But sometimes.

And why was this? I am still not certain. Perhaps it was because I wanted to believe in the chance of a perfect, everlasting world. Decay made me anxious, and still does. It reinforces the understanding, which we so often ignore, that our lives are balanced precariously at the edge of disorder and chaos. Entropy is ever increasing, beyond our ability to control. Even our memories are not safe forever, and so we must try to preserve them as best we can.

On a trip back home, I decide to drive the forty miles from my mother's house to the small town where I spent my childhood years, where one of my brothers still lives. I want to show my friend the house I grew up in; the schools where I learned and played and made friends, some of them for life; the streets down which I rode my bicycle and on which I learned to drive a car. I want her to see the place that did more than anything else to make me who I am, the place that forms the backdrop for so many of my memories, good and bad.

We drive along a two-lane country blacktop that runs straight for many miles toward town, through broad fields with curving rows of maturing cotton. In the distance, the white towers of a grain elevator and the silver tank of a water tower stand like sentries above the plain, reflecting the morning sunlight. We drive a few miles farther along the highway, and the low profile of the town itself comes into view, at this distance appearing as an aggregation of trees and rooftops, still far enough away to seem ordered and tidy. I think of how many hundreds of times I have seen this view, from this exact place.

We slow for the curve at the edge of town, where a hospital seems incongruously out of place at the edge of a wheat field, like a ship in a desert. We drive past the hospital, a clinic, a dental office. Now the road straightens again and we drive on into the town, passing small houses, a retirement facility, a funeral home.

Impulsively, I turn off the main road onto a brick street that will take us past my high school. We drive along over the rough bricks. My eyes scan left and right. I see homes along the street that I remember from my childhood. Something is different, though, and for a few minutes I am unable to find an explanation. There is something about the light, I think. There is more light? That doesn't make sense... then suddenly I realize what it is: many of the trees are gone. The tree lined sidewalks and shaded rooftops, the dim recesses of front porches, so clear in my memories of this place, are gone. The light now casts everything in bolder relief, sharpening the images and adding a brittle quality that clashes with my remembrances of softer scenes.

It has been as many as forty years since these memories were formed, and I am reminded here in a poignant and personal way, that trees, like people, have only so much time. The trees I remember from my long-ago childhood were already mature, and now they are gone. It looks now as if they were never here at all. I feel a sadness rising from somewhere, threatening to envelop my mood. Up until now, I was soaring, ebullient with expectations of seeing again the parts of my past, and revealing their many wonders to my friend, who I notice has donned her "Jackie O" sunglasses against the too-much light.

"There were trees here, along this street," I try explaining to her, pointing a finger to the left and right of our car. "It wasn't so... empty-seeming." I begin to realize how badly I wanted her to see what I had seen, to feel what I had felt so many years ago; how I wanted for her to see for herself and feel for herself some important part of what it was like to be a growing-up me.

We drive slowly past the middle school and then the high school, where a new building has replaced the ancient one of my school days. I say, rather inadequately, "Well, that's where I went to high school." I tell her about the old building, its high ceilings and creaking floors; about my memories of hallways filled with echoes of youthful voices. But I am disappointed that I can't point to a third-story window and tell her that it was behind that very glass where I first heard about, but was not allowed to read, The Catcher in the Rye.

We turn right and drive some blocks to my old neighborhood. Here, too, there is the absence of the splendid old trees of my memory. Where I remember there were once houses, there are in some places only littered weedy lots, some of them showing the black and gray of old soot. We turn a corner and drive slowly along the dirt street at the side of our old house. The garage that had been next to the road is gone. A tree my parents planted in my pre-school years towers next to the house, but other trees are gone. I once knocked a sparrow off a branch of this tree from more than twenty yards away, with a rock fired from my slingshot, the greatest feat of my childhood, if not of my entire life. I remember it now, as we drive past the house: how I rose slowly and stealthily from behind the freshly painted fence, aimed, and fired; how I watched the rock all the way.

The fences my brothers and I helped my father build, and which we painted white over the course of a long hot summer, are gone. As if in a dream, I remember wearing my baseball mitt and bouncing a rubber ball against a section of fence for hours. I replayed, over and over again, the games of the 1967 World Series, in which my heroes, Carl Yastrzemski and Rico Petrocelli of the Boston Red Sox, lost to the St. Louis Cardinals in seven games. The sidewalk at the front of the house, where I once set a family record by bouncing on a pogo stick for an hour without stopping or falling, is cracked and broken.

Overall, and in every respect, our old place is a relic of what it once was. Someday I will come back and it will be gone, like so much else. My friend peers over her sunglasses to survey the sagging roof of the little house. She narrows her Irish eyes against the brightness. I wonder what comparisons she is making, if any, to her own upbringing in the affluent suburbs of a northern city far from here.

I want to explain that the problem is the Second Law, that what is here now is not part of me or of my memories. I want her to see something, just any little something, that might help her to understand how I love what this place once was for me.

"Well, this is so different from what I remember," I finally say. I am thinking again of irreversible, immutable, ineluctable laws.

She turns the Irish eyes on me, and I see that she senses my disappointment. "Then show me your memories," she says.

Bones

R othwell, or "Rowell" as the locals pronounce it, is a small town in Northamptonshire, a county about seventy miles north of London. Mostly rural, famous for its shoe industry (now mostly outsourced to other countries), it's called the county of "spires and squires" because it had, and still has, both in abundance. Trinity Church in Rowell lost its spire in an earthquake in the eighteenth century but still manages an imposing presence on account of its size and beauty. Built in alternating layers of ironstone—one a warm bronze, the next a liquid honey—it stands squarely at the top of a small rise, the Manor park on one side, the Rectory and Manor house on the other. The approach divides at the church door then runs on either side, hugging that warm stone and fencing off the graveyard to the north and south. These paths, like little tributaries, run into the Market Square behind the church, revealing other lovely old ironstone buildings like Jesus Hospital and the Market House, both built in the sixteenth century, as well as shops and pubs and other essential services of a small town. It's the inhabitants in the churchyard on the south side, though, who caught my attention decades ago and who continue to absorb me now.

We moved to Rothwell in 1972 just three weeks before my youngest child, Peter, was born. It was a necessary move—we needed the extra space to accommodate a growing family—but I loved the town we had lived in before, my first experience of small town life. We had made many friends there and were part of a warm, lively church community. Rothwell church seemed very different. We sat in the fifth pew to the right of the main aisle as we had done in our previous church, but this was a very different Sunday experience. This was "low"

11

church for one thing—no incense, no bells at the consecration, no singing of the Mass. The people were friendly, but more reserved, initially at least. The interior of the church, though, showed off the magnificent skills of the twelfth-century craftsmen who built it and those who, coming after in the fifteenth century, added beautifully carved misericords, those masterfully constructed hinged choir seats that allowed monks to half-perch when the seat was in an upright position. Just to the right of our pew was a pillar decorated, like all the others, with small sculptures—faces carved by the masons all those centuries ago, perhaps using each other or themselves as models. Some of these little characters were melancholic, some rather scary. Ours, though, had a very friendly face; he smiled almost as if he were winking. His hair, long, wavy, and in what had no doubt been a fetching twelfth-century style, was kept in check by a horizontal band much favored by hippies. I thought how modern he looked—like my dad who in the fashion of the 70s was wearing his hair longer, or one of the protesters of the 60s involved in love-ins.

Whenever I walked the pathway back to the Market Square I noticed a row of gravestones, some small, some large and imposing, belonging to a family called "Burdett." I marked this particularly because it was my grandfather's Christian name. I had no idea it could be a surname as well. When I told my grandmother about the gravestones, she said "that's because your grandfather's family come from there for generations back." I was amazed. Even living in Northamptonshire came about by accident because a job became available, but to find myself in a place to which I had family connections was amazing. I grew up in Birmingham, the second largest city in Britain, where no one apart from the Welsh and the Irish who proclaimed themselves by their accents, came from anywhere. We kids seemed to think, if we thought at all, that we just sprouted in the city, Brummies by birth and ancestry, and we had no idea of a family history beyond its boundaries. If our parents knew such a history, they were either too tired or too incurious to relate it. Unlike most of my friends, though, I never felt quite at home in the city. It was too grey, had too many pavements, too few trees, and not enough history.

Using the dates on the gravestones, I traced the Burdetts in the parish registers and fleshed out the bare facts later in the County Record Office. This was, indeed, my grandfather's family, an amazing fact in itself considering that all the Burdetts ever born seemed to have lived in that town. The earliest gravestone, of Joseph Burdett, showed that he was born in 1699. A will revealed that he was a maltster, as, I found out later, were generations of his descendants. A maltster! The man who made the malt, that essential ingredient in beer and whisky. So that's why generations of my family have been, shall we say, connoisseurs of good ale and its stronger cousins!

The inscription on Joseph's gravestone reads:

A loving husband and father kind
In his business bore a faithful mind

A simple sentiment and a laudable one, but I've since pondered that line about his business. I knew that maltsters were often in trouble for "engrossing," that is, holding back grain in times of poor harvests, disobeying laws that mandated that the making of malt be suspended until barley became more affordable for the poor. Many maltsters bought grain by the field and long before it was ripe; this was a benefit to the farmer who had a buyer in hand but disastrous for the poor if the harvest then failed. There was even a riot earlier in the seventeenth century in Northamptonshire, in part prompted by the activities of some maltsters buying up and hoarding grain, although they were doing nothing more than futures traders do today with impunity. Good for Joseph, I thought. Fight back—in stone!

Wills of other family members gave vivid details of their lives, their possessions, and their relationships to other family members. One will, of a great-great aunt, Catherine Ann Burdett, who died in 1844, showed that she left "an oak bureau" to her nephew Thomas Austin.

One of the Churchwardens holding office in the 1970s was Harold Austin, a bit of a curmudgeon and an expert on when to sow peas in the spring (as well as many other matters). He was also someone of whom I became very fond. I told Harold about the will. He said, "We've still got that bureau—or at least our Brian has." Sure enough "our Brian" and his wife did indeed have that bureau, and I was duly taken round to see it, marveling at such a survival.

This same will posed many more questions than it answered. Why, for instance, did Catherine appoint as executor a "Mr. Carpenter, Surgeon," leaving him "all [her] Household Furniture, Goods, Chattels, China, Glass, Plate, Linen and other effects, and all other [of her] Personal estate whatsoever absolutely and for Ever"? It seems unlikely that this was payment for medical services, as she obviously had some modest financial resources, as well as surviving parents and siblings. Were she and Mr. Carpenter friends? Was this bequest to help him weather the storm of his impending bankruptcy, which occurred in the same year that she died? Unlikely but possible, I thought. Sadly, in the year following Catherine's death a notice appears in the newspaper:

CARPENTER, MARY, ROTHWELL
DIED ON THE 3D INST., AT ROTHWELL, MARY, THE BELOVED WIFE OF MR. CARPENTER, SURGEON, IN HER 47TH YEAR, LEAVING A NUMEROUS FAMILY TO LAMENT HER LOSS

So my initial thought that perhaps they were, but for my aunt's untimely death at the age of 34, an "item" was wrong. He was probably much older than she and obviously had an extensive family as well. So perhaps it was simply that she was grateful for his care in her last illness, or a blend of many of these reasons.

Mr. Carpenter's woes only worsened after his bankruptcy and his wife's death. Four years later, in 1848, he is accused of malpractice in treating one Robert Shortland, a patient "on the sick list" (the "sick list": charity cases paid for by the parish). A battered contemporary pamphlet, one page missing, recounts the charges and counter-charges in a case that would have roiled this small town to its core. Another doctor in town, one Dr. Brighton, called in by the Vicar, had found the patient suffering from "inflammation of the liver" and in a "very debilitated and dangerous state . . . . [and] had not been bled either by the lancet, cupping or leeches, neither had any blister been applied." Mr. Carpenter, obviously outraged to have his medical decisions questioned and his patient now treated by his rival, responded, according to the Vicar, by threatening to stop Robert Shortland's parish dole. Mr. Macpherson, the Vicar, reports:

> *I met Mr. Carpenter and his assistant on the street; the former accused me of unhandsome conduct in interfering with his practice, to which I replied, I had no wish to interfere, if he would attend to it as he ought to do, and I walked on.*

In an exchange of letters, Mr. Carpenter questions Dr. Brighton's medical qualifications, to which Dr. Brighton responds by enclosing notice of his degrees and threatening to sue. Poor Robert Shortland, caught in the crossfire, has already died, no doubt leaving behind a family bereft of support. What would Catherine have thought of all this? She must have known the actors in this drama and heard the story from all sides: Her family was, as they say in Northamptonshire, "big Church people" so she might have sided with the Vicar and Dr. Brighton. On the other hand, she was obviously close to Mr. Carpenter.

And another puzzle: How did Catherine have the financial wherewithal to leave Mr. Carpenter anything? Where did the "Furniture, Goods, Chattels, China, Glass, Plate, Linen" come from? She was unmarried and her parents not obviously wealthy. Her sister Ann's will provides the answer. Ann also died young and single—in 1838 at the age of 42. Her will shows that she was relatively affluent, leaving parcels of land to be sold to provide annuities to her parents and siblings. A little digging revealed that she, Ann Burdett, had been housekeeper for a wealthy wheelwright in town, a Thomas Butcher; her sister Catherine had also been a servant in the house. When Mr. Butcher died, he left almost everything to Ann, including land and household appurtenances as well as small gifts of money to her sister, her siblings, and parents. Like many wills, Mr. Butcher's offers a glimpse of his household. He leaves her his "Furniture, plate, Linen, China, Brewing Utensils, Wines, Liquors and Coals and half the beer that may be in or about [his] premises." (No mention of where the other half was to go!) He also leaves her all his books except his business ledgers and his copy of "Brown's Bible." This latter work goes, together with fifty pounds, to his business partner's son. His reference to Brown's Bible suggests that Mr. Butcher was a nonconformist, probably attending the Independent Chapel in Rothwell. This is probably why in her will Ann makes a small bequest to their Sunday school fund while reserving her place in the Church of England graveyard with the rest of her family! This story branches out into others in the same way that Catherine's story involves the town doctor and the vicar. That's one delightful and surprising aspect of getting to know one's ancestors; their lives open out into those of others—and those lives and their contexts illuminate the whole.

I've always loved history, taking bare facts and making them into stories and following up the questions that inevitably emerge. As a child I imagined the people who built the Elizabethan manor house that I passed on the way to school (and even got invited in once to see the size of the fireplace that was big enough to roast an ox). Now, though, in Rothwell, as a result of sheer serendipity, was a history that was mine, and it was real. I liked being descended from these people. They had lives and jobs that I could understand, and I saw occupations and traits traceable to my own generation. It was like finding a treasure chest that had infinite and interlinking compartments.

In the early eighteenth century, workmen digging in the graveyard on the south side of the church literally fell into a crypt that had been boarded up and long forgotten about. It held the partial remains of about fifteen hundred people—the skulls and crossbones considered in past centuries as essential for salvation. Some thought that these were the relics of people who died in the great plague of the 1340s, others that they were from the Civil War in the seventeenth century. Expert opinion, though, says that they were the remains of people whose graves had been disturbed when the church had been extended at various times over the centuries. These days the "bone crypt" as it's called, is open to the public on Sunday afternoons. Church members volunteer to act as guide and guardian. (A "guardian" is considered necessary since someone once tried to make off with a skull, making the excuse that he was in a production of *Hamlet*!) I often took my turn, watching people from neighboring parishes and beyond pick their way cautiously down the steps into the dim light, some putting handkerchiefs to their noses, afraid of the moist, musty, organic smell. One woman looked horrified, said, "Oh, no!" and scrambled back up the stairs. Children were fascinated. Scientists asked scientific questions. Sometimes no one came, so I was down there by myself with the bones. Knowing that my family had been inhabitants of the town for centuries, I looked at the rows and rows of neatly stacked skulls and imagined which ones they might be. Some skulls, small and narrow in form, looked as if they'd been varnished, the effect of tannins in oak coffins leaching into the bone. The other discernible group was white and larger in size. The Burdetts were much more likely to be among the white bones, I thought. My father and grandfather and his siblings had broad faces and high foreheads, reminiscent, come to think of it, of that cheery twelfth-century character on the pillar in church, fifth row from the front on the right.

We lived in Rothwell for eleven years, long enough to put down roots and enjoy the benefits of living in a small town, especially the kindness and warmth of its inhabitants. We were thoroughly involved in local happenings, as absorbed in the minor turbulences and pleasures of parish life as Great Aunt Catherine and Mr. Carpenter the Surgeon must have been. As I searched the records of previous centuries, looking for more interesting stories about my Burdett ancestors, I noted the same names cropping up over and over—the Cheneys, the Shortlands, the Austins, for example—names of people who now own shops or teach in the schools or run the daycare, people whose families, unlike mine, had not left to find work in large cities. When I was tempted to feel envious of their long association, I reminded myself that though their families had fleshed out the generations, I came from the bones: There was something satisfying and steadying in knowing that.

PART II

Miss Mabie's Babies

My third grade at Hubbell Elementary School in Des Moines in Miss Thelma Mabie's class was special. Her big, smiling face was rimmed with short, curly gray hair, and she reminded me of my Grandma Holmberg, with her abundant stature and her warm expression of love for me and other people, too. I loved to watch Miss Mabie write on the blackboard at the head of our classroom. Her handwriting, with the white chalk, matches the Spencerian Script on the long black cards she pinned, A through Z, along the top of the blackboard in our classroom.

The highlight of third grade was when Miss Mabie took our class on a field trip to her house to eat our bag lunches and look for her baby robins. We took turns looking through the window of her tiny, sunny yellow breakfast room with the starched, white frilly curtains that we were allowed to pull back for our search. Outdoors, the robin's nest seemed dangerously close to the house, but we were lucky that day. When my turn came, I slipped into one of the two wooden chairs at opposite sides of the tiny breakfast table, and I saw a mother robin delivering bits of bug to the loud cluster of wide-open yellow beaks that filled her nest.

We were all like those fledglings, circled around this kind woman, finding our places in her nest. Miss Mabie lavished her love on everyone she taught.

But to me, her kind knowing was distinct and dramatic, if subtle. One day, when our Civil Defense movie directed us to "Duck and Cover" under our desks, I headed for my spot under the low blue table in the back of the room, and Mikey K. came to sit beside me. He hesitantly pressed his silver Cub Scout ring into my palm, well within

21

Miss Mabie's view. When Miss Mabie invited the class to emerge from under our desks, I expected ridicule and punishment from her.

But Miss Mabie overlooked our secret as she announced to the class, "Now, each of you, please take out your own library book for free reading." She let pass her opportunity to embarrass me more than I already was, and I never forgot her for it.

But in 1951, I have risen to fifth grade, and Miss Mabie has reason to retract her sympathetic affection for me. This morning, like any other, my homeroom class meets with Miss Divine, the Physical Education teacher. She's in her clean white Keds sneakers, gray pleated skirt, and soft, white sweater, a long-sleeved one today for spring. How does she fix her pretty, brown hair, making it lie smooth, under control? Miss Divine's hair is just the opposite of my stringy blonde hair that Mom keeps torturing with the newest Toni Home Permanent with the probably poisonous ammonia smell.

Our classroom is located in the balcony overlooking the floor of the big kids' gym. I plop down into my auditorium seat that has a small, lift-up desk arm. We all sit down, and each of us overzealously slams our books on our tiny desks. Directly below our class space is a miniature kitchen, where parents and teachers are making green ice rings for the lime-sherbet punch for today's Parent-Teacher meetings. This particular morning I am curious about the excitement down in that tiny kitchen, and I crane my neck out over the rail, fidgeting. We kids watch party preparations for today's gathering. Adults carry platters of food from the little kitchen below, out past the walls of monkey bars and onto white bed sheets stretched as tablecloths over the long tables arranged across the gym floor. Back and forth they walk, into the kitchen, out to the gym, like ants to a picnic. Wonderful aromas waft upward to our lookout—ummmm—tiny wienies swimming in ketchup and butter on their tray that's heated underneath with the little Sterno can.

My classmates trickle in for our homeroom period. Kenny B. is too tall to fit into his assigned chair in the back row, so he sits at the end of his row where he can stick his long legs and blue jeans into the aisle. I notice his black, high-top Converse All-Star sneakers. And here comes Kenny J.—last week he sailed his black-and-white high-tops over the basketball backboard and had to go to the principal's office. Principal Toohey is no friend of Kenny J., even if he *is* the crossing guard where I cross Pleasant Street on my way to school.

Is it 10 feet or 20 feet down to the gym floor that Mr. Frasier waxes each summer? The mellow scent of that wax mingles with the food and somehow soothes my nerves today. But inevitably, my fifth-grade boredom and curiosity overtake me, and I lean over the gray-painted iron pipes that keep us from falling out of the balcony, balancing in my ugly brown-and-white leather saddle shoes on the lower railing.

From the kitchen emerges a parade of big punch bowls— glimmering glass carefully toted in the loving arms of the parents and teachers who are in charge of the day's party. Unconsciously, I collect some moisture in my mouth and curve my tongue around a fluffy, white blob of spit, and let it lilt into that glorious open space above our gym floor. I watch it stretch into a long cloud, floating softly downward to measure the height—gravity at work.

At the end of the procession appears one more punch bowl, swirling with its green ice ring and frothy lime sherbet—the punch bowl held by Miss Mabie. My floating thread of spit lands with a soft splat, right in the center of my dear Miss Mabie's fuzzy gray hairdo, centered in the bird nest of hair that circles her cowlick, that flat place right above the ring where her hair starts to curl.

Oh, NO! I quickly retake my seat and start my serious inspection of the gym rafters. Although I cannot say exactly what happens next, I can say that with suddenness and subtlety, our homeroom class becomes the stage for a great showdown: Me vs. The Rest of the Kids.

Eventually, after what seems an eternity, Miss Divine announces, "Class, we need your truthfulness to resolve this incident. Does anyone want to say now that he or she spit down on Miss Mabie's head?" We all look at each other. We all remain petrified and silent.

Time slows to an itch. She continues, *"No one?"* Then each of you will put your head down on your arm, and then the person who did this can raise a hand; no one else will know. So reach down, pull up the writing-pad arm of your desk, put down your head now, and cover your eyes."

Class is dead silent for the entire twelve-minute period, a torturous time span for any boisterous fifth-grader and unparalleled in my memory.

"How disappointing. Not one of you is honest enough to confess. Very well. We will do this for every class period until we reach the truth."

For four agonizing days, my entire homeroom remains trapped in a cruel time warp, with heads down on desks, waiting for the culprit to confess to that descending demon of spit. I can't do it. I can't raise my hand. The kids in class whisper and fidget. And after my fourth day of dogged despair, my perplexed parents elicit my tale of woe.

After another kind of long and equally agonizing silence, Mom simply intones, "Your father and I" (which always bodes ill) "encourage you to go Miss Divine tomorrow morning, before school, to admit your guilt." I'm doomed, and I know it.

The next morning is the Friday that I meet with my Hubbell School troop of Girl Scouts of America. I glumly get into my green Girl Scout uniform, which reminds me of my Girl Scout Promise to uphold all that is true in my whole natural life, forever and ever. I put this green sash across my chest to tell the world that I have achieved proficiency in many things, that I will be honest and true. But today I must tell my wonderful teacher that I am a liar, a dishonest fifth grader, probably even a teacher-hating brat.

Dad drops me off at the northeast door of Hubbell School, half an hour before the rest of the kids arrive. He watches me slumping toward the building to make sure I keep climbing up the steps and all the way through the door into the life-threatening, gaping maw of the hallway.

There stands Miss Katherine Divine, far down that long hall, with her pretty, long, brown hair curled just so and her gray pleated skirt and white socks and clean white gym shoes. She is serenely tacking up the day's announcements inside the glass case on the wall outside our classroom as I approach. My tongue anxiously wrestles the glue that seems to coat the inside of my mouth. Next, I inspect my silver braces, both the inside caps and the outside wires and posts, even the rubber bands that link the upstairs braces to the downstairs braces. Those braces seem to connect every tooth in my mouth this year, and still my very dry mouth will not open. Miss Divine sweetly smiles toward me. All I see is that little silver pendant on the dainty silver chain around her neck, that oval medal with the carving of a tiny Virgin Mary, before I look back down at the gray and black stones that pave our marble hallway.

"Hey, Virgin Mary, I need you now," I think, struggling to find courage for what I must do next. I try not to be nervous, but my ankles start to itch under my white bobby socks. My knees find each other, rubbing together for comfort. Miss Divine calmly staples more little colored flags to the bulletin board. Will I ever summon the courage to do my good deed here?

Finally, I make myself lift my head a little and look up at her: "Miss Divine, I-am-very-sorry-I-did-it."

She doesn't let me off easy. "Why Susie, what do you mean?" But I know she knows.

I am dying inside, but I have come too far to back out. "I did it. I spit over the railing. I'm sorry that Miss Mabie was down below, and I am done spitting from railings above anywhere, ever in my whole natural life."

Miss Divine seems relieved, "Thank you for confessing this, Susie, and now you must face an even more difficult task."

"What's that?" I ask, although I know what else I have to do. Dad already had told me. He had said, "You must confess, face-to-face, to Miss Mabie, and apologize." I feel sick.

25

The next day is Saturday. Mom drives me to Miss Mabie's house and parks in front. I slowly and reluctantly climb the steps onto her front porch and press the buzzer. Will this torture ever end? She answers the door. She is taller today, and her usual fullness has somehow expanded to fill her doorway, menacingly. I can't look at her face. My own face is flaming hot. A long time passes before I break my sudden and fierce examination of my shoelaces.

At last, I can say it. "I'm-sorry-I-spit-over-the-gym-class-railing-onto-your-hair, Miss Mabie." I already feel better. Time is speeding up again.

When I have nerve enough to look up, she smiles with her wide face and big teeth that are meant for smiling, "You are brave to come and tell me, and I know you are a smart girl who will not do it again."

Miss Mabie softly puts her big hand on my shoulder and guides me back out to her front steps. "Do you know, that mother robin and her newly hatched babies are in the nest up there, above the doorway. See that pile of twigs? Now, listen carefully, and you will hear her babies chirping for their lunch."

Down Mexico Way

My brothers and I are surprised to learn that our family will be taking a little vacation. We don't ever take vacations. Our father says we are going down to Old Mexico, and that it's a long drive. We all pile into the Ford station wagon, the one with the wood paneling on the sides – except it's not really wood paneling, it's just vinyl stickers that look like wood until you get up close – and head out of town toward Abilene. At Abilene we get on the Interstate, where a sign says it's more than 400 miles to El Paso, the last place in Texas. Old Mexico is a long drive.

I sit in the back seat next to a door and lean my forehead against the window. Cotton fields and pastures roll by for hours. We stop at a little motel next to the Interstate sometime after dark. We don't ever stay in motels, and I had looked forward to stopping. As it turns out, staying at the little motel isn't that much fun. Our room is just a paneled box with the type of carpet people put on their patios. A black-and-white television with rabbit ears sits on a metal stand against one wall. My mother doesn't like the bathroom very much. An air conditioner in the window hums like a jet aircraft.

The next day I sit by the car door and lean my forehead against the glass again for many hours. The cotton fields and pastures give way to ranch country, and then the ranches give way to desert. Finally, we climb through the Guadalupe Mountains and down into El Paso.

"Tomorrow we're goin' into Old Mexico," my father tells my brothers and me as we pull up to another little roadside motel.

My brothers and I find out that my parents have a reason for going to Old Mexico—it's not just a vacation, after all.

"We got to rent us a trailer somewhere hereabouts," my father announces.

My father and mother have been thinking about buying a new table for the dining room, and have discovered that the prices of tables big enough for all of us are way too high. "Highway robbery," my father says. So my parents want to buy an Old Mexico table and bring it back to Texas in a trailer.

First, though, we have to make a scouting trip across the border and see if we can find a table and chairs we like. We pile into the station wagon again and make it across the border. The border is a busy place, with armed guards and police on both sides of the bridge over the Rio Grande. My brothers and I stare out the windows while my father and mother try to figure out which way to go.

A boy younger than me waves to us and points the way to a place where we can park our car. He runs along first one narrow street and then another, motioning for my father to follow him. My mother worries that he is leading us off into Old Mexico where we might get killed or something. We follow the boy until he finally directs us to a weedy lot. He tells my father to give him a dollar to watch our car until we return.

My father knows the boy will likely run off in search of other cars as soon as we are out of sight. I know my father is thinking this because that's what he himself would do. My father grew up hard and learned how to do the hustle. Taking advantage where you can is something you learn early when you grow up like my father grew up. I know that this is something in which I will never be like my father. I feel shame that I haven't learned to distrust people, and I think my father would think more highly of me if I did.

My father says he will give the boy a dollar when we return, but the boy shakes his head. This is confirmation enough, in my father's way of thinking, that the boy doesn't intend to stay here and watch the car at all—dollar or no dollar. This is beginning to seem strange, standing here in a rough neighborhood in Old Mexico watching my father haggle with a six-year-old. My father acts as if he were buying a set of used tires from the old man at the Gulf station back home.

My father decides to offer the boy a quarter to watch our car. The boy insists on a dollar, showing his dissatisfaction by spreading his arms and lifting them toward the sky, as if asking for heaven's help with this unreasonable Gringo. The boy assumes my mother will be easier to persuade. He makes his case to her in broken English, opening his eyes wide and affecting what I think is an expert portrayal of innocence.

"Just give him the dollar," she pleads with my father.

The boy understands her perfectly, and extends an open, expectant hand toward my father. My father places a quarter in the boy's little brown hand.

"Mucho dinero," my father laughs. I think my father admires the boy, in a way. But he shows him no mercy. My father never pays the asking price for anything. We turn and walk away, retracing our route through the narrow streets.

We see other Americans browsing at storefronts and haggling with street vendors. We find a few furniture stores and my father and mother decide on a table and chairs they like. My father says the table kind of reminds him of the table the Cartwright's have at the Ponderosa. We know he's talking about the television program *Bonanza*, which my brothers and I regard as a true story. We all wish we were Cartwrights.

A good amount of time is spent discussing the price of the furniture, with my father pretending to go into shock and the shop's owner acting offended. Much of the talk is in English, but my father insists on throwing in some Spanish.

"No, no bueno!" he says, shaking his head and pretending he is going to leave.

"Come on boys. Let's get the hell out of here. Mucho dinero, loco!" he tells the Mexican man, shaking his head.

The shop owner decides to throw in some lighting fixtures, and this gives my father the idea to look around the store a little. My father decides it would be nice to have some artwork to hang in our house. He and the shop owner argue over a framed image of Elvis painted on velvet. The shop owner seems especially fond of the Elvis painting. He stands back from it and opens his arms toward the young Elvis.

"Hermoso!" he says.

My father looks at the Elvis painting as if he were in the Louvre admiring the Mona Lisa. I can tell he is thinking it would look pretty good in the glow from those new lighting fixtures.

"Now that does look like real velvet," he whispers to my mother. My mother is one of Elvis Presley's biggest fans. In the painting, Elvis is young and thin, the way she likes to remember him. She's thinking how nice it would be to have Elvis to look at every time she walks through the living room.

Finally, our father is able to make a deal that includes a table, eight chairs, various lighting fixtures, the Elvis painting, and some other velvet masterpieces, to boot. He is very proud. He tells the shop owner he will come the next day with a trailer, and that he will pay him then. The shop owner asks for a deposit, but my father tells him, "Loco!"

When we get back to the parking lot we find that our car has a broken windshield. It makes my father angry, but I can tell he understands.

At the border the next day, our father tries to convince the armed guards that the table and chairs and stuff he bought in Old Mexico aren't supposed to be taxed.

"Look here, I got all these kids and this woman, and if you divide the cost by all of them it's under the limit for taxes," he says to one of the guards. "And look here at this windshield."

"Now, sir, you can't take a carload of kids and a trailer into Mexico and come back with half the furniture in Juarez and not pay United States duties," the guard says. The guards are unmoved, and there is no question about the asking price.

My father pays the fees eventually, mumbling, "Loco, mucho loco," under his breath.

Rooster's Demise

One typical, adventurous, early summer day in western Kansas, I was tagging along after my sister, brother, and uncle. We headed down the alley, past the milking barn, the pig pen, and the shed, up to the fence with barbed wire strung along the top. My uncle, at nine years old, flew up and over like lightning. My brother, at five years old, climbed quickly behind him. And my sister, at six years old, didn't waste any time crossing that fence either. At three years old, I tried to follow across.

"Help!" I yelled.

Generally, my sister would help me, but this time she slowed, looked back at me, and yelled, "You can do it!" as she raced on. She did not want to be last yet again because of her baby sister. I struggled time and again to get over that fence, but I was afraid I would fall or get cut on the barbed wire. Finally, I had to give up and trudge back up the alley to Grandma's house by myself.

From the edge of the yard, I stood looking at the back door of the house on the corner of "A" Street. The pump and the bench with a metal water bowl for washing up waited by the back door. Suddenly the safety of the house and the cool water seemed a hundred miles away.

I knew I was stuck. I scanned the yard for the rooster—the big one that had pecked me before. *It hurt.* I didn't want it to happen again. I looked and looked, but I didn't see him. I looked down the sidewalk that ran by the street to the two huge lilac bushes on each side of the walk that led to the front porch of Grandma and Grandpa's house. Two saddles rested on the porch railing. If any of my uncles were outside, they would let me sit in the saddles. They seemed a long way away, too.

31

While trying to figure out what to do, I noticed two huge ant hills that had pushed the sidewalk up and red ants busy tunneling in and out of the sand. I would dig down and see where those ants were going another day. Now I had to figure how to get across the yard to that back door before the rooster saw me. I could see the chickens scattered across the yard pecking for worms and bugs. They were always loose during the day. The spotted goat that pulled the cart my uncle made was staked out near the pigeon coop, munching on a bush. The cows were far out in their pasture, but no grown-ups or older kids were around to help me. I was all alone.

I looked across the street to the railroad tracks with the box cars that we sometimes played on. No workers were there today, and I wasn't supposed to cross the street alone. Behind me at the other corner stood a two-story white house where two old-maid sisters lived. They were probably forty years old, but they were not outside, and their lacy curtains were silent and still. I stood in the alley between the two houses, beneath the mulberry tree that I loved to climb when the berries were ripe and juicy. I always tried to wipe my hands clean of the purple stain after feasting on those yummy berries. The berries weren't ripe yet, so I wasn't climbing trees today. How could I make it across the yard through Grandma's back door to safety?

Halfway across the yard was a mound of dirt with two wooden doors that I could slide down—the storm cellar. That day a bear hide was stretched out on these doors to dry. We all went to the storm cellar when a tornado was coming. It was musty and smelled of dirt and potatoes. But there was no safe haven there today.

Flowers were everywhere. Grandma had iris, petunias, hollyhocks, and a beautiful old-fashioned yellow rose bush, but she wasn't outside tending them today. I stood there in my sun suit that Mama had just made me. It was a yellow print with bloomer pants, a bib front with two white buttons that fastened straps that were crossed in the back. What should I do?

I looked again. I didn't see the rooster, so I finally decided to make a run for the back door. My first step into the yard, I saw him looming before me like magic. That big red rooster was bigger than I was and three times the size of any of the hens. He had dark reddish brown feathers on his wings and body; golden reddish brown feathers covered his head. His red comb stood up and a red gobbler hung down his neck. His yellow legs ended with huge talons. He looked like a monster to me.

He would strut around with his chest stuck out, protecting his flock and domain, ruling the roost. He hated everybody except Grandma. My uncles said that was because she fed him. Grandma and the hens loved that big Rhode Island Red Rooster. She said that since she got him, the hens were laying more and bigger eggs, often with double yolks.

I turned to run for the white house. I didn't make two steps before he caught me. His talons pierced my bare back, his beak pecked hard on my head, and those wings encircled me, flailing, hitting all around me. His weight was staggering. I believe he was trying to fly and carry me off. I shrank and let loose with a banshee scream. I turned and twisted, but my short arms couldn't touch him. I could hear the awful sound of those wings flapping, but I could no longer see. This attack was much worse than before. I had no defense. He hated me and wanted to kill me. Talons, wings, beak—all at the same time, over and over. I could feel the blood running down my face, my back, and into my eyes.

The old maids heard me. They dashed down their back steps and came running. The rooster flew away at their approach. They swooped me up. They took me in the house and stood me in the sink. Then they poured pitchers of water over my head to clear away the blood. Then they carried me home to Grandma's. She inspected me with love and thoroughness. Iodine was poured onto the open wounds. I cried some more. Then I got lots of tender hugs and kisses from everyone.

Years later, my sister and I sat together trying to see who could remember the earliest events of our childhood. When I mentioned that

33

rooster, my sister told me the rest of the story.

My sister, brother and uncle had heard my screams and had seen that the rooster had me. They burst through the back door of Grandma's house yelling, "The rooster got DD again!"

My other five uncles were in their teens and early twenties at that time. They were tall, lean, lanky, and handsome. Dressed in their Levis, cowboy boots, and white T-shirts, they busted out the back door yelling, "I said I'd kill that rooster if it ever touched that child again!" They all chased that huge rooster around the yard, trying to catch and corner it, periodically making a dive for it, landing in the dirt as it flew out of their reach, squawking in panic.

Grandma was chasing behind them brandishing a wooden spoon, yelling, "Don't kill my prize rooster!"

My sister, brother, and youngest uncle were chasing after her, back and forth and around in circles, not wanting to miss a minute of the ruckus. My sister waved her arms as she described the scene, making circles and figure eights to show how the procession progressed. It was one of the craziest memories of her childhood, too.

"There were too many uncles for that rooster to escape for long. They soon circled up and caught him. He promptly got his neck wrung," my sister concluded. "His feathers were plucked and the rooster was put on to boil, while Grandma rolled out the homemade egg noodles. We young'uns had a safe haven again."

My sister grinned as she finished telling me about the rooster's demise. "That was some good chicken and noodles, even if that bird had to be boiled a long time."

I remember making a pact with myself that I wasn't going to be afraid to do whatever it took to keep up. I didn't care how big the fence, rocks, or fallen trees were that were in my way, after that I never got left behind by the big kids again. I also remembered being eager to learn how to kill a chicken. I soon learned several ways: wring its neck, stand on its head and pull until the head separated from the body, or put its head on a block and chop it off with a hand axe. From the time I was about nine or ten years old, if we were having chicken, I got to wring its neck and watch it flop around before I plucked the feathers. Someone else could do the cookin', I would do the killin' and eatin'.

The Other Shoe

My brothers and I have come home from church, where we don't much like to go, and a fight involving a few of us breaks out in a bedroom as we are changing out of our Sunday clothes. I stand on one leg to yank off a hard-soled shoe and throw it at a brother. At the last second, he ducks away and the shoe crashes into the window behind him, shattering the glass. Instantly, there is a profound silence, one in which each of us replays the incident in slow motion, and during which our stomachs begin to churn at the thought of what our father will say and do when he finds out.

The differences of opinion which had provoked us only moments before into throwing fists and shoes at one another now dissolve, and we are transformed, by fear, into a unified group. Whatever our problems with one another might have been that morning, they are forgotten. We now have a much bigger problem: we have to keep this broken window a secret from our father until we are grown up and have moved away, or until our father is buried somewhere.

How many times have we been reminded not to break things? Many, many times we've been told. The broken window, along with the fact that it occurred in the course of a fight, will warrant severe punishment in our father's way of thinking. There will be no explaining allowed, and even if we could try to explain, the truth is we were fighting in the house (not allowed), we threw something in the house (also not allowed), and we broke something in the house (definitely not allowed). Our prospects for acquittal are nonexistent. After considering our immediate futures, we conclude that we are as good as dead. But maybe, just maybe, we can find a way out.

First, we examine the window to see if the damage might go unnoticed. No, it could be seen from outer space. Our father will surely see what we've done when he walks by outside the window, and we know him as a person who notices everything. Next, we think we might assemble the shards of glass into an approximation of an unbroken window, then hope for a storm with high winds—or better yet, hail—that we can blame. We try for a minute or two, careful of the razor-sharp edges. No, it is impossible, we decide.

Finally, out of ideas and growing more anxious and desperate by the minute, we decide to tell our mother, hoping to enroll her in the cover-up and get the benefit of her ideas. It is a bit risky. Our mother will not be happy about the broken window, and she will likely remind us yet again of the rule about breaking things. She might tell our father. But she, too, will know and dread the consequences to us if she tells him. We figure she will help us. In any case, we think she is our best option, and we are probably going to be dead anyway. We have nothing to lose.

Our mother does remind us of the rule about breaking things, in a voice that shows a bit of the strain of raising so many children while working a full-time job. She stands looking for a moment at the carnage with a furrowed brow, hands on her hips. But she notices we are afraid, and this helps to persuade her. She will buy a piece of replacement glass from the lumber yard on Monday and help us fix the window, she tells us.

Until then, we are not to breathe if there is even the slightest chance our exhalations might break something else. We hope that our father will not notice the broken window before it is fixed. If he should notice, our mother will tell him not to worry, that she has already dealt with it. We will hope for the best and try to stay out of sight for a while, just in case any guilt should show on our faces. My brothers and I are not very good at keeping secrets.

The following Sunday, we arrive home from church and see that our cousins Tracy and Charlie are parked in front of our house with their parents. My brothers and I are happy to see our cousins, and we run into the house with them and into our bedroom to change clothes. As we strip off our Sunday shirts and pants, I begin telling Tracy about how we broke the window the week before, and how we didn't even get into big trouble because our mother helped us fix it and our father never found out. This was, after all, one of the great victories of our collective childhoods. It was not often that we found salvation, but we had found it this time, and by plucking it from the very depths of despair, at that.

"I was mad, and I threw my shoe and it broke the window," I tell Tracy. I reach down and remove my shoe, illustrating how it had happened. I lob the shoe gently across the room toward my brother. At the last second, to my great dismay and astonishment, he ducks as he had before.

There is a moment of déjà vu, in which I think my life has entered a sinister, endless loop of church and broken windows and idiot brothers. The shoe tumbles slowly, turning in the air beyond my outstretched arm, repeating more or less its trajectory of the week before. Open-mouthed, I watch it strike the window. There is the familiar, agonizing sound of breaking glass.

Boxes

When I was a kid, we had boxes of stuff. When there are a lot of kids in a family, there's a lot of stuff to put in boxes. The oldest girl in my family had already moved out of the house before I was born. Mary went to learn how to be a nurse. Pat, who was the youngest of the nine, was born one year after me. I remember my next oldest sister, Ruth, when she still lived with us, which is kind of remarkable, as I was only four when she left home. The next eight years of my childhood I recall clearly. If I ever doubt a memory, I can ask my siblings and they usually agree with my recollections.

One of the boxes we had was the box of boots. When it snowed, we tromped down thirteen stairs to the basement to the boot box. There were at least twenty black boots in there. Some were galoshes, made to go over shoes, some were rubber rain boots. Others had good tread on them for snow. We sorted through the pile, first trying to find two boots that matched, then trying to find ones that fit. I don't know which was more difficult. There was trading and arguing and last-minute jockeying. Maybe I had one good boot, only to find brother Mike or Pat holding the other one. We'd fight, and eventually one would surrender. It was a chore to work out, and it always happened in a big pile at the last minute, with Mom yelling down the stairs that we were going to be late to school.

If the boot went on over the shoe, which was ideal, it was darned difficult to get your foot and shoe out once you were *at* school. I remember being given dirty looks by a nun, who was faced with thirty-eight wet and cold children in the same predicament.

But if you needed boots just to play in the snow, the whole thing was easier. Just find a couple of boots, and you didn't need your shoes. Sometimes there might be two right-footed boots or two that were different styles, and that was okay.

Another thing we had a box of was wheels—wheels salvaged from old tricycles, lawnmowers, skateboards, and wheelbarrows—from the last twenty years of kids. This box was the one we went to when we wanted to make a go-cart. We'd try to find four wheels roughly the same size. Then a brother or a neighbor boy plus a brother would find some crappy wood and axles from some other cast-off project and fashion a rickety platform for the wheels. Sometimes they succeeded—I remember using the go-carts before they fell apart. That was often on the first run.

Then there was the box of costumes in the attic. On Halloween night we would eat dinner and go to the attic and start pulling stuff out of *that* box. By the time I came along, it was filled with leftovers—mostly rags and small, outgrown store-bought bottoms of costumes. There were tiny leotards and cheap plastic masks, cracked and uncomfortable and useless in building a good disguise. I remember the leopard suit Mary made for Pat when he was little. The idea was that they would be used as pajamas after the holiday. He wore it so much that Mom cut the feet off, and it lived on way past its reasonable usefulness.

There were some scarves in the costume box, too. Usually we were just "hobos" for Trick-Or-Treating. After all, we had mainly rags to decorate ourselves with. There were old stretched-out garments, too, unidentifiable by that time. I remember an old skirt that we safety-pinned on a brother one year. He was too little to "get it," and he was sent simply as "a girl."

We also got boxes from Aunt Phyllis, who wasn't an aunt, really. She had two girls who were just older than my sister Joan and me. They had nice clothes, and these hand-me-downs were golden. I remember the cool bathing suits and the go-go boots. Joan and I were in heaven.

Wearing a school uniform every day and coming home to put on play clothes got boring. My clothes were nice enough, but old. Aunt Phyllis' girls had style.

As the sixth girl in the family, I had a number of little dresses with matching panty covers or ruffled drawers. I loved these. I looked forward to choosing which of them to wear on a summer day. I'm pretty sure they were leftovers from my sisters Joan and Jean. When the first grandchild, Kate, was born, her mother told me that even she had her daughter wearing some of those tired old little-girl dresses. They must have been twenty years old by 1973. I got handed down Joan's saddle shoes, too. They were big on my feet, but I liked them. Vaseline applied on the black parts would make them shine, and white shoe polish spruced the shoes up nicely.

Then there was the box of mittens and gloves. It wasn't actually a box, but a mothball-smelling Charles Chips can in the living room closet. Finding a pair of mittens or gloves that fit was much like finding a pair of boots—frustrating. When I was about ten years old, I remember when we went out to play in the snow. Our poorer neighbors used socks for mittens. We thought, socks? Jeez. Now that was harsh. At least we had the correct outerwear. And even if they didn't match, they were meant to go on hands, not feet! On Christmas, Santa put oranges in our stockings. How pedestrian! We had oranges whenever we wanted them. But Debra and Mary Miller thought oranges were a treat. It was, like anyone knows, all relative. I used to let the Miller girls hold my newest doll, feeling that it was a cheap little soul—a small addition to my doll family, which numbered well past twenty-five. I remember that Debra and Mary were reverent, as they had no new doll.

At fifty years old, I find again that boxes are thematic in my new life. I made my own box. When my husband and I split up after twenty-two years, I felt like I needed a new thing to do, so I enrolled in the arts center class for beginning ceramics, Handbuilding For Beginners. I took the beginner class three times because I was so hard on myself, but I loved the clay, too. Most of all, I just wanted *one* good thing to come out of that class. Something I could use. I learned not to call my works "bad" or "poor," but instead, "primitive." In the last class I produced a box—a slab construction. Recently enamored of birds and nests and themes of peace and safety, the instructor suggested I incorporate this bird theme. So I crafted the top handle to look like a young bird. I was extremely pleased with my creation. So far it doesn't hold anything, but it gives me joy.

The other thing boxes now mean to me is moving.

In August of 2011, my husband handed me down my boxes from storage to clean out the attic in preparation for my moving out of our house and out of his life.

There was a little yellow wooden box with a hinged lid. When I was five or six years old, my sister Ruth gave me this box. She understood that I needed a place to keep my treasures in our chaotic household of too many people. She helped me cover it with kitten decals. We soaked them in warm water for a bit, then slid off the backing paper and stuck them on. I can still feel her as I describe it, even though Ruth is gone now. Its contents were telling: a rabbit's foot, a book on leaves native to Kansas City trees, letters from John, my first-kiss boyfriend of twelve years old, among other things.

In another box, I found correspondence spanning my entire life. Yes, I have kept every letter ever written to me. Letters from my grandmas who wrote me birthday cards, letters that were charming and bittersweet, letters from lovers in my college years. Reading them all late that night in private, I knew I would be okay, that I was a survivor.

My husband and I split up after twenty-two years. As part of my recovery I began writing. Enormously grieved, I wrote, recorded, and journaled every single thing I could. Notebook after notebook. Hundreds of pages. It was therapeutic. Now I have *them* in a box, too. Somewhere.

Through the Blue

My three young brothers and I share a spare little room with hardwood floors and bunk beds, two sets of them stacked two-high. They are placed along adjoining paneled walls with a shadowy space for an old chest in between, where an assortment of dusty, mostly broken toys lie unused and neglected: G.I. Joe's with missing arms, baseballs with ripped covers, misshapen green Army men wounded in their battles with our dogs' jaws, and pieces of metal and plastic from forgotten who-knows what. My bunk is a top bunk. A wooden ladder can be hooked on the rail at the side, but I mostly climb up the end of the bed, next to the old chest. I use the wagon-wheel spokes of the headboard for hand- and footholds, pretending to make the first ascent of some icy miles-high peak at the end of the known world.

The little bedroom shares a wall with the den, where a television, an ancient couch, and my father's battered recliner squat in a close circle above a stringy oval rug. And an odd thing, a window is cut into this common wall, a hole through which you can see—and even climb—from one room to the other. It is a narrow window, but tall, about four feet high, reaching nearly to the ceiling.

The first time my parents saw our house, buoyed though they were by the dream of buying something of their very own, this window cast some doubts. My father assumed the existence of anything and everything was due to some rational, though not always good cause. He narrowed his eyes and looked the window up and down. For the moment, at least, he was lost to the window's purpose and the intent of its maker.

"By God, there's a window in this wall," he said thoughtfully. My father did not like things that had no purpose in the world. "Now, what in the hell…"

"It's decorative," my mother said, and then added, "I guess." My mother did not assume that all things must have a purpose. They could be decorative.

My parents stood in their future den that day, my mother with her hands on her hips, thinking she could hang a plant in the window between the rooms, my father with his arms crossed, thinking he could rip everything out and build a proper wall. But in the end, they covered the window with a piece of particle board, which was decorative in its own right, with a pattern of holes cut through it in diagonal rows. I could peak through the holes, but I couldn't climb through the window anymore.

My parents soon realize that from my top bunk I can watch the television through the holes in this divider, though the images appear as a disjointed kaleidoscope of gray and white, a jigsaw puzzle of shifting light. So at night they hang a dark blue sheet over the window. I lie awake and look at the pieces of my mother's face through the pattern of holes, as she smiles at me and raises the sheet between us. But the sheet is no defense against sound.

In the near-darkness, in the bluish, radioactive-like glow created by the sheet, I lie awake and listen, trying to identify the sounds that come leaking through, each of them oddly more distinct in the still half-light: my father pulling a chair back from the dining room table, my mother saying something to him in a low soft voice, my father replying with a grunt and an "I guess."

I watch television with my ears, straining to listen through the blue barrier. I imagine James Arness as Marshall Matt Dillon, Raymond Burr as Attorney Perry Mason, and Jack Webb as Sergeant Joe Friday, conjuring up faces and places to go along with the soundtracks. Through the blue I hear hoof beats and footsteps and police sirens, the tinny pianos of saloons, the gavels of courtrooms, and the radios of squad cars. And of course there were the voices.

Matt Dillon touching his cowboy hat: "Mornin', Kitty. Tell Festus I'm ridin' out to check on a rustlin' . . . "

Perry Mason divining the truth in the nick of time: "And wasn't it you, and not my client, who poisoned your husband . . . "

Joe Friday about to change names to protect the innocent: "We were working the day watch. It was hot . . . "

Of course, it isn't all make-believe. Real life seeps through the blue sheet, too. It is through this gauzy curtain that I hear of my parents many worries and hopes, hear my father's quiet sobs during the nights after my mother died, hear little bits of who is doing what and who is doing who—my veiled window on the world of grown-ups. On such nights, I count the holes and the diagonal rows, up and down, and side-to-side, over and over again; I add and subtract and multiply these carriers of fuzzy light and mixed sounds, of television fantasy and real life truth, turning them into numbers and pushing their meaning away, wanting to never grow up and for everything to just be alright.

But I do continue to grow up, as do my brothers. We eventually outgrow the world of our bunk beds with their Western motif. The old chest of broken toys disappears somewhere along the way. I watch Matt Dillon and Perry Mason and Joe Friday from another couch, in another den, in another house my father and step-mother buy, this time with my eyes as well as my ears.

Tell Me A Story

G randma, tell us a story about when you were a little girl in the
"olden days," the grandchildren begged. I laughed and
remembered when I use to beg my Grandma for a story.
"Crawl up here on my lap, and I'll see if I can remember back that
far."

*Once there was a little girl with a little curl right in the middle of her
forehead. When she was good, she was very, very good, but when she was
bad she was horrid.* I always tried to be good, but there were so many
interesting things to do back before television or cars. Actually, we did
have a car, and we could stand up behind the front seat to watch
everything that went by—horses, trains, and telephone poles. We
always waved at the train men, and they would blow the train whistle. I
would listen to the grownups talk or play the alphabet game with my
sisters and brothers. When I got tired I would crawl over the seat and
fall asleep in Mama's arms. The car was used for going from town to
town out on the highway. If it was full, with eight or ten of us in
Daddy's sedan, I would sit on an uncle's lap and fall asleep. Sometimes
I would pretend to be asleep. If they wanted to know for sure if I was
asleep, someone would say, "There's a horse," and I would pop my
head up to see it because I loved horses.

My Grandpa worked for the railroad, and so did some of my
uncles. Grandma and Grandpa's house was generally full of people. We
went there often and so did my uncles, aunts, and cousins. The railroad
tracks ran by the north side of the house. We young'uns were not

allowed to go on the north side of the house. We had to stay away not only from the tracks but also from hobos that might get us.

A grab to a tummy elicited a squirm and a giggle.

When the train roared by, Grandma would sit all of us on the floor in a couple of semicircles in front of the big picture window facing the tracks. We would watch the train, then sit there and be quiet (kind of quiet) waiting for Grandpa. He would park the train and walk down the tracks when his run was over. He would come in, get an apple, peel it, and get a spoon before he sat down. Then we could sit in front of him (I liked to crawl on his lap) while he scraped apple with the spoon and fed pieces to each of us.

When Grandma had the meal ready, the chairs around the big wood table would fill up. The only time it was relatively quiet was when the prayer was said. After I got too big for the high chair, or if a younger baby was there, the Sears Roebuck catalog or Montgomery Ward catalog would be stacked up so I could reach the table. I liked sugar. If I wanted sugar they would put it on my food, like tomatoes, hominy, and even beans. I got about three tablespoons in my tea. At bedtime Grandma had a huge couch that made out into a bed that we young'uns would sleep in. Sometimes there would be eight or ten of us. Some of our heads were at the top and some of our heads were at the bottom, but no one had to sleep on the floor.

We walked everywhere, summer and winter. We walked to church, to school, the grocery store, to ball games, the movies, and picnics. Our town, Phillipsburg, Kansas, was built on a square around the courthouse. There was a doctor's office, a cafe, furniture store, insurance office, bakery, dry cleaners, photo shop, the movie theater, a hotel, and the bank. I can't remember all of the stores. I was only three.

There were schools, churches, a feed store, a grocery store, a gas station, but these weren't on the square.

Dr. Mary's office was where Mama taught me to read when I was three. Mama would always read all the magazines while we waited at Dr. Mary's. The *McCall's* magazine always had a children's story with pictures. I watched as Mama read, and I got to name the pictures when Mama paused.

One time I heard a baby crying. "What's happening? Is the baby hurt?" I asked.

"No. That baby was just born," my mother explained. "The doctor holds the baby by the feet and spanks its bottom."

"Why?" I asked.

"It makes the baby take its first breath," Mama answered.

Soon someone walked by the door with the baby wrapped in a blanket. Mama murmured "It's a girl."

I think my Mama is the smartest person in the world. "How do you know, Mama?"

"Dr. Mary ties a pink ribbon in girls' hair and a blue ribbon in the boys'," she informed me.

"What if they don't have hair?" I asked.

"She tapes the ribbon on. It will soon be our turn. If you're good, you'll get a prescription."

The prescription was good for one free ice cream cone or pop.

Martha's Café, across the street, was where we took our prescriptions after seeing Dr. Mary. Dr. Mary and Martha were sisters. In our county, we not only had a lady doctor, but a lady also owned the café, and we had a lady post mistress. Sometimes I got to ride with the postmistress to deliver the rural mail. Several ladies that had lost their husbands continued to farm, ranch, and rodeo.

We went to Martha's Cafe at other times, too, with Daddy, my aunts, uncles, or friends. I would stand in the seat and eat the butter pats until someone spotted me and took the dish out of my reach. They always told me, "No!" But butter tasted so good!

The next year the pats didn't taste so good. "Why don't these taste the same, Mama?"

"It's not butter anymore. It's oleo margarine."

There was a big sign on the wall. "What does it say?" I asked.

"We have the right to refuse service to anyone."

"Why? What does that mean?" I pestered.

"The restaurant does not have to serve someone that's dirty."

"Mama, those farmers have mud on their boots and up their coveralls."

"Child, it doesn't say they won't, it says they don't have to."

I was in high school before I learned the racial connotation to the sign.

The bank was on the other corner. I would stop when we went through the doors, it was so immense. Past it was a dress shop where we would look at the new fashions. Then we got to go the drug store where Mama would have a Coca Cola and draw the dress designs on a napkin. She would go home and make a pattern and sew us new clothes.

Actually, I usually got my sister's hand-me-downs. Her panties had to be pinned on me because they were too big and fell off me. One time I got to pick out the 50-pound flour sack I liked best. The one I picked had dainty purple flowers. It became my favorite dress. We took turns picking out the flour sack. Mama could get a dress, a shirt or kitchen curtains from a cotton flour sack.

One of "the boys" worked at the dry cleaners. "The boys" refers to my uncles. Mama had six brothers. The dry cleaners had a funny smell. There was a big press that ironed shirts and pants a section at a time. The steam would waft up each time the top part came down on the clothes. Those presses were nothing like the irons at home. There were also big machines to clean the clothes.

At home Mama had a wash board and tubs. Later she would get a wringer washer that you had to be careful not to get your fingers or hair caught in. My sister was running clothes through the wringer and I wanted to help. I pulled up a chair and climbed up. I was four or five years old and small for my age, which would have made Myrna, my sister, seven or eight years old. Myrna said, "You're too little. Get down!" Of course, I didn't listen and leaned over to grab some clothes. I got too close to the wringer. It grabbed my long black hair. We were both screaming.

52

My sister thought I was going to be scalped. Mama came running. She hit the release bar to stop the wringer. I was barely touching the chair with my tip toes by this time, and my head was against the rollers. I don't know how she finally got my hair untangled from both rollers with me screaming at the top of my lungs, but she didn't have to cut too much. Later, when Mama wasn't around, my brother teased that a minute later and I would have come out like a paper doll.

Mama could take apart and fix anything that wasn't working right. It might be the waffle iron, electric iron, furnace, or a sprung screen door.

I spent my days at Grandma's on A Street. I was not to walk to town by myself. Grandma would send me home at the end of the day. We lived on C Street in a house down from the road. I saw my Mama walking home from work and decided to walk home with her. But she disappeared. I walked clear to town and never found her. I made it to the movie theater and was looking at the posters of the cowboys on their horses before I realized I wasn't going to find her and I had better go home.

When I finally got there, Daddy was really mad. I got a bruising spanking with Daddy's bare hand. When Daddy spanked me, I howled louder than any newborn baby. I hoped the doctor's hand wasn't as hard as Daddy's. Later that evening, Mama and Daddy decided to go to Grandma and Grandpa's with my sister and brother. I was told I couldn't go with them, which was heartbreaking, because Grandma and Grandpa's was my favorite place in the whole wide world.

"You get in that bed and stay there," my father ordered.

I did.

I don't know which was worse, not getting to go to my grandparents, having to stay in that big old house all alone, or the spanking. The three together made a lasting impression.

After awhile, my youngest uncle was sent to tell me I could get up and come to their house. "No way!" I refused. I wasn't getting out of that bed until Daddy said so. Uncle Punk (age nine) went back home and told everyone that I wouldn't get out of bed. He was sent back, and we played on the bed until I fell asleep.

Getting spanked was common enough in the olden days. My brother, sister, and several other kids talked about what was the best thing to do when you had got caught doing something you weren't suppose to do and you knew you were going to get it.

Some suggestions were humorous:

"Stuff your pants with a pillow or something!"

"Don't cry!"

"Cry quick and loud!" or

"Squeeze your butt together!"

Mama's spankings didn't hurt, and the teacher's spankings weren't bad either—except I would get another one from Daddy when I got home. When I realized that, I never got another spanking from a teacher.

"That's enough stories for one night. It's bed time for you, you sleepy-eyed young'uns."

Billy, DD, and Myrna, 1943

Angels and Goblins

L ike most folks, once upon a time I had two grandmothers. We lived with my maternal grandmother for a good part of my childhood and, together, my divorced mother and my long-widowed Grandma Carver were father, mother, uncle, and grandparent to me and my sister, Nancy. Of the two grandmothers, Grandma Freel was the one that always seemed more like a grandma—the kind you see in movies or read about in storybooks. She was paired with a grandfather, for example. She was the girlier grandma, always dressed in simple shirtwaist dresses, seamed stockings, and low-heeled shoes. She wore an apron when she cooked to keep the spatters of grease from staining her dress. She baked cookies and she fried chicken. She was pleasant and always generous with kisses and hugs. Of the two grandmothers, she also seemed old, the way a grandmother should be. She used a hair bluing rinse— a chemical added to rinse water to bleach the yellow from graying hair—that made her hair a pale, violet white. Her body was soft and rounded. She had lacy wrinkle lines on her paper-thin skin that reminded me of an old Valentine. Today when I look at photos of her taken when we were little, I realize that she was the age that I am now. Even though she was the more traditional grandmother, she was still the more exotic one to us, probably because we didn't live with her. Their house was a big, old, two-story house perfect for curiosity-driven exploration by two small girls. When we went to visit her and Grandpa Freel, we entered an entirely different world.

While Grandma Carver viewed housework as just one more chore, Grandma Freel elevated it to a vocation. She was cook, housekeeper, and servant to my grandfather, a retired plumber and handyman. She also worked as a cook in one of the women's dormitories at Washburn University. She didn't learn to drive until after Grandpa died. Every day he drove her to work and picked her up and took her to the store when she needed to go. He would wait in the car, smoking his pipe and reading the funnies in the *Topeka Capital-Journal* while she shopped for groceries.

There were other differences between my two grandmothers. Grandma Carver allied herself with the Methodists and considered herself a Christian, but didn't spend much time in church, thinking, I suppose, that God would know where to find her when the time came. Grandma Freel was a devout Baptist and never missed her Sunday service at the Seward Avenue Baptist Church two blocks from their house. When Nancy and I spent Saturday nights at their house, we packed our Sunday clothes so we could go to church with her on Sunday mornings. Grandma would roust us early on Sunday morning so we could have breakfast before church, and off we'd go in our Sunday finery—matching dresses that our mother had made, white anklet socks, and patent leather shoes. Grandma wore white gloves that smelled like the powder in the compact she kept in her purse. She also wore little hats with fancy netting and sequins. She accessorized with clip-on earrings matching strands of beads. On warm days, we walked along the brick sidewalk, Nancy and I skipping along to keep up with her. When the weather was bad, Grandpa drove us there and picked us up after the service. He never went inside. I heard him tell my Uncle Larry that he'd been preached at enough for one lifetime.

Grandma couldn't get enough preaching. She loved to hear the Word of the Lord. She gave each of us small bibles bound with white leather, and embossed with gilt letters that read *Holy Bible* at the top of the front cover and *New Testament* at the bottom. The pages were thin and parchment-like with bible verses printed in black and red letters. I liked the pictures of Jesus inside those bibles. Jesus had pale, white skin, long brown hair and a beard, and flowing robes of white and gold. A halo blazed around his head like sparklers on the Fourth of July.

Even though Grandma was Southern Baptist, she wasn't all fire and brimstone about it. She believed in the New Testament and a God of love. She liked to talk about the blood of the lamb being spilled for our sins and told us about how the angels would sing when we were received into heaven. Grandma and Grandpa had a piano where we played and sang hymns. The upright piano was old, and every note was a hollow, off-key "plunk" that sounded like it was played under water.

> *Jesus loves me, this I know,*
> *'Cause the Bible tells me so.*
> *Little ones to him belong;*
> *they are weak, but he is strong.*
> *Yes, Jesus loves me! Yes, Jesus loves me!*
> *Yes, Jesus loves me! The Bible tells me so.*

I liked the exclamation marks.

When I was a sophomore in college, I became a Roman Catholic. Nancy told me that when Grandma Freel heard the news she said, "I'll love her no matter what she does." I had deserted the fold of the True Christians, but she was willing to forgive even that. I learned only recently that my gay cousin came out to her when he was in high school more than 30 years ago. She told him the same thing; her love was unconditional. She also wished him a partner with a lot of chest hair so he would have a soft place to rest his head at night.

Grandma and Grandpa Freel lived in Oakland, a quiet neighborhood in the northeastern corner of Topeka. To get there, you had to drive over a bridge that spanned the Santa Fe shops, one of the major hubs of the Atchison, Topeka, and Santa Fe Railroad. The Santa Fe Railroad company, chartered in 1859, was originally intended to run from Atchison, Kansas to Santa Fe, New Mexico. Ironically, it was known mostly as the Santa Fe Railroad even though rough terrain prevented the line from actually reaching Santa Fe.

The Santa Fe shops in Topeka included several large, red brick warehouse buildings adjacent to the hub of tracks near the station. Although the number of workers varied depending on the economic conditions of the day, the shops helped keep thousands of workers employed in the business of repairing and maintaining steam and then diesel engines and their boxcars. The plaintiff in the famous *Brown vs. the Topeka Board of Education* case was a welder at the Santa Fe shops. Because these were railroad jobs, the neighborhood was a mix of religious and ethnic groups: Little Russia, north of the river, for the Volga Germans, East Topeka, for the African Americans, and Oakland, for the Irish and the Swedes and the Mexicans. The area was typical of the hypothetical melting pot; each group had their own baseball teams and choral groups, their own churches, and their own identities.

My grandparents' house was a simple two-story house, like a child's drawing, with a front porch and a swing. There was a barn in the back by the alley. Most people in the neighborhood had gardens; some even had chickens. Grandma grew hollyhocks and four o'clocks and Grandpa grew corn and cucumbers and tomatoes. The four o'clocks put out small, round, black seeds that looked like peppercorns. These seeds collected on the ground beneath the plants, and Nancy and I spent hours harvesting these and storing them in empty pickle jars. We could have started our own four o'clock farm. Grandma showed us how to make dolls out of hollyhock blossoms so the petals resembled beautiful evening gowns. It's a lost art.

Their house had a sleeping porch. A sleeping porch is a room, usually on the second floor at the back of a house. Their sleeping porch had windows on three sides with storm windows in the winter and screens in the summertime. Sleeping porches were popular before air conditioning became a standard feature in Midwest homes and often were the only rooms in the house that allowed for sleep on humid summer nights. With the storm windows off, an occasional wisp of air would come through the screens and lift the heat for a brief moment, bringing respite from the oppressive, muggy air. The screens let the air in and kept the bugs out. City streets were quieter then, and the only sounds coming through the screens from the damp, still night were the chirps and squeaks of a gazillion bugs. At night, when the indoor lights were still on, June bugs and moths, fatally attracted to light, would carom off the screens as they tried to get inside. The June bugs would buzz and click angrily after they thumped into the screen and fell onto the pavement.

Grandma Freel was a wonderful cook. Her meals were traditional—fried chicken, mashed potatoes and gravy, sweet corn in cream, and biscuits—all made from scratch. In the summer we would have watermelon and cantaloupe with lots of salt. Her kitchen had galvanized steel cabinets and counter tops, all painted off-white. Grandma let us help her cook, mostly by letting us stir things with wooden spoons. She tied aprons on us that hung to the tops of our shoes and stood us on chairs so we could reach the countertops. I liked to roll dough for cookies or pies. At Christmas time we made sugar cookies and frosted them with red and green icing or sprinkled them with colored sugar. That was the best because we were allowed to roll out the dough and use aluminum cookie cutters to cut out trees and angels and bells. Grandma Freel's kitchen was a factory of flour and steam and warm smells.

Grandpa loved to tease her. After we had taken our places at the round table in the center of the kitchen and Grace had been said, he would begin passing the platters of food around the table. He would wink at us and then start the gravy bowl around first, leaving the mashed potatoes for last. He never tired of this, even though Grandma got exasperated by it every time. He kept up this prank until my Aunt Janice bought them a set of melamine dishes one Christmas that included a divided serving bowl to hold both potatoes and gravy.

After dinner in the summer, we washed and dried the dishes while Grandpa went to the front porch to smoke his pipe and watch the neighbors stroll past. We joined him when the last of the pans was dried and put away and the dish towels were hung to dry. We sat on the swing with Grandma while he sat in his rocking chair. Grandma moved the swing back and forth with one leg as we sat on either side of her, begging her to go faster. She never did, preferring to move us forward and back in a meditative rhythm while Grandpa rocked his chair slowly. Any movement of air felt like a cool breeze on our steamy, damp skin. The conversation was slower by then as dusk settled around the neighborhood. Grandpa drew on his pipe from time to time, making the bits of tobacco spark and pop as he pulled the hot smoke into his mouth. When neighbors walked by on the red brick sidewalk, we waved and smiled and said good evening. Sometimes, after someone passed out of earshot, Grandpa would say, "That's the old Swede," or "He's eye-talian, you know." That was ethnic diversity in those days.

Grandma didn't let him smoke in the house. He chewed tobacco sometimes, and she didn't allow that indoors, either. I remember the smell of his pipe tobacco. He bought Prince Albert tobacco in red cans and, when we were inside for the evening, he spent time packing his pipes for the next day. The tobacco was sweet and rich, with a fragrance that saturated the air. It never smelled as nice when it was burning. He chewed tobacco when he was working or walking around because smoking a pipe required silence and contemplation. When he was in the house, he chewed gum. He and my grandmother had their own chairs in the living room. Hers was an overstuffed upholstered armchair; he had a recliner. He had a pipe stand with two drawers next to his chair. In the top drawer he kept his pipes and tobacco, along with pipe cleaners, a Zippo lighter, flint replacements for the lighter and a can of lighter fluid. Zippos used naphtha as a fuel source, a petroleum distillate that had its own peculiar sweet smell, set aflame by the rotary action of a wheel that caused the flint to spark so that the naphtha-soaked wick would light. In the bottom drawer of the pipe stand, unbeknownst to my grandmother, he saved every piece of chewing gum he ever chewed, sticking each piece onto the growing wad of gum before going to bed each night. He showed it to us from time to time. It was our secret.

On those peaceful Saturday nights, after it got dark and we had come inside, we watched the *Grand Ole Opry* on NBC. When the news came on, Grandpa would tell us stories while Grandma caught the headlines and the weather. We liked to sit on his lap and listen. Up close, his teeth were stained from tobacco and his breath stunk to high heaven, a mixture of ashtray smells and Wrigley's spearmint gum. His favorite bedtime story was the James Whitcomb Riley poem, *Little Orphan Annie*. He knew it by heart.

Little Orphan Annie's come to my house to stay.
To wash the cups and saucers up and brush the crumbs away.
To shoo the chickens from the porch and dust the hearth and sweep,
and make the fire and bake the bread to earn her board and keep.

The poem made it clear what happened to children who didn't behave:

Once there was a little boy who wouldn't say his prayers,
and when he went to bed at night away up stairs,
his mammy heard him holler and his daddy heard him bawl,
and when they turned the covers down,
he wasn't there at all!

He told us about the goblins who came after recalcitrant children.

Once there was a little girl who always laughed and grinned
and made fun of everyone, of all her blood and kin,
. . . And as she turned . . . to go and run and hide,
there was two great big black things a standing by her side.
They snatched her through the ceiling fore she knew what she's about,
and the goblins will get ya if ya don't watch out!!

He had us convinced that goblins were holed up in the attic space next to the sleeping porch. He showed us the scuttle hole in the closet that led to the attic. All we could see was a dark opening and the vague, skeleton-like ribs that were the beams of the roof and the floor. Nancy thought it was funny, but I was terrified and flew past that closet whenever I had to pass it, sure that the goblins were going to come shrieking out at any moment.

When the news was over, Grandma would run our bathwater. She filled the tub with warm water and bubble bath and let us splash around together for a while before she came in to do the scrubbing. When we were clean and glowing pink, she lifted us out and wrapped us each in big, thick towels. We'd run to her room and jump onto her chenille bedspread. Before we pulled on our pajamas, she dusted us with talcum powder out of a round canister, using an enormous powder puff. It smelled like roses and we choked and giggled as the cloud of sweet and flowery talcum surrounded us.

While Grandma got ready for bed, we rummaged through her dresser drawers. We were fascinated by what she kept in the top left drawer—a jar containing her gallstones, whatever those were, and the foam rubber inserts for her bra which she had to wear since her left-sided mastectomy in 1933. We had no idea what all of this was; we just knew that the stones were brown and strange and irregularly shaped and that the foam rubber inserts looked funny when we put them inside our own shirts. She knew we played with them, but we stashed them away and jumped under the covers when we heard her open the bathroom door.

Grandpa's bedroom was upstairs. He would clomp up the stairs after we got in bed and, for his last laugh of the day, drop one Redwing boot onto the wooden floor next to his bed. We waited in silence so that we wouldn't miss the sound of the second one dropping. His patience was endless, and he would sometimes take forever to drop the second boot onto the floor. Only then could we go to sleep.

Before the lights were out we had to pray one more time.

Now I lay me down to sleep,
I pray the lord my soul to keep;
If I die before I wake,
I pray for God my soul to take.

This could put me over the edge. I found little consolation in the idea that God would take my soul when I was done with it. I wasn't really keen on the idea of separating from it, even though I had no idea what a soul was. So there I was, wide awake, worrying about my own demise. This plea for salvation wasn't reassuring in the face of the continuous goblin scare. Would God and the goblins fight over who got what? I often lay awake for quite a while contemplating the death and dismemberment I'd been told was possible.

Today, as an adult, I no longer believe in goblins, and I don't spend a lot of time worrying about when death will come because I am certain it will come soon enough. I have a whole new set of anxieties, brought on by a lifestyle full of stress and uncertainty. What seemed alien to me as a child, in retrospect looks ordinary and comforting. The memories of fried chicken with mashed potatoes and gravy on a Sunday afternoon, a sleeping porch on a hot summer night, or a parade of neighbors every evening are as distant now as another galaxy. When I long for the past, I think about those solid routines, the time spent preparing and eating meals with family, the washing up afterwards, and the endless hours of slow conversation on a front porch on a summer evening.

A Train and the Water

I hear something in the distance. But I am not sure what it is.

"Something is coming," I say to my brother.

"Huh?" my brother stops and turns toward me. He is walking just in front of me.

"Hush! Shut up!" I put a finger to my lips. I listen.

"You shut up!" my brother tells me.

"No, just please shut up," I plead with him.

"No, you shut up!" he yells back.

"For God's sake, you idiot..." Again, I hear something.

The sound is pitched so low that it seems to move the air, rather than move through the air. I bend and touch the rails, and I feel something—or is it my imagination? Whatever it is, the sound seems to grow louder. It is not imagination. Now I am certain I feel it in the rails. My brother shouts, and points. I stand and follow his gaze down the tracks.

The train emerges from around a bend and speeds toward us. The engineer sees us on the tracks. I see his head in the front window of the engine. I see a face behind dark glasses. His mouth opens. I know he is looking at us. Suddenly I am hit, as if with a hammer, by a wall of sound. The engineer has blasted the train's air horn at my brother and me. He blasts us a second time. The sound is long and menacing, an unrelenting bone-cracking scream. It is so loud that it paralyzes. I have heard countless train whistles, but never from directly in front of an oncoming locomotive. I feel that my forehead is being tattooed by the sound of the horn. I can't think. I can't move. Now the rails rattle and hum, and I think the world is shaking to pieces. The engine is 75 yards away. My brother and I have not moved. Our eyes are wide and our mouths are open, but we have not moved.

Then we do move and run into one another. My brother is knocked down, and I trip over him. I reach for him, missing his flailing hand. The engine is 50 yards away. I scramble to my feet. I begin to panic. Another blast from the air horn, even louder, slams into us. I grab my brother's shirt and pull him. He has caught his shoe beneath a railroad tie. He kicks and screams. There is a sound that I imagine is like the ripping of the universe. The train's wheels lock tight and hundreds, or perhaps thousands, of tons of steel slide and grind down the rails toward my brother and me.

We know that we must never go onto the bridge. But like other forbidden things, it has an allure that pulls us, in spite of its dangers and the threat of losing our hides to our father's belt. We are wary, but we are drawn.

"Let's go across," my brother says. But he is not completely sure. It will be up to me. We stand at one end of the bridge and look across; then we look down. There is water far below.

"Only a little ways," I say after a moment, though I am reluctant. Because he has suggested it, I can't say no. This makes me angry with my brother. I give him a stern look that tells him not to push too far his luck of being younger. We both know that if we are caught it will be me that suffers most.

We step onto the bridge, careful to place our feet directly on the ties. Looking between my legs, I see the water below, a distant ribbon, foaming and brown. We find loose spikes in the ties and carefully stuff them in our pockets to take home. My pants grow heavy with their weight. My hands are dark from the iron and the rust. Soon I realize we have gone too far. And that is when I hear something, when I tell my brother to shut up, when I bend to feel the rails.

The locomotive's massive wheels grind the rails toward us, and then my brother's foot comes suddenly free, and we are falling. My heart leaps into my mouth, and then it stops. I do not breathe; I do not blink; I make no sound. I am twisting in the air. I think of the time I fell from the garage roof and knocked the air from my lungs, and how I thought I would die in the seconds before I could breathe again.

As through the lens of a camera, I see the bridge, the train, the smoky exhaust, parts of my brother. I look toward the ground, and then my face is hit very hard, and I feel a thousand needles in my skin. And then I feel nothing. I sense that I am still falling, but that I am falling so very slowly. My eyes come open. It is dark, but a light shimmers above me. I move my arms, and they seem not to want to move. They are heavy, and very cold. Without thinking, I breathe in, and the thick air burns. It, like my arms, is heavy and cold. Something shrieks in my head, and I know it is not air I have tried to breathe. I am under water.

I panic and thrash about. I feel something bumping beneath me, the ground, I think. All around and above me the water goes brown-black. The weight of the railroad spikes in my pockets pins me down. I see flashes of my hands, my arms, my shirt. I paw frantically at the pockets of my pants. I struggle to not breathe. I must not breathe, yet I have to breathe.

My greatest fear has always been of drowning. I am afraid of water. I don't tell anyone, because I am ashamed of being afraid. It isn't a matter of disliking water, like when a person dislikes peas. It is a morbid and desperate instinctive dread. It is a fear embedded deep inside me, and I don't know why it is there.

I have fallen from the bridge, where I was forbidden to go, and the water has me now. But I will not drown here. I will not die here. I will find my brother and make sure he doesn't die here. He will tell our mother what we have done, because he is young, and our mother will tell our father. Our father will be relieved that we are alive, and he will take a few moments to think of what might have been. He will shake his head and wonder how he could possibly bear the loss of his children. He might want to hug us, but he won't. After awhile, he will emerge from his thoughts. He will loom large above us, his mouth agape with incredulity, that we could have been so stupid. And has he told us to stay off that bridge, by God he has. And by God he ought to beat the hell out of us, and by God he thinks he by God will.

Anger will build inside him until he shakes. It will twist his face into a rictus of futility and rage, and then it will claw its way out, uncontrollable and screaming like the locomotive, covering me like the water, and I will not be able to breathe. Later my father will be sorry to have punished us so, but he will not say he is sorry. He loves us and wants us to be safe, and so he feels he must do what he must. I know that the rage is not him, but that it is in him, even so. He is powerless against it.

I feel myself slowly rising, weightless. The blackness brightens to gray. I think I see the source of the light above me. I feel something hitting my chest.

"Wake up, wake up, Momma says to wake up," I hear. I see a pajama-clad brother sitting on my chest, knocking on my ribs with his chubby fist. I am lying in my bed. Through my mouth, I inhale great gulps of morning air, light and warm with the taste of sunshine. My dream dissolves into oddly angled contorted images, disconnected from meaning and context. The images fade somewhere behind my eyes. I grasp at them, but they have become like air, and one by one they elude me. They seep through tiny leaks in my consciousness, into spaces where they hide until some other night, when they reassemble themselves and come up for air.

Three Ages of the Soul

1

Almost bedtime. I'm sitting in the bathtub, warm suds flowing over the small white mound of my stomach. My hands are busily soaping, soaping, soaping. The lather builds steadily, layer upon layer, until my belly is glistening with snow-like foam. Suddenly—my brain reels in panic. My fingers, slippery with soap, fumble at the tiny chicken bones of my neck. Is *it* still there?

Yes. Yes. *YES!* I nearly convulse in my relief. I am saved once again from eternal damnation. My scapular, with its relic (perhaps a minuscule bone fragment from some long-dead Saint?) is still hanging around my neck, protecting me like an ironclad insurance policy. At seven years of age, I never take that scapular off, not even to take a bath. What if I should drown? What if Death should catch me off-guard while I'm scrubbing my stomach and I plummet to Hell even before I can rinse all the soap off? It is best to be prepared.

I am well prepared. With great earnestness, I make my first Confession and first Holy Communion at Our Lady of Sorrows Church. I am dressed all in white, from the miniature bridal veil atop my blonde head to the shimmering white satin underpants, expressly purchased for this special day, which feel so good against my skin. They were expressly purchased for this special day. While I am waiting in the front-row pew with the rest of my second-grade class to march up to the communion rail, Sister Teresa, who almost never speaks in a tone of voice above that of a whisper, bends over from the pew behind me and clears her throat. I glance up at her—her wrinkled old face is practically glowing. The single black hair sprouting from the mole on her chin is quivering with excitement. It's as if she has a 100-watt light bulb shining inside her head like a jack-o'-lantern.

Sister lowers her voice to an absolute hiss—the sound of steam escaping from a particularly quiet teakettle—and she tells me a story that I can never forget. According to Sister, a little girl (the same age as me) had just walked out the doorway of a church (Catholic, of course) after making her first Confession and Communion and was immediately struck by a speeding car. Instantly that little girl died and, because her soul was spotless from the cleansing grace of the sacraments, she just as instantly went straight up to Heaven. No long, boring, painful stay in Purgatory—for *her*.

Sister Teresa smiles broadly, her dark eyes crinkling at the corners, as if a seven-year-old child getting killed by a hit-and-run driver is a cause for celebration. "This was the best thing that could have happened to her," the nun confides, in a whisper as soft as an angel's wings. A thrill runs up my spine and, as I start up the aisle to receive the sacred Host, I begin to get a stomachache.

Unfortunately, no car driven by a reckless driver comes careening around the corner to kill me right after my first Communion, so I am left on this Earth to continue committing sins. And I commit plenty. My Confessions to Father Ryan are always the same. "I disobeyed my mother and father six times. I got angry at my father and mother two times. I fought with my sister ten times. I am sorry for these and for all the sins of my past life." I can never actually remember how many times I have committed all these sins (or even any specific instances of committing them), and sometimes I vary the number of times each crime was committed just to alleviate the monotony of making the same exact Confession every week of my life.

 howdy howdy howdy

Seven years old. My thin white anklets continually spiral downward to sprawl around my ankles. I shift from one knobbly knee to the other on a hard, unpadded "kneeler" in a dark confessional. My breath comes in quick, hard gasps. My tummy hurts, as it always does whenever I am frightened. Breathing in the damp, musty air, (thickly scented with the smells of hundreds of other sweating penitents and the overriding odor of Father Ryan's Old Spice aftershave), I wait.

The little door in the window slides open with a faint creak that almost startled me off the kneeler. Now I am supposed to recite my litany of sins. But I can't. I have to ask my question first. I have gotten hung up on a technicality of life in Heaven, and it torments me daily. Father Ryan has to help me. *He has to!*

"Father, if we don't have our bodies—" I blurt out. I am beginning to break down.

"Yes, my child?" Father's voice sounds a bit impatient.

"If we don't have our bodies when we're up there in Heaven, how will I recognize my friends and my mom and dad? I mean, if we don't have bodies . . . " My voice trails away and, to my embarrassment, I begin to cry, right there in the confessional, with my stomach now doing leapfrogs inside me.

"My child, that is a mystery," the priest tells me. There is a sharp edge to his voice, so sharp that it makes me almost doubt that I am hearing it.

"But, Fa-Father, if we don't have our bodies!" I am really sobbing now, and my nose is starting to run.

"Now, go in peace and God bless you," comes the hurried reply, and the little door in the window between us slams shut.

I stumble out of the Confessional, still crying. My parents are waiting for me in a pew and, as I look at their faces, I am acutely aware that they are angry at me for "making a scene." My heart is thudding behind the white cotton undershirt on my skinny chest. What if someone in one of the occupied pews—Mrs. Beasley, for instance, with her black lace chapel veil drilled so securely into the middle of her skull with a bobby pin, and her mouth set in such a thin, pious line that she is no doubt thinking extremely holy thoughts—should see my tear-stained face and runny nose and think that I have just confessed some horrible crime?

It's so unfair! How could I even *see* people up in Heaven, if I don't have my body and, therefore, have no eyes? What is the point of going to Heaven, anyway, if all you do up there is float around airily, a bodiless soul drifting amid millions of other bodiless souls?

I know what souls look like. There are pictures of them in my Catechism book. They are circular and white, shaped a bit like the thin white Hosts that always stick unyieldingly to the roof of my mouth after I receive them. (This sticking business always creates another dilemma for me. I'm not allowed to remove the consecrated Host from the roof of my mouth with my human and, therefore, unclean fingers, because It is the Body of Christ. So I have to push against It mightily with the tip of my tongue until It finally, after many anxious moments, becomes unstuck. One day I commit the very grievous sin of actually vomiting up the Host right after Mass. I am convinced, between bouts of nausea and diarrhea, that if I die, right then and there, of the stomach flu, I'll be damned forever.)

Of course, some souls are not shining bright, washed nice and clean like our white-tiled kitchen floor right after my mother scrubs it with Ajax. *Some* souls are dirty black through and through—like the souls of criminals and gangsters, people who have committed horrible crimes like murdering stray cats with axes. And some souls (like mine, if I haven't been to Confession in more than a week's time) are littered with little venial sins—things like telling your little brother that he's adopted when he really isn't, just to get him all worked up.

And then there are mortal sins—great big black spots on your soul more indelible than the ink from a black magic marker that might stain your favorite white school blouse. These black marks might appear if you do something truly dreadful, like kill someone or miss Mass on Sunday. The only way to get rid of these spots (which make your soul look like the skin of a Dalmatian puppy) is to go to Confession and then say your penance. (I always pray double the Hail Marys and Our Fathers that are assigned to me in the Confessional, just to be on the safe side.)

All the rituals of my religion are so oddly comforting to me. The heavy smell of incense billowing through the church, receiving the ashy imprint of Father Ryan's thumb on my forehead on Ash Wednesday ("Remember, man, that thou art dust and unto dust thou shalt return"), the interminable length of the litany of the rosary, crowning Mother Mary during a May Queen procession ("Queen of the Angels! Queen of the May!"). All those things, and yet I am not quite sure that they will save me.

They hadn't saved my little brother.

ଋ ଋ ଋ

Six years old. My sister wakes me up from a sound sleep, screaming, "William Edward's not in his crib!" I don't know why, but my stomach seems to knot up in fear. Together my sister and I run into my brother's bedroom and peer through the hard wooden slats, pitted at the top with tiny teeth marks.

It is true. William Edward is not there. Where could he be this early in the morning? We burst into our parents' bedroom, dancing with excitement, and then stop short at the sight of our dad's face.

My dad—my big, strong Dad—is crying! He is sitting in bed with my mother and tears are glistening on his big man's face. He hasn't shaved yet, and the tears are mingling with the dark stubble on his chin. My Dad, with the big shoulders and strong arms and great, booming, radio-announcer's voice, is dissolved in tears! What kind of thing has happened to reduce my powerful father to such a state?

And then—to see the look on my mother's face—a look so raw that it hurts me somewhere deep inside. The smell inside the room is that of grief—a thick, overpowering sort of odor that I've never smelled before. My mother tells us, with a catch in her voice that makes my heart grow cold with dread, "Dr. Bryan came in the night and took your brother up to Heaven."

This is a really disturbing idea. If doctors go around in the night taking innocent children from their beds and hustling them up to Heaven, then why do people go to them for help? So many sleepless nights after that I cry into the thick, manly smelling hair of my father's broad, sweaty chest, "I don't want to die!" How can people walk down the street every day; how can they smile or chat or laugh, when sooner or later, they will all end up six feet under the ground?

In bed each night, after I say a prayer to my Guardian Angel (who is always watching over me, despite his invisibility), I hug my boy doll to my chest, willing him to be William Edward. I pretend so hard that he is my brother that at times I even fancy that the doll is crying, in the same infant voice that William Edward used to cry.

And every night before I go to bed, I soap and soap my stomach. It never seems quite clean enough.

2

"You are a very, very old soul." The words are spoken with a firmness that I find very unnerving.

I am squirming uncomfortably in my seat in a small, dimly lit office. It is a business office, with all the requisite business paraphernalia: a clunky old Royal typewriter, metal filing cabinets, and a large wooden desk littered with papers.

Yet seated at the desk, facing me, is a person who looks very unbusinesslike: an elderly woman with flowing white hair, and such heavy, makeup that it appears theatrical. I have come to her for help. She is a psychic. I found her in the Yellow Pages.

She doesn't have a crystal ball. Yet it is amazing to me that she knows so many things about me already, things that I haven't told her: my favorite food (lemons), my favorite color (purple), and even my deepest fear (that my boyfriend and I won't get back together).

The psychic does not want to talk about my ex-boyfriend, although I keep trying to lead her back to the subject. (After all, that is what I am paying her for.) Instead, she persists in focusing on my "very old" soul.

I feel very uneasy, as uncomfortable as if she is watching me while I'm getting undressed. Her eyes are blue and very penetrating. It feels as if those eyes are peeling back layer upon layer of me, exposing my very core.

There is a burning sensation in my gut, and I've forgotten to bring any Tums. I wonder if I can dare ask for my fifteen dollars back. My stomach gurgles ominously, and I quickly decide "no."

I stand up to leave (the air in the room is so stifling that I need to escape before I faint), and the woman repeats, "You are a very, very old soul. Your soul has been around for a long, long time."

"Really?" is all that I can manage, and my voice comes out in a shrill, high-pitched sound, sort of a cross between a sob and a giggle.

"You are destined to keep coming back, until you get it right."

A fly is buzzing in the air above me. It flies so close to my left ear that I worry that it will actually burrow inside my ear, but there is not a whole lot that I can do about it, since my body is twisted up like a pretzel in the Lotus position, and it is all that I can do to maintain my limbs in the required angles.

৪৩ ৪৩ ৪৩

"Relax." Miss Temple, the teacher, says the magic word. The next order of business is the Relaxation Exercise, the part of the class that I love best, the part that keeps me coming back each week to the large, rank-smelling YWCA gymnasium where these Yoga classes are held.

Ten other women's bodies in the room are falling to their exercise mats in unison as Miss Temple dims the lights. Sighing with relief, I drop down, too.

It is very quiet. Even the pesky fly seems to have stopped buzzing.

"Let your toes gently relax." Miss Temple's command is spoken very softly in the stillness of the room. I feel my toes curling inward, as if in obedience, until I hardly feel connected to them anymore.

"The beautiful feeling of relaxation is traveling slowly up your body." Miss Temple's barely audible instructions carry the warm, peaceful feeling of relaxation from my legs to my spine, from my neck to the top of my head. My entire body lies limply on the mat, as heavy as lead.

And then, all at once, I am startled to find myself floating, flying, soaring above my body. I am on the ceiling, looking down at the whole class. And there—I can see myself! There I am, on my mat! I can actually see my own eyes closed in concentration and my mouth hanging open in blissful repose.

How can this be happening—right here at the stinky YWCA?

❦ ❦ ❦

"He won't feel a thing," the vet assures me. Yet Spunky, my beloved and seriously ailing Cairn terrier, is pacing back and forth on the examining table, and his expressive brown eyes are wild with terror. I can't bear to meet those eyes as Dr. West holds the hypodermic needle just above the skin on Spunky's neck.

But at the last moment (before I can even scream, "Stop!"), Spunky's eyes lock with mine, and the look he gives me conjures up the unthinkable.

He knows. *He knows!*

Then—things seem to be happening now in slow motion, or maybe I'm just getting very hot and dizzy—Dr. West's fat, hairy thumb presses down hard on the plunger, and Spunky's body just crumples into the air, just goes flat. I hear a faint hissing sound, as if air is being let out of a bicycle tire. Then Dr. West hands me a full box of Kleenex, pats my hand awkwardly, and hurries out of the room.

And, for a very long moment, there is something else. Something almost indescribable, and certainly almost unbelievable.

There is a palpable sense of something—or someone—in that tiny examination room with me. A sensation of intense energy that seems to have escaped from my dog's limp body. It fills the whole room, crowding out all my uneasy thoughts, all my misgivings.

Whatever it is, it reassures me.

Whatever it is.

3

It is nearly 3 a.m. My muddled thoughts refuse to let me sleep, so I am sitting at the kitchen table with pen and paper, feeling compelled to write a poem. Until I begin writing it, I am not at all sure what the poem will be about.

The solid black fountain pen flies back and forth across the paper, seemingly with a mind of its own. My fingers fly with the pen, letting the ink flow and bleed across the paper.

When the pen seems to be quite finished, I pick up the white sheet of paper and read.

The words on the page at first seem strange to me, but soon they take on the satisfying comfort of the familiar. Of the very, *very* familiar—more familiar than the air I am breathing or the cold tiles of the kitchen floor beneath my bare feet, more familiar to me than my own bones and muscles and the blood beneath my skin.

I am, I realize, looking deeply into the reflection of my soul.

And finally, I think, I am getting it right.

Mixed Blessings

M
y life began in southern Missouri, and until right before I started school, we lived in a small unpainted shack without water and heated by a wood stove. The land around it was beautiful and full of woods and hills, all reminiscent of the Arkansas Ozarks of which they were an extension.

Our shack was on a dirt road, hilly and rocky like the rest of the land. But it was located at the top of the long descent to my mother's relatives' places along Possum Trot Holler. Seven miles or so of bumpy roads with lots of woods and greenery around them. They were also lined with my father's family. First came Uncle Pros and Aunt Almeda and their children. Then Grandma and Grandpa Wimpey's house, Pat and Wilma—related in some way—then my Grandma's brother and his wife, Uncle Frank and Aunt Effie. Five miles or so later was the farm of someone we called Aunt Zill, although I don't know if she was a relative or just called Aunt because she was very old.

Of course they were all Christians, but they didn't make a big deal out of it. They said blessings before meals, and my Grandma always came in to say my evening prayers with me when I stayed there. But mostly they just tried to live right and do the right thing. Grandma Wimpey truly lived by the rule, "If you can't say something good, don't say anything at all."

My mother's mother was a different story. Southern Baptist to the core, she had strict rules and used the Bible or some other religious stick to beat people up. She had her favorites among her children, and my mother was not one of them. I have speculated on why this was, wondering if it was because my mom was intelligent, which was not always good for a woman in that culture, or because as the oldest child my grandmother expected her to stay home and help her raise the younger brood. Instead, she married my Dad at an early age and started her own family.

I'm sure one of the reasons my Mom insisted on church for us was to please her mother, which didn't happen. Grandma could forgive and love the son who abandoned his wife and five kids and took work out of town, only to start a family with another woman. But she could find no reason to praise my mother, even though mom insisted we go to the Southern Baptist Church and she followed all the good Christian rules. She did the same with her grandchildren. Some were pampered and excused, others could do nothing right. Some were welcome in her home, others were not.

Being Southern Baptist in southern Missouri was serious business in the 1950s. There were so many evils to avoid: drinking, makeup, dancing, and all manner of activities were full of the devil and his constant temptations. And you didn't even have to actually do anything bad or be a party to evil activities. Just thinking the wrong thing was as bad as sinning. God saw and knew every evil thought or dark spot in the heart. I must have learned this all before the age of 5, because we were still living in the little shack at the top of Possum Trot Holler when I began to hate going to the outhouse. And not just because it was cold or drafty or housed spiders and perhaps even snakes, I just didn't want God to see me going to the bathroom. But from what I had learned in church, there was no way to hide anything.

There were only two churches in the nearest small town— Methodist and Southern Baptist. I remember later years watching the movie "A River Runs Through It." The minister father (Presbyterian, I think) said that Methodists were like Baptists except they could read. At first it seemed funny, in a snobby sort of way, but I took offense to this negative spin on my religious experience. There were a lot of good people in the church, and they were really trying to do the right thing. And just because I might have some negative interpretations about what happened there, I didn't feel that the whole congregation needed to be lumped and dumped like that. It's kind of like being angry and disappointed and upset with a family member. I can complain and rail about something they had done, but no one else had better criticize or condemn them.

Our preacher was Brother Johnny. All the grownups loved him and thought he was wonderful. They hung on every word, and everyone wanted to be part of his inner circle. On Sundays he moved back and forth around the pulpit, circling and gesturing. His voice held the cadence of fire and brimstone, slow and gentle at first. But gradually he would walk and talk and his hands would begin to pump and wave. He would jump and sweat and yell. He tried his best to scare us into being good and into staying away from the Devil's ways. We were born evil and often lost our way, but JE-sus was there to save and heal us. JE-sus.

Vacation Bible School was a very uncomfortable experience for me. I must have known some of the other children, but all I remember is feeling that I didn't know where to go or what to do and that I felt very alone. It seemed we had to sit still for a very long time, and the walls just pressed in upon me. I longed to be outdoors in the woods, the only place I could go to find comfort and joy and peace.

But Vacation Bible School was indoors, and we were supposed to learn how to become good. I didn't like knowing I was bad. I went along and did the best I could with the stories and questions to be answered after the stories. It was invariably humid and hot, and any effort led to a sticky tiredness. I can still sing part of the songs I learned, like the names of the books in the Bible: *"Matthew, Mark, Luke and John, Acts and Epistles to the Romans. First and Second Corinthians, Galatians and Ephesians."*

After drinking red Kool-Aid and eating sugar cookies, we had a brief recess, and then we finished our day singing our hearts out. We could really go to town on *"Onward Christian Soldiers marching as to war, with the cross of Jesus going on before."* We sang loudly as we marched around in the aisles. The music and movement and sugar did lift my spirits, sometimes to a fevered pitch.

But then, on the way home, the excited fever and enthusiasm cooled down, even though the car did not. There was lots to think about on the dusty ride home. I knew that my Dad had been to the War, and he seemed to think it had not been a good thing. And there was all of the "Thou Shalt Nots" to figure in. One of them had to do with not killing. How could you go to war without killing? We also learned some about the Golden Rule: Do unto others as you would have others do unto you. But turn the other cheek. It was all very confusing and probably complicated by the heat and the dust and the waning effects of all the sugar.

In church on Sundays, Brother Johnny railed and exhorted and put all of his fire and feeling into letting us know the perils of bad behavior. The gates of hell were always open and the devil was trying to lure us in. Taking the Lord's name in vain was a terrible sin.

My Dad's conversations and stories were sprinkled with curse words he had learned during the War. My mother corrected him and tried to tone his speech down, but it was also understood that his circumstances were special. Those who Fought the Good Fight perhaps slipped in other areas as they protected us from the Nazis and the horrors of which they were capable. We kept his vocabulary as secret as possible, and gradually he did totally abandon taking the Lord's name in vain.

I think Brother Johnny's last name might have been Philemon, but in these later years I think of him as Brother Johnny Philibuster. He has been renamed in my memory. He sure could keep things going on and on, and many Sundays I thought he would never quit heaping words upon us, trying his best to keep us on the straight and narrow.

One hot summer day in Vacation Bible School, having listened to stories and answered questions and sung our sugary day away, a bunch of us tired and squirmy kids were packed into Brother Johnny's station wagon to be driven home. We all lived on various and scattered dirt roads up and down the hollers, and no possible route would have made it a short and easy drive.

I was the last one in the car, and just after we turned off the highway to make the last mile and 1/4 to my house, he had a flat tire. I have no idea what else was going on in his life, but the Devil definitely got ahold of his tongue. And the Devil managed to get some really bad words out of his mouth. An outright tantrum of curses and foul language. *Jesus Christ* and *Son of a Bitch* and *God Damn It All to Hell.* Brother Johnny had a well-developed set of lungs, with all his enthusiastic preaching, and he pushed his volume to the limit on that dusty dirt road. I sat stunned in the back seat. What a revelation!

After a time he slowed down, apologized, and asked me not to tell my folks. He asked me to promise. It was very important to him. A secret between the two of us. I had not wanted to go to Vacation Bible School. I was already feeling uncomfortable about so many things, and now the preacher was telling me not to tell my parents something that had happened. Wasn't that a little bit like lying? And weren't sinners supposed to confess before the congregation and ask for forgiveness?

I told him it was okay because my dad cusses all the time so I had heard the words before. But now here was something else to work into my confusing religious experience. Keeping the secret that Brother Johnny sinned and then tried to hide it.

Several Sundays later the church service was very different. Brother Johnny was not flying and soaring and posturing on the wings of angels and dive bombing the devil. Everything was operating differently. He was explaining, almost pleading, even. There was a whole different rhythm and pitch to his voice. The tone and posture and gestures were different. The cadence was broken.

I asked my mom about it, and it never really did make sense to me. Brother Johnny was seen at the Holiday Inn in Joplin, about 40 miles from our home, having dinner at a place that served liquor. And members of the church were upset. But no real details were given to explain what was going on with the congregation. There was a lot of whispering and a lot of stopping whispering when I happened upon a group of grownups. Tongues were wagging but I couldn't hear what they were saying.

Soon Brother Johnny was off to another church. And for a time I was free to roam the hills and woods, getting my sermons from the wind as it filtered through the trees and flowers. Eventually Brother Johnny and our secret became a memory I seldom visited, because when I did it made me feel bad.

And then I am 12. My mother is always talking about whether or not I am saved. How do I feel? Do I want to be saved? It is important. When I am saved, my life will never be the same. Everything will change. And it needs to happen or I am in danger of losing my immortal soul.

Push has come to shove. Today is when it is supposed to happen. Brother Bobby—or whatever his name is—is doing that walk and talking that talk. His arms are open. The music is playing, *"Just as I am … without …."* I already heard that same spiel quite a few times, and I must confess I am prone to cry when the music is playing and the preacher has softened his cadence and is inviting the sinners down to accept Jesus. I hold out through that one, but then the choir begins singing, *"Softly and tenderly Jesus is calling… Calling for you and for me."*

I have the feeling that Brother Whoever-it-is can keep those songs up indefinitely and likely will until he gets his quota of sinners, which more than likely includes me. He and my mother have contrived to force me down the aisle. The warming weather makes the river and baptizing a possibility, if enough sinners can be rounded up.

I am scared, but somehow I manage to stand. I am stuck for a while, dreading the walk down the aisle. It seems that I am being pushed, but no one is shoving me. Gradually I make my way down the aisle to the front of the church, and the preacher is rejoicing and praying over me.

So many people congratulate and welcome me. They hug me and take me aside and tell me how their lives changed and how they have become different people since they accepted Jesus as their savior.

We do not believe in the sprinkle business. No baptismal pool for us. We all sing, *"Let's all go down to the river, there's a man there who's walking on the water…"*. And so we make our way to the river. The whole congregation is there. Several of us are lined up. My time is coming. Brother Whoosit puts his hand on my back. His other hand grasps mine and he tells me to pinch my nose shut. And trust in him. I go backwards and the water washes over me. Somehow I get a nose full but it is all okay. It is all worthwhile to change myself and the world. Everything will be different.

I sit on the bank wrapped in a towel. Cold and shivering but ready to experience this new world. Behind me I hear Myrtle, one of the old women who has witnessed to me and told me how my life would change.

She is whispering, and I suppose she thought that would prevent others from hearing. She is saying something unkind. Hurtful. Gossiping about another member of the church. And that is my first experience in my new "Christian" world.

ജ ജ ജ

When I was 35, I got a call from my grandmother, telling me she was worried that my mom might kill herself. My mom had driven 4 hours to pick up Grandma and her husband and take them a considerable distance to Oklahoma for eye surgery. Along the way, Mom had a migraine headache, and her mom said something along the lines of "You're more trouble than help" or "more trouble than you're worth." This caused my mom to talk about killing herself. Anyway, Grandma said that she was worried about her, but because she had told me, she felt she could relax. This prompted me to wonder where her God and religion were in all of this. This was not the first time I had wondered this about her.

I remember visiting my other grandmother, Grandma Wimpey, when she was dying in the hospital. She was blind, and sometimes she thought she was at home. As soon as I would get there, she would tell me where I could find blankets and ask me if I was hungry and tell me that Uncle Raymond would find something for me to eat. Her thoughts were always on helping others and making sure they were comfortable.

These days, I find myself running from people who get all preachy on me. I am drawn to the ones who are quietly helping others, those who show love and compassion as their way of life, and those who set a good example of "Do unto others as you would have them do to you."

TONY R. PIERCE

Oliver

1. School Days

My mother walks with me the block-and-a-half to my first day of school at Oliver Elementary. I am wearing stiff Levi's with legs that are rolled up at the ends because they are too long, and a shirt my mother has made at her sewing machine. She always makes four shirts with the same material and pattern, in different sizes, and when we go anywhere she makes my three brothers and me wear the same shirt. We feel ridiculous and don't want to look like one another and it makes us want to fight each other, but my mother likes it for some reason and she makes us do it. On this trip to Oliver Elementary there aren't any brothers, and I am happy they are too young for school and must stay at home.

My mother carries the things we bought for school, a Big Chief writing tablet and a cigar box containing paste, blunt scissors, Crayons, a rubber eraser, and two fat pencils.

The week before, my father had taken me downtown to get the cigar box from a blind man who sells newspapers, candy, and cigars from a little shop. My father explains to the man, whom he calls Ambrose, that his boy is heading off to first grade and needs a cigar box. Ambrose sits behind a low counter with his cane between his knees. His shop is dim in the dusky light of a bare low-wattage bulb that hangs from the ceiling behind him. A little electric fan hums at one end of the counter, ruffling the pages of a magazine laid near it. I smell old newspapers and the sweetness of tobacco. Ambrose is wearing dark glasses and smoking one of his cigars, which he carefully places in an ashtray on the counter.

"Ah, the first grade!" says Ambrose, holding up a finger. "Yes, yes." He moves his cane aside and reaches under the counter. He grunts and moves his hands about until he finds an empty cigar box, which he holds in the air with an "Aha!" He shakes it lightly next to an ear and then holds it close to his nose and sniffs.

"Oh, I like the cigars that came in this box," he says. "Ten cents each, and worth every nickel." He and my father laugh, and I think this must be some kind of cigar joke. He extends the cigar box, and my father takes it from him.

My father buys a newspaper, which I think is strange because he never reads a newspaper, and he allows me a candy bar, which is truly strange.

"All I have is a five, Ambrose, I'm sorry," he tells Ambrose.

"I can trust you," Ambrose says, and he extends his hand. My father places the five-dollar bill in his palm. Ambrose rolls his chair forward and opens a drawer. He finds a roll of tape and carefully places a piece on the bill near one end, then puts the bill into the drawer. He moves his hands around in the drawer, not looking down. Then he gives my father his change, some one-dollar bills and some coins.

After we leave, my father hands me the cigar box. "You see Ambrose put that tape on the five-dollar bill?"

"Yeah, how come he did that?"

"Ambrose only takes one-dollar bills, usually. He put the tape on the five so he would know it's a five later on," my father tells me.

"How come he only takes one-dollars?" I ask.

My father stops walking. He gives me a familiar look, the one he gives when he is about to explain something that he thinks I should already understand. Standing there with a mouth full of chocolate, I try to think quickly, but I can't think of anything. I just look up at my father.

He shakes his head. "Close your eyes," he tells me. He takes the cigar box from me. Then he tells me to hold out my hand. Soon he has put something into my outstretched palm and I close my fist around it.

"Keep your eyes closed," he warns. "Now, tell me if that's a one-dollar bill or a five-dollar bill."

"I don't know," I say through the chocolate. I rub the paper between my thumb and fingers, and hope I don't have chocolate on my hand.

"Well then," says my father, and he takes the bill from my fingers. I open my eyes and he shows me a ten-dollar bill. He raises his eyebrows, and I nod that I understand. He starts walking again. I wonder why everyone can't just tell Ambrose if they have a one-dollar or a five-dollar bill, like my father had done. I decide to think about it for a while before mentioning the idea to my father. My brothers and I have learned that it's best to suggest only good ideas.

My mother and I walk into Oliver Elementary, a long single-story building stretching along Oliver Street from one end of a block to the other, with classrooms on both sides of a central hallway, and a cafeteria at one end. The first grade rooms are down the hallway to our left as we come through the doors. I stay close to my mother as we walk down a dim corridor that smells of bleach and floor wax and chalk, but I don't hold her hand. During the summer, Oliver Elementary has been scrubbed and waxed and buffed like an old table. The woodwork gleams. The dark floor tiles are polished to a shimmering, shining onyx. Looking down, I see a hint of my image reflected in their glow, vague and featureless, like a shadow.

A jumble of voices, younger and older, mixes with footfalls and the scratching of my new Levi's as we wind around clumps of teachers and mothers and boys and girls. We skirt a bouncing, chattering knot of girls bigger than me, all talking at the same time about their summers and which teacher they have. One of them looks at me and I quickly look away. I see a snaggletooth boy with jug-handle ears that will one day become my college roommate, a dark-haired brown-eyed girl that will become, in a few years' time, the object of my first crush. I see faces whose names I will learn and remember for nearly half a century. There is the tough kid in the scruffy clothes that will tell me on the playground that this is his second time for the first grade, and that he doesn't much like school. There is the girl who will get pregnant in our junior year and drop out of school and disappear. There are the boys who will take over their fathers' farms, and the girls they will marry. Their children will someday walk this very hallway.

There are three rooms for first-graders, with lists of printed names taped beside their doors. My mother stands with other mothers to scan the lists, and finally she sees my name.

I am to be in Mrs. Cole's room. She is tall and very thin, a bony, wrinkled woman with papery skin, a hint of lips, and a stern squint. I think she might be the oldest woman I have ever seen. I take the Big Chief tablet and the cigar box of school supplies from my mother and look for a place to sit. There are five rows of desks running from the front of the room to the back, with six desks in each row. I think it best to sit in the middle row halfway back. I see other children putting their Big Chief tablets and their cigar boxes in a hollow space below their seats, and I do the same. My mother waves goodbye to me and I do a quick little wave and wish she would just go and not make a big thing out of me going to Oliver Elementary. I try to sit still in my desk while other mothers and kids arrive and meet Mrs. Cole. Dried chewing gum is stuck to the bottom of my desk and I pick at it with a finger. I look around. At the front of the classroom Mrs. Cole's desk sits next to a bank of windows spanning the length of the room. A blackboard is built into the front wall. Above the blackboard, shapes are printed on colored cards that are affixed to the wall in a row.

I stretch my neck and look out the windows and see my mother walking back toward home. I feel something in my throat and have the sudden urge to run after her, but I don't move. I have begun to notice that my mother is uncommonly pretty. She is small and dark-haired and thin. The summer sun has turned her skin into gold. On our rare trips downtown I walk close to her along the sidewalks and feel the eyes of the men on us. I shoot the men sullen looks under knitted brows, but they aren't looking at me. I don't know if my mother notices their stares, but she looks straight ahead and walks with purpose, her gold calves shining below her skirt.

I know the boy who sits in the desk to my right. His name is Louis. He lives across the street from my brothers and me. I am happy to see him, a familiar face in a sea of strangers. But I soon grow anxious and try to ignore him. Because he has taken the bottle of paste from his cigar box and is eating the paste, looking at it closely and licking it from his fingers. He takes the new Crayons from their little box and smells them, then removes their paper sleeves. He takes the blunt scissors from his box and begins cutting Blue into small pieces, squeezing hard on the little scissors with both hands. Then he cuts Brown into small pieces, and puts the pieces into his paste bottle. He takes a little bite of Red and grins at me.

There was a problem with Louis during the summer. He developed the habit of running away from home. From across the street in the evening, we would hear his father marching around outside and yelling, "Louis!" over and over, and sometimes "Goddamned, Louis!" Then Louis' father would stomp off into their house, and come out again with Louis' mother, the both of them cursing and stomping. They would get into their rusty old car and slam the doors and drive around the neighborhood looking for Louis, the car exhaust smoking and the engine making a terrible racket. They always found him, because there he would be the next day, outside digging in their front yard with a little shovel and filling a toy dump truck with dirt.

Sometimes we would hear shouting from across the street and know that Louis' father and mother were fighting again. His father had a job working on cars and his mother stayed inside their house for the most part, and sometimes when the father came home he and the mother would start shouting. Louis would come tearing out of the house and run off somewhere and they would have to go find him. Sometimes Louis' parents would come outside in the evening and get into their car. "Louis, you stay here and don't run away again or I'll beat your ass good," his father would say, pointing at Louis, and they would drive away and Louis would keep digging away in the front yard, filling his toy dump truck.

Mrs. Cole wants to find out if we know something called the alphabet. She takes a long stick and moves to the blackboard. She has sharp bumpy shins under thick nylons that sag with little wrinkles near her ankles. She is all neck and arms and elbows and feet, like someone stuck a wig and a watch on a pair of stilts. She points the stick at the girl in the first seat in the first row, and then she points at the first shape on a card above the blackboard.

"What is this?" she asks the girl. She gives a stern look.

"A," says the girl in the first seat in the first row.

Mrs. Cole moves the stick to the next shape.

"B," says the girl.

Mrs. Cole moves the stick.

"C," says the girl.

Mrs. Cole points the stick at the boy in the second seat in the first row. She points to a shape above the blackboard.

"What is this?" she asks the boy. She gives a stern look.

"D," says the boy in the second seat in the first row.

This goes on for a while. I have no idea what the shapes are. I know Mrs. Cole will soon progress to the middle row of desks, and then halfway toward the back of the room, and to me. My heart beats hard in my chest. What am I to do? I don't know these shapes. I feel panicky and want to cry. Already on the first day at Oliver Elementary I am no good at school and everyone else knows everything and I know nothing at all. I am going to be one of the dumb kids, just like I knew I would be.

When Mrs. Cole reaches the end of the row of shapes, she walks to the first shape again. She points to the boy in the desk in front of me.

"What is this?" she asks the boy. She looks stern.

"A," says the boy in the desk in front of me.

She moves the stick.

"B," says the boy.

Mrs. Cole points her stick and her pale arm at me.

"What is this?" Her stern look blazes.

I remember the girl in the first seat in the first row.

"C," I say.

She moves the stick.

I remember the boy in the second seat in the first row.

"D," I say. But I know that is all I can remember. I don't know what I will say when she moves the stick again and looks at me with her stern look. But she points the stick at the girl behind me, and I can breathe again.

At night my father comes home and asks me about school. I tell him I am one of the dumb ones and I don't know this alphabet like everyone else in the class. I tell him I don't want to go back to Oliver Elementary with the stern teacher with the bumpy shins and Louis who ate his paste and Crayons, and whose mother had to come for him before school was over. He tells me that's what school is for, to teach me things I don't know, and by God I will be going back to Oliver Elementary, and for a good long time, and that's that.

My mother tells me that some kids went to kindergarten last year and that's why they already know the alphabet. I have never heard of kindergarten. She tells me it doesn't matter. She tells me I am smart and I will learn fast, and she reminds me that I should not be eating my paste and Crayons like Louis, by the way.

"That Louis is an idiot," my father mumbles from his chair in the den. I look over my shoulder and see him sitting in his recliner, the outline of a big arm lifting a beer can, a silhouette in the gray-white glow of the television. My mother ignores him.

"You know the song about the ABC's, you just don't know you can write down the ABC's," she says. She tells me the ABC's are what words are made of, and anything at all you can say you can write using the ABC's.

I know about words and books, but I don't know they are made of the ABC's. Could this be true? I ask her if she is sure. I don't want to make a mistake at school.

"Yes," she laughs. "I'm sure. Let me show you." She takes a pencil and writes something on a piece of paper in large shapes. She spells it out aloud, pointing to each of the shapes, giving each a name. I look for a minute.

"That's your name," she tells me.

"That's me?" I look at the paper and then at my mother. She nods. I like the way my name looks. There are straight lines and rounded lines. They go across, and up-and-down, and at a slant, and one bends and another goes all around. I think it looks very nice. I trace the ABC's with a finger.

"Yes, that's you." She sees that I like the look of my name. My mother has many types of smiles. She does the one that is real and rare, that I am careful to watch for, and I am happy.

2. Seeing the Light

The school nurse knocks on the door of Mrs. Reed's room at Oliver Elementary, where I am in the third grade. The nurse is called Mrs. Markham. She is a plumpish woman, old like Mrs. Reed, and when she opens the door I see she is dressed in a nurse's white uniform with a white cap and white shoes—her usual attire. She pokes her head into the room. I see she is wearing glasses with dark frames and has her graying hair tied up beneath her cap. I have seen her in the hallway from time to time in my years at Oliver Elementary, and she has never looked especially friendly. I realize that I have never seen her smile. Maybe she thinks if she smiled, all of us children would pretend to be sick and want to come see her and then she would be too busy. None of us likes to be sent to Mrs. Markham, so she is not usually very busy.

Today, she has come to take our class to the cafeteria, where she will give each of us an eye test. She does not look happy.

We follow Mrs. Markham down the hallway toward the cafeteria in single file. She looks back along the line at frequent intervals, giving us warning looks to remain quiet. Mrs. Markham has cleared a corner of the cafeteria to use for her eye test. She has placed two pieces of blue tape on the floor, twenty feet apart. She has drawn and cut two letter "E's" from a piece of poster board and colored them black with a marker.

Still in line, we move forward to one of the pieces of blue tape. She gives the first boy in the line one of the "E's." Then she walks to the other piece of tape. She holds up her letter "E" and the boy holds out his "E" in the same way. She will hold it out sideways and backwards, not the way an "E" is supposed to look, and the boy will move his letter to match. Then the boy will give his "E" to the boy or girl behind him. This process continues until I am handed the "E."

I squint toward Mrs. Markham, trying to see her "E." I hold out my "E."

"No! Now pay attention," Mrs. Markham calls out to me. I can see she is moving her "E," shaking it emphatically at me. I make another guess. Classmates near me in the line snicker. Mrs. Markham yells for them to be quiet. My guess is a bad one.

"No, you are not paying attention," says Mrs. Markham. She decides to give up on me.

"Next!" I hand over the "E" to the girl behind me.

I get out of the line and stand with the others who have completed the eye test, all of them except for me doing well enough to satisfy Mrs. Markham. I feel embarrassment and shame for not being able to see the "E". I am angry at Mrs. Markham. She is testing my eyes, but when I can't see the "E" she thinks I am only stupid or inattentive, not that my eyesight is poor. I decide I don't like Mrs. Markham.

A few days after the eye test, Mrs. Reed calls me to her desk. I stand next to her chair as she points to one of my papers, which she has laid

TONY R. PIERCE

on her desk before me. I see a math paper, one containing addition problems we copied from the blackboard the day before. I love to do the math problems Mrs. Reed writes on the blackboard.

"These are not the numbers I wrote on the board," she tells me sternly. "You wrote down every one of these numbers with at least one or two of the digits wrong. You must learn to pay better attention."

I am very embarrassed. Classmates look at me from their seats. I worry that they think I am dumb.

She tells me, "Now, when you added the numbers you wrote down, you did get correct answers, so at least you know how to add. This makes me think you are not careful. You must look closely at the blackboard. You must try harder."

I don't tell Mrs. Reed that from my seat near the back of the room I can't see the numbers she writes on the blackboard. I think if she just moved me closer to the front of the room, I could see and everything would be fine. But she doesn't suspect my eyesight; she thinks I am only inattentive. This makes me angry, like I was with Mrs. Markham about the eye test. I do try hard at school. I know school is important.

I am bothered enough by these things to tell my mother that I cannot see Mrs. Markham's "E" and Mrs. Reed's math problems. I worry that she might be disappointed in me for my eyes. My mother smiles and tells me she expected I would need to wear glasses someday. She herself has worn them since second grade, she tells me. "You got your eyes from me," she says. I don't know how this could have worked, but I am happy that having bad eyes is not my fault.

My mother takes me to see Dr. Cromwell. Like Mrs. Markham and Mrs. Reed, he is also very old. I sit in a chair and he swings a big machine in front of me. He turns out the lights in the room. There are holes in the machine for my eyes.

"Look through the holes," Dr. Cromwell tells me. I look through the holes and see a big "E" like Mrs. Markham's, and some smaller letters on the far wall. Dr. Cromwell moves his hands about on the

96

machine and the letters become more distinct, until finally they blur. I tell the doctor about Mrs. Markham's "E".

"Yes, you take a size twenty letter and view it at a distance of twenty feet. If the letter is clear, you have what we call 'twenty-twenty' vision, which is normal eyesight. You need glasses," he tells me.

"I got my eyes from my mother," I tell him.

A week later my mother and I return to Dr. Cromwell. He places my new glasses on my face, then removes them and fusses with them for a while. After repeating this a few times, he seems satisfied and turns out the lights.

"Read the bottom line," he points to the far wall. I read a series of letters and numbers, and he switches the lights on.

As we walk home from the doctor's office, I realize I have emerged into a new world. I see the tiniest details in the sidewalk under my feet. I see grains of sand in the old cement. I resist the temptation to count the blades of grass that now jump out of the ground with amazing clarity. The trees have uncountable numbers of distinct, individual leaves; street signs are startlingly vivid; clouds high in the sky above captivate me with their shapes. I read every car license plate, every storefront and traffic sign that I see on our way back home. For the first time, I see that there are words painted on the town water tower. I announce this to my mother, who tells me, "Well, of course." For the remainder of the afternoon, I point out to my mother the many wonders of everything around me, causing her to laugh and shake her head.

"Wait until it is dark and I will show you something," she tells me.

I cannot wait until it is dark. I want to know why I must wait until dark for her to show me. My mother tells me to wait until dark, and I will know why. Finally, after supper is done and the daylight is gone, I pester my mother to show me.

"When I got my glasses, my mother showed me this," she says. We walk outside into the backyard, where she looks up and says, "There they are."

I follow her gaze and see the stars, but not as the fuzzy, faint patches that I had known for as long as I could remember. I see them for the first time as brilliant, blazing points of light.

3. Know, Knew, Known

No one remembers how they learned to talk. There is never a time when you first realize, hey, I know how to talk. No one remembers how they learned to understand what someone says, never a time when you first realize what is meant by "hand me that hammer," or "watch it, that's hot."

Speaking, and understanding what is said, seem to just happen, somehow. But not so, writing and reading. I know this from Mrs. Cole's first-grade class at Oliver Elementary, where I grip a fat pencil and sweat mightily to make A's and B's, T's and U's, under the constant threat of Mrs. Cole's red pencil, which she brandishes like a sword in an eager bony hand.

"Messy!" she writes at the top of my papers, where she knows my mother will see it. "Pay Attention!" she pens, in a perfect script, precise and evenly spaced in strawberry beneath my wobbly name.

"Needs Work!" she declares.

I am distressed to learn that there are two A's, one big and one little, and the same for B's and C's and all the rest. This seems unnecessary, and at least a waste of paper, when I must write both the big and the little, one after the other between the lines, again and again, always aware of the merciless red sword. There is a top line, a bottom line, and a dotted line in the middle, where the big "A" must be crossed and the little "a" must curve. Mrs. Cole is very serious about this dotted line.

Finally, there is a time in the first grade when Mrs. Cole puts only a red check-mark at the top of my work, though I think my writing has barely improved. I think she has decided I have caused enough red marks, and that she will pass me on as a burden to other teachers. But

Mrs. Cole is not done with other things. She tries to teach us to read. We are divided into groups, with names of colors like Blue and Red and Green. I am in the Blue group, and when Mrs. Cole calls for us we sit around a low table at the front of the class to read.

"See Spot rrr . . . rrr . . . ," one of us will begin.

"Run," says Mrs. Cole.

"Run," says the reader. "See Jack. See Jack rrr . . . rrr . . . ," he reads on.

"Run," says Mrs. Cole.

"Run," repeats the reader. "See Janet. See Janet rrr . . . rrr . . . ," he continues.

"Run! For goodness sake," says Mrs. Cole.

"Run," he says, then in a confused way, "for goodness sake."

I find that I am able to read in a way that is okay for Mrs. Cole. She will only occasionally correct me or tell me to pay attention. Most of her time is spent with others who do not seem to take to reading, and for this I am grateful.

But it is not my reading that causes me trouble: it is the way I talk. I bring a paper bag of wild plums to school for show-and-tell. I give everyone a plum and tell about how we went to my grandparents' house and there is a plum thicket on the side of the road along the way, by the big bridge. And how my father stopped on the side of the road and told my brothers and me to pick as many plums as we could in ten minutes, after which he would drive off and leave to the bobcats anybody not sitting in the car with their mouths shut. I tell about how we arrived at our grandparents' house and showed our plums to our grandfather, and how he was very happy with us and told us he had never seen anybody that could pick plums like us. He knows how much we like the plums.

"What did your grandfather say?" Mrs. Cole asks, as I stand at the front of the room clutching my paper bag.

"He said 'I ain't never saw nobody pick plums like you boys'," I say proudly, happy to repeat my grandfather's praise.

"You mean he said, 'I have never seen anyone pick plums like you'," Mrs. Cole tells me.

"No, he said 'I ain't never—'." But Mrs. Cole stops me.

"That is incorrect. You must learn to speak correctly or no one will listen to you."

I don't know if this is right. I can listen to my grandfather talk all day long. Over the next months I find that speaking correctly is harder than you might think.

I think, I thought, I have thought, I am thinking.

It is not easy to see patterns. I see, I saw, I have seen. I find out how little I know about language. I know, I knew, I have known. I speak, I spoke, I have spoken. It is, it was, it has been, it shall be.

Spot *runs*, but I *run*. But Spot *ran*, and I *ran*. Spot *has* run, but I *have* run. Spot *is* running, but I *am* running. All of this is very confusing. The people who made up words have made up too many, and I don't like it that there seem to be exceptions to all the rules. But after a time, I accept this, and begin to realize that language, beyond its rules that are so mysterious, might have possibilities that I cannot imagine.

One day Mrs. Cole gives us a book that we will use to learn arithmetic. There are pictures of oranges that show how two oranges and three oranges put together are five oranges. But this is true not just for oranges. I am happy to learn that two apples and three apples put together are five apples, and that two bananas and three peaches make five, too. I realize this means that two and three of anything is always five. Always. There are no exceptions to the rules of arithmetic. They are absolute and beyond the reproach of Mrs. Cole. Two Spots and four Spots make six Spots. Two of me and four of me make six of me. I like this very much. I begin to realize that arithmetic, like language, might have its own unimaginable possibilities.

Many years later, I will lie on a bed in a dorm room and read the words of men and women who have taken language and used it to create meaning and feeling I could not have thought was possible. I will sit in a university lecture hall, where a man writes on a blackboard an equation that changed the world. I watch and listen as he explains that without this short sequence of symbols a man would never have walked on the moon.

I will realize how little I know, knew, have known. I will again think of Mrs. Cole, see Spot run, and add oranges and apples on the pages of a little book with pictures.

Christmas

1

My sister Nancy pulled me aside one night after dinner a few weeks before Christmas. I was almost nine years old and she had just turned seven. "Do you think there's really a Santa Claus?" she asked.

I knew enough to hedge. I didn't want to shatter any beliefs she might still have and ruin it all for my baby sister. On the other hand, I didn't want to look hopelessly gullible in case she knew the truth. "What do you think?" I asked.

She was on the fence, but not because she harbored any uncertainties or fantasies. "I think we get more presents if there's still a Santa Claus," she said. "If Mom thinks we think he's real, we get presents from her *and* from Santa!"

With that impeccable reasoning, we agreed to keep the scam alive at least one more year so we could cash in on the presents.

In my memory, Christmas is a time of magic and lights and packages against a background of glitter and music and snow, an image culled from many years of experiences. There is no such thing as the perfect Christmas season. Over time, as we distill experience into memory, what we recollect becomes a compilation of what we choose to recall. My memories are often colored more by the way things were supposed to be than the way they actually were. In the case of Santa, for example, I picture Santa as a jolly, rosy-cheeked, gentle man bearing gifts and spreading joy. The Santa I conjure up in memory is the Santa of the image. The Santa I actually experienced was frightening and large and just too much for the shy, small child that I was. No way would I march up to this larger-than-life man in a red clown suit with an improbable beard, sit on his lap, and tell him what I wanted for Christmas. I was terrified.

My grandmother loved all holidays. Christmas was definitely the best because it had its own long season with its time of preparation, seasonal cheer, and, even then, before the protracted commercialized season it has become, a build-up unmatched by other holidays.

She didn't really kick things into full gear until after Thanksgiving, but she was busy planning her projects even earlier. She loved to decorate and she loved to make things, and the Christmas season was tailor-made for these activities. I think being a special education teacher gave her a certain license to purchase industrial amounts of craft materials. Her classroom was her own crafter's test lab, where projects that showed promise were brought home for us to implement. If her students could make something, we were certainly capable of making it, too. She saw to it that we were well supplied with felt, fabric, glue, clay, buttons, ribbons, Popsicle sticks, cotton balls, and glitter.

The mega-hobby stores like Michael's or Hobby Lobby didn't exist then, but she made do with Woolworth's and Duckwall's—the "five-and-dime stores," as she called them. Women's magazines like *McCall's* and *Woman's Day* and *Redbook* were mined for ideas for homemade decorations and handcrafted gifts. She was a diamond-in-the-rough version of Martha Stewart.

Every year she picked one major decorating project and one or two gift ideas, and we were off and running, shopping for supplies and setting up our home Christmas factory. The days after Thanksgiving, when we were out of school, were ideal. "Let's get the ball rolling," she'd say as she set up the card tables that would occupy our living room until only a few days before Christmas. The sewing machines would be brought out and threaded, patterns would be traced and cut out and pinned to fabrics, and each of us would be assigned a task. I liked using pinking shears to cut things out with jagged edges. I didn't like gluing things because I preferred not to get sticky.

One year we made pincushions using Mason jar lids: red and green velvet pads filled with emery sand, and a decorative ribbon around the edge of the jar lid to finish it off. "Everyone needs a pincushion," she announced. All of the relatives, friends, teachers, hairdressers, and secretaries on our lists got handmade pincushions that year.

Our little factory would hum—one of us cutting fabric, another gluing ribbon, another measuring and pouring the sand. As I was a perfectionist, I got frustrated easily if the ribbon wouldn't glue on straight or if the fabric had a wrinkle when I pulled it tight. Grandma kept an eagle eye on her crew. She'd let me struggle for a while until she sensed I was ready to throw the piece across the room, and then, very softly, with her big, gentle, gnarled hands, she would take it from me and say, "Here, let your Uncle do it." She always referred to herself as our uncle in these more paternalistic moments. I don't know why. It was comforting though, and I had the sense of being protected and loved. When I anthropomorphize God, I envision a large, happy woman with her wig on backwards, her big hands sticky with glue and covered with glitter.

As a subsidiary enterprise to our gift factory, we also produced decorations and ornaments. These ranged from simple construction paper chains and strung popcorn to more elaborate themed trees and table centerpieces. We made snow villages out of sugar cubes and angels out of corn husks. We glued strings of beads onto Styrofoam shapes and hung them on trees. One year she made a sleigh out of a turkey breastbone. It was spray-painted gold, and the tableau included eight reindeer figurines, a stuffed Santa made of red felt, and his bag of toys, which was a burlap bag stuffed with cotton balls. A length of cotton batting served as a cover of snow.

The very best of these crafting ventures was the year she decided to make a partridge tree she had seen in *McCall's*. She cut birds and pears out of felt fabric, stitched them together, and stuffed them with cotton. Then she enlisted the services of her squad, and we all started decorating. We had boxes of beads and buttons and ribbons and feathers to glue onto the birds to give them eyes and wings and plumes of color. They were spectacular, and when they were finished, we hung them all on a silvery aluminum tree. To cap off the effect, she positioned a rotating color wheel light at the foot of the tree to bathe it in alternating red and green and blue and yellow. It was splendid.

2

Second only to her delight in making things was my grandmother's hunt for the perfect gifts. It was essential that each gift be perfect, and each one a perfect surprise. She was furtive, spying on conversations to figure out what someone might want, scrutinizing us closely while we watched toy commercials, taking note of the items we lingered over when we went shopping. She loved the element of surprise and took great pains to trick us every chance she got. She would put rattles in boxes to fool us when we shook them. She thought it was fun to put small gifts in enormous boxes so that no amount of guessing would yield the right answer. A rock or two could make a pair of socks feel like a camera, maybe.

Downtown Topeka, Kansas, in the 1960s was a thriving retail area, not far from the state capitol and state office buildings. Topeka had two large department stores a couple of large clothing stores, two jewelers, shoe stores, a leather store, and a camera store. Today, downtown Topeka has the feel of Soviet cities before the Iron Curtain fell. These buildings now house an occasional office or apartment and sometimes a restaurant, but, more often than not, they sit vacant.

In their prime, the two department stores—Pelletier's and Crosby's—were each several stories tall. Each floor was dedicated to departments such as home furnishings, better dresses, lingerie, menswear, sportswear, shoes, and cosmetics. Crosby's had an elevator operator who announced the departments as the doors opened. Both stores used pneumatic tubes to carry payments from the customer to the cashier and to deliver change and a receipt back to the floors. The sales clerks wrote up the tickets in fancy secretarial handwriting, using carbon paper between the store copies and customer receipts. Like the grand department store in cities like Chicago or New York, these aspired to be elaborate and elegant. They were carpeted and well-lit places with bronze fixtures, large mirrors, and discreet sales clerks waiting near fitting rooms with tape measures across their shoulders, ready to fit women for brassieres and other undergarments designed to make any figure look good.

They were especially fun to shop at during Christmas. The streets would be wet with new snow, the air would be brisk and cold, and then we'd step inside one of these retail icons with their high ceilings and soft carpets and muted Christmas music. It was warm and inviting and full of interesting merchandise.

Today's malls are noisy collections of shops where sounds echo and voices carry. Going into one of the old department stores was like being invited into a grand palace. The larger department stores in U.S. cities, such as Lord & Taylor in New York and Marshall Field's in Chicago were veritable cathedrals of commerce. The famous Marshall Field's slogan, "Give the lady what she wants" was indicative of the marketing force that made department stores successful. They catered to women, who were the life force of American consumerism in their drive to furnish homes, clothe families, and provide comfort for their loved ones. They were cathedrals of commerce, each one ostensibly self-contained, often housing restaurants and tea rooms to give shoppers a chance to rest and refresh. There was nothing casual about the experience, either. Women wore heels, and jewelry, hats and gloves to enter one of these places. No one would dare wear slacks or sandals.

One year Mom was excited because she had not only figured out the perfect gift for Grandma, but she had engineered a surprise that none of us could match. They had gone shopping downtown to look at dresses. "Look," Grandma said, as she stopped by a rack of winter coats. "Isn't this gorgeous?"

She was rubbing the fabric of a blue wool coat. It had a soft, white fur collar and double-breasted buttons. She lifted it off the rack and held it up to examine it more carefully.

"Try it on," Mom said. Perhaps she had found the perfect gift.

Grandma took off her old, brown nubby wool coat with bone buttons. She draped it on a nearby chair over her pocketbook and slipped on the coat. The lining felt cool and silky. It fit perfectly and made her look tall and elegant. The blue brought out the sparkle in her eyes.

A sales girl approached. "That looks lovely," she said. She smoothed the fabric over Grandma's shoulders with an expert hand. "It really couldn't be a better fit."

Grandma turned from side to side to view herself in the mirror. "I haven't even looked at the price," she said. "Oh, dear," she said. "I can't pay that right now."

"We have a lay-away plan," the sales girl said. "You can put ten percent down today and we can hold it for you for 60 days."

Grandma took off the coat and handed it to the clerk who put it back on the hanger. My mother suggested she think it over. Mom was planning her strategy. She could come back later and buy the coat, slip it under the tree, and wait for the grand surprise.

"I'll take it," Grandma said.

So Mom watched as Grandma filled out the lay-away paperwork and made the down payment. As Grandma took the envelope with the lay-away agreement and receipt and put it in her purse, my mother got another idea.

That night at home, when Grandma was in the kitchen washing lettuce for dinner, Mom went into Grandma's room, pulled the envelope out of her purse, removed the lay-away agreement, and put the envelope back. The next day after she left work, she went to the store and paid the balance on the coat. She hesitated when the clerk offered to gift wrap it, but then remembered she would have to carry it past Grandma when she got home. Better to have it already wrapped, she thought, as she agreed to pay the exorbitant fifty cents for the heavy, gilt-flecked wrapping paper with a gold chiffon ribbon. She could hardly contain her excitement. Nancy and I were more than curious about the contents of such an elegant package.

On Christmas morning, I woke up first. I jumped onto Nancy's bed and whispered close to her ear. "Let's go see what Santa brought us." She was immediately awake and springing out of bed. I think even now, with both of us well into menopause, I could still rouse her out of a deep sleep by whispering those words in her ear. I tried it a few times when we were in high school and it worked like a charm.

We thundered down the stairs, opened the door to the living room, and then stopped to take in the transformation that had come to pass while we had slept. Dolls and games and toys were arranged in a magnificent display around the tree. Stockings stuffed with oranges and apples and trinkets were draped on the sofa. And miraculously, the shag rug had been carefully vacuumed.

As we moved toward the tree, Mom appeared out of nowhere and said, "Wait just a minute."

We had to wait for Grandma to get her instamatic and Mom to get the eight-millimeter movie camera. We had posterity to think about. Amid the blinding lights of the movie camera and the incessant flash of the instamatic, we tore into the gifts.

Later, after we had played with and rearranged and examined our toys and pulled the trinkets out of our stockings and put them back for safekeeping, we were invited to eat breakfast. Grandma, who really couldn't cook, did have a knack with homemade bread. Every year for Thanksgiving and Christmas she made a mound of soft, white bread dinner rolls with a yeasty dough. She always made enough extra dough to make cinnamon rolls for breakfast—gooey things that were spirals of bread filled with brown sugar and cinnamon and covered with pecans. We ate them warm with large glasses of cool milk.

Then it was time to open gifts from family. Uncle Bernard usually played Santa. We ripped paper in spite of Mom's repeated requests to keep it intact and save it for another present. The living room became a nest of festive paper, ribbons, and boxes as we all tore into our gifts to see what was inside. When Grandma was handed her fancy package, my mother sat back with a smug smile and a special twinkle in her eye. She had certainly won the prize for the most perfect gift.

Grandma took the package and said, "Oh my, isn't this fancy?" She ran her hands along the chiffon ribbon and tugged at the bow until it fell away from the box. She very carefully pulled open the paper, careful not to tear the paper with the Scotch tape. Then she folded the paper, smoothed it out, and set it aside to save it. She shook the box a little then. "I wonder what this could be?" she said.

My mother had her Kodak Instamatic ready. She wanted to capture Grandma's face at the right moment. Grandma popped the tape loose from the box, one side at a time. She set the box on her lap and remarked how heavy it was. She slowly lifted the top. When the box was opened, she admired the tissue paper for a minute. It, too, was expensive looking. She slowly opened the paper. My mother raised her camera, her index finger poised over the shutter release. Grandma lifted a deep red coat out of the box and held it up for us to see. "Well look at this!" she said. "Isn't this just gorgeous?"

Mom was stunned. What on earth had happened to the blue coat she had purchased? She thought for a minute that the sales clerk had wrapped the wrong coat, but then remembered she had watched her put it in the box and wrap it with the paper. Then she looked at Grandma who was bursting with glee. "I wish I had my camera ready to take a picture of the look on your face, Wilma," she said. Then she started to laugh.

It didn't take Mom long to figure out that the surprise was on her. Grandma had pulled off a stunner.

Maple Memories

Our simple farm home was nestled on 640 acres, seven miles south and west of Goff, a small town of 100 people in Nemaha County, in northeastern Kansas. There was always plenty to do on the farm, and the four of us worked together. Mom and Dad always did the field work and milked the cows. Mom was usually the disciplinarian because Dad was usually involved in any mischief, but he was also the protector of his girls. Susie, my blond-haired, blue-eyed, dimpled sister, and I were responsible for feeding the chickens, gathering eggs, and bringing in the cows. Susie was timid and cautious; she would hang back and let me try things first, which proves she was smarter. I was the brown-eyed brunette, and more adventurous. Of the two of us, I was the risk taker.

Our farm was home to animals galore. We raised dairy cows, Herefords, chickens, dogs, cats, and horses. All of the animals either worked to complete a necessary farm job, such as gathering cows, were sold for profit, or were raised for our own food. The horses were always my favorite. Susie and I rode the horses to bring in the cows for milking. We would always grumble about being stuck with this job, but secretly we both delighted in riding, even when the cows were stubborn. But even more than the horses, we loved the old maple tree in our huge front yard.

Maple trees are not usually considered the best or most significant works of God, but when I was ten years old, I thought our maple tree was His best work yet. It stood atop a ten-foot bank beside the road— huge, full, and loaded with leaves. The leaves were shaped like a child's hand with the fingers extended, except the fingers were webbed. Beneath the tree was a lush, green, bluegrass carpet that provided a cool base in the shade of this mammoth memory-maker. Etched in this grassy base was a well-worn path where we children dreamed and played. The great trunk had even bark that was ideal for climbing. The trunk was so big that Susie and I could stand with our arms outstretched, fingertip to fingertip on either side and never touch each other. Its main trunk split into a fork about three feet off the ground. It was a perfect design—one side of the fork for Susie and one for me.

Among the abundant limbs was a special one shaped like the capital letter "L." The base of the L rose from the split part and snaked straight out over the dusty, hard-packed, country road that formed the edge of our front yard. This was the "swing" limb. Dad had formally entrusted this fat limb with our safety when he ceremoniously tied a thickly braided, jute rope onto it and tied a knot on the end of the rope for a handhold. At first Susie and I tightly gripped the rope, barely lifting on tippy toes, as we cautiously lifted our legs and swung three to four inches from the solid, safe ground. With each new turn on the rope, our confidence and trust in our new steed grew; we rushed faster and farther each time.

In July and August, Kansas temperatures are in the high 90s to 100 degrees, and when we were growing up air conditioning was unheard of on a farm. There was never any relief. At night we would lie on the floor next to a window or sleep on the porch just to catch a breeze. Summer was also the time when the four Carlton cousins came to stay on the farm with us. Elaine was the oldest, 2 weeks older than me, very responsible but always ready to laugh. Joyce was the clown of the group. Karin, affectionately known as "The Boss," always knew how to organize us, regardless of our activity. Dean was the only boy, a lovable, big ole teddy bear. We six entertained ourselves outside for the long summer days, year in and year out.

As the hot weather droned on, the joy of riding the knotted jute rope over the road became monotonous and hot, hot, hot! We often made up games. We would race to the Ford tractor to see who would get to drive after the cows since we did not have enough horses for all of us to ride. It was tricky to fit the six of us on one small tractor, but we did it. We played in the freshly stacked hay in the barn, even though Dad told us we would stink it up so bad the cows would never eat it. (They always did!) We swam in the freshly harvested wheat as it was dumped into the truck. I remember the smell of the earthy, floral perfume and the feel of sun-warmed mounds of those golden kernels lifting and lowering us in a soothing, billowy sea.

We often played in the creek down the long hill behind the house. Where the idea came from, none of us can remember. It was a small, wandering creek that ran through the back pasture from an unknown spring miles upstream and watered our cows. The tepid water ranged from 6 to 24 inches deep. Huge old elm and cottonwood trees towered over the creek, providing an inviting respite from the scorching sun. We tromped through the muddy, tadpole-ridden water 3 to 4 hours every day. We slid down banks, had contests to see who could hold their breath the longest, and caught tadpoles in canning jars. We were always exhausted by the time we had to think about the uphill climb back to the house. The trek was made less tedious as we found cool rocks along the way and filled all of our pockets and hands with them. Mom received all six of us dirty children, clothes, towels, and rocks in the pockets back at the house day after day, and she never complained. But when the cousins left, playing in the creek was no longer fun with just the two of us sisters. The boredom of summer oozed over us.

One hot day soon after the cousins left, still feeling adventurous from weeks of romping together, I had a great idea! What we needed was a new game that would be exciting and challenge our rope-riding skills. When a car, truck, or tractor would approach, which was not common on our dirt road amid vast Kansas farmland, we would charge the road on our trusty rope.

I was eager to test the new game and wished the Carlton cousins were still with us. Susie stood by anxiously, waiting to see if this game would provide the spine-tingling excitement we suddenly lacked. With exhilaration, I grabbed the throat of that old rope and ran with all my might to the edge of the bank by the road. *Wahoo!* The ride had just enough daring and challenge! As my ride swung to an end, I returned to the bank, and I noticed Mom standing there. She was definitely unhappy—and scared.

At supper that night we had a lively family discussion about whether we got to keep our rope swing. Mom was ready to take it down. She kept repeating, "It is just not safe for you girls to go flying over the road on that ole' rope; not only that, you are beating a path through the beautiful bluegrass."

Dad, in his usual calm way, said, "School starts in a couple of weeks. How about if we let the girls keep it until then? Besides, the fun they are having outweighs the danger, and the grass can grow when the girls are grown and gone."

Hesitantly, Mom considered the proposal and reluctantly agreed. Susie and I were back in business!

Over the next couple of weeks, we charged the road at least a hundred times, and for ninety-nine of them, we achieved the desired effect. I grabbed the rope just above the knot, ran across the grass, gave a gigantic push, lunged skyward, and enjoyed the flight. But on the hundredth time, I watched the hay truck roll by out of the corner of my eye as I ran for the road and my feet left the ground.

Just before I reached the road, I heard a ripping sound. Suddenly, the rope went limp in my hands and the limb snapped back dramatically—without me attached. I flapped my arms and legs as if I might take flight and escape the inevitable. Chest-first, I crashed onto the dusty, hard-packed road.

Instantly I was starving for air. I fought to catch my breath and began a mental checklist of body parts. Each arm and leg began to move slowly; all were okay. I recalled the farm truck bulging with bales of alfalfa hay rolling by just moments before. The smell of alfalfa still lingered. As I lay there gasping for breath, I recalled Mom's warnings about "flying over the road on that ole rope." I opened my eyes to see Susie disappearing up the hill toward the house.

After a long moment my breath returned, and Mom and Susie appeared. One look at Mom, and I knew my rides on the rope swing were done forever. My dreams of sharing the joy of flying over the bank with the Carlton cousins next year dissolved into the Kansas road dust.

"No more rope swing rides," Mom said simply. I was already rehearsing reasons we should continue riding, but her eyes filled with tears and melted my protests.

After this episode, our trusty steed—or any other—was never retied to the L-shaped limb of the old maple tree. Instead, Dad took it down and retired it to the garage for far less worthy work.

Today, when Susie and I visit Dad, we get to see the mighty maple. Nearly fifty years later, I again ponder that same maple tree, with its smooth bark and the perfect limb for swinging. Susie and I can easily stretch around the beloved maple tree's trunk, even with partially extended arms. The trunk and limbs have healed from scuffs and cuts from children's shoes. Only the leaves still look the same—like children's hands with webbing.

The maple tree has not changed, but I have. I can see the magic in that old tree begin to awaken when my grandchildren eye it. I envy their youthful visions. Where does the magic go when we grow up?

Somehow the years have replaced the feelings of excitement, fear, and curiosity with memories of pleasure, peace, and sadness. I feel a knowing kinship with the mighty maple tree. It's an old childhood friend that shares some of my favorite secrets.

And Dad was right. The grass under the mighty maple is beautiful, bluegrass carpet again. And if you close your eyes and listen carefully, you can hear the gleeful laughter of two little girls under a loving old maple tree on a dusty Kansas road.

Sidearm

Our father has enrolled a brother and me in a summer baseball league. I don't think our father has asked us if we wanted to play baseball. One of his friends is coaching our team, and I figure that's why we are going to play. My brother and I ride in our father's pickup out to a dilapidated practice field carved out of the weeds next to the old National Guard Armory building. There is a swampy pond nearby, optimistically called College Lake, where teenagers come at night to park and smoke cigarettes and drink beer. At one end of the lake is an area called Motorcycle Hills, a spider's web of undulating dirt trails that wind through red clay gullies and around mesquite trees. The kids who aren't old enough to park and smoke and drink ride their bicycles and minibikes here.

The baseball field is an expanse of rocky ground bordered on the west and south by the dirt road leading to the Armory, and the Armory's parking lot; and on the east and north by mesquite trees and cattails that lead down to the lake's edge. The town sends out a few men occasionally to mow the field, but it is not one of their top priorities. The backstop behind home plate consists of rusty chicken wire strung across three long metal pipes inserted into the ground. The wire droops and sags tiredly on the pipes; it has been hanging here in this lonely place for a long, long time.

Our coach retrieves three canvas bags of sand from his pickup and places them at what he thinks are the correct locations for first, second, and third bases. Home plate is a rubber mat cut into the proper shape: a square with a triangle added to one side. It, too, is retrieved from the coach's pickup and plopped on the ground a little distance in front of the backstop. The pitcher's mound is not a mound at all. It is just an area where the weeds have been worn away a little, roughly on a line between home plate and second base.

I know only a few of the boys on our team. The few that I know have, like me, just finished the second grade at Oliver Elementary. Most of the other boys on the team are bigger boys from the third grade, and there are a couple of first-graders, like my brother. Some fathers decide to stay and watch us practice, and they stand off to the side talking with one another. They yell at their sons when a fly ball drops behind them or a ground ball goes through their legs, which is often. Our players are not very good at baseball. The fathers must have been great baseball players when they were boys, because they yell out to us everything we are doing wrong.

The coach wants to know if I can pitch. He takes me to the pitcher's mound that's not really a mound and says, "Let's see how you can throw."

I'm not sure what he wants me to do. I throw the ball to the boy who is playing second base, which surprises the boy. He throws the ball back to me and looks at the coach.

"No, no, throw it to the catcher," my father yells from outside the third base line.

I can't remember which one of the players is the catcher. I throw the ball back to the second baseman.

"No, for God's sake, throw it to the catcher!" my father yells, exasperated. I've never heard him say the word "baseball" before today, but he always wants my brothers and me to be good at whatever we are doing.

The coach gets the ball from the second baseman and walks back to the pitcher's mound.

"Right there," he points to a third-grade boy who is crouching behind home plate and frowning at me. "Throw the ball to him, he's the catcher." He hands me the ball.

I throw the ball to the catcher, and the catcher throws it back.

"Keep throwing the ball, and throw it pretty hard right to the catcher," the coach tells me. He stands behind me and watches.

I throw the ball to the catcher for a while. The catcher holds up his mitt and I try to hit it with the ball. It's not that hard to do. I've thrown a lot of rocks at empty beer bottles and through the windows of the old bus parked in back of my grandparents' house, and it's just about the same thing.

After a while the coach stops me. "Where did you learn to throw like that?" he wants to know.

I can't remember ever having learned to throw. Throwing is just something everyone can do, although I know some people are good throwers and some people are bad throwers, like my mother. "Don't know, I guess," I tell the coach. I think I must be doing something wrong.

"You throw sidearm, did you know that?" the coach asks me.

I don't know what sidearm means. "No," I say. "Is that okay?"

He smiles. "Oh yeah, that's just fine. Lots of kids that start throwing balls and rocks at a young age throw sidearm because they can throw harder that way. Best way to skip a rock on water, ain't it?"

I know this is true. "Yeah," I say.

"Fellow name of Walter Johnson, a long time ago, won over 400 games in the big leagues, second all-time to a fellow name of Cy Young. Threw sidearm like you," the coach tells me.

By the time we play our first game, against a team with some other boys I know from Oliver Elementary, I am one of our team's pitchers. I have learned to wind up and throw the baseball as hard as I can. Over the course of the summer I learn that throwing sidearm scares some of the batters on the teams we play, and some of their mothers yell out for our coach to tell me to stop throwing like I do.

"He's gonna hit my boy!" they holler from the seats behind the backstop, their embarrassed husbands wishing they would sit down and be quiet.

My coach yells out to them, "It's alright. He only hits every other one!"

And people laugh.

Imagination at Play

A new generation of kids exists today. With a flip of a finger they can bring up Bangkok or with their thumbs they can destroy virtual alien hordes. In my youth, the world was all out there... across a frozen pond or down the train tracks. Our world was material, but it was shaped by our flourishing imaginations as well.

When scientists are concerned about the extinction of a species, say the Spotted Owl in the old-growth forests of the American Northwest, they are really speaking of an entire habitat that is endangered, not just a generation of owls. If I talk about imagination and a particular kind of childhood, I find that it, too, existed in a particular time and space, more or less extinct now.

I grew up in Hillsboro, a small community in central Kansas during the period after Eisenhower and before Nixon. But I thought little of that world outside my habitat, beyond the fact that the streets running north and south on the east side of Main were named after presidents. I lived on Lincoln until I was nine. Then my family moved to Wilson.

Hillsboro in that era was not an extraordinary place. The population hovered around 3,000. The town was largely filled with people of Mennonite extraction: church-going and conservative. There was a small, church-affiliated college, but the economy was largely dependent on the surrounding farms. These details might have been otherwise. And I do think, for many of my generation—let's say for kids who lived in a coherent urban neighborhood—they were indeed quite different, if we shared the quality of imagination because of certain cultural characteristics we had in common.

As a child and a youth, while I knew more about any of the world that existed outside my rural Kansas town than a Spotted Owl does of the world outside its old-growth forest, certain elements in that isolated time and place that led to a flourishing of imagination—and ultimately human development—among many of my generation.

Consider ice skating and hockey on the pond near my house. When temperatures dropped well below freezing for several days, my brother and I would go get the small sledge hammer from the shop and walk across the highway to Vogt's pond to check the ice. After breaking though, we would take off our gloves and stick our hands into the ice-cold water to check with our fingers and thumb just how the thickness of the ice was progressing. Eventually the ice would strengthen, and we would venture onto the pond, sliding carefully away from the edge. And finally, we were jumping up and down on the ice, where it was still shallow in case we broke through.

I learned to ice skate wearing the white, cast-off figure skates of the older sister of my best friend. Starting with the skates we had and with sticks broken to length from branches on the bank, we played hockey. Shoes dropped six feet apart were goals. A smashed beer can (or whatever was handy) made a puck. We played for hours at a time.

We made our play from what was at hand. Vogt's pond became Klassen's pond in time. The body of water itself was perhaps a little smaller in area than a football field, shaped like most Kansas ponds in some variation of a teardrop, heavier at the earthen dam end, thinning to nothing where an intermittent creek drained into it.

The creek bed, dry, except when it rained, coursed underneath the highway. My friends and I played in that culvert. You could follow the creek upstream, so to speak, as it ran through a vacant lot. Willow trees large enough to clamber up to grew along the drainage. We played in that lot and sledded on its short slopes when there was enough snow. The creek continued back into our yard, and under a bridge, mostly put there for the idea. That bridge itself was little more than two heavy wooden planks spanning the line where the stormwater flowed. After passing the hedge on the north edge of our yard, always a good spot to hide for numerous games, the creek finally passed upstream, through our neighbor's yard, until it came to the street, where storm gutters fed into it. We played in the gutters, too. They were a special playground for engineers with childish minds. We built our own earthen dams, creating teardrop-shaped ponds in those gutters.

Some of what we consider imagination, I suppose, is simply a recognition of patterns and a play on endless variations to notice—even if somewhat unconsciously—what interests us in our world. Water, in its many forms, including how it shaped the ground as it followed its natural course, was of significant interest to us. Perhaps that interest itself is instinctual.

But today the words "ice" and "hockey" conjure up many images of bulky men, smashing each other into boards that define a rink.

As innocents, we simply started with frozen water, a surface that was smooth, slippery. Our place to play was unlike the earth we ran on in other seasons. Skates, the simple idea of a metal blade attached to the ends of our legs, gave us purchase on the ice. We could skate fast and turn sharp, all while remaining upright—once we got the knack. And getting the knack was part of our fun.

The sticks and whatever we initially used for a puck were just what we took to make a game of it all. Ice hockey was not something we made up entirely. We'd seen the game played on TV. But hockey itself was in truth little more than the germ of an idea. And we most emphatically did not start by being driven to a designated building and placed under the supervision of a coach. We made up most of our own specifics.

Probably after the first winter when we started playing on the ice, my brother and I got real hockey skates for Christmas, opened early that year. We got real sticks and hard rubber pucks. As technology often does, these things increased our reach, our ability to manipulate our environment.

But that's what the broken branches were to begin with, an extension of our arms to play with a thing—in our case a beer can or maybe another chunk of wood. Those things became a way to focus our energy and interest into an objective. The rules—as we mostly made them up—became a way to contain the game so that it became more than just flailing on the ice. We moved from the simplest of elements, frozen water, and added layer upon layer until we reached the level of game. Its function was to create purpose, even though we barely managed to keep score at times. Our life was largely made up of whole cloth. And playing hockey, as we called it, was but a swatch of it. In our play, we went from things to purpose, and importantly, we made it up as we went.

So I have been working up to this: Imagination was a key ingredient in our play. Most of what we did came from within ourselves. No adults told us what to do or how to do it. We created our own rules to make the game fair and interesting by our own measure. If there were only a few of us, the pairs of shoes were dropped closer together. If it was just me and my brother, we set up only one goal, one of us skating the puck out beyond an imaginary line before coming back hard at the other, who was now the defender.

Certainly we must have spoken of rules at times, but often they formed naturally. No slap shots, for example, where a player brings the end of his stick hard onto the ice just at the edge of the puck, slapping it into the air, a hard-flying missile. No one wanted a painfully, bruised shin, or worse, so we didn't do it. It wasn't exactly the Golden Rule, but it was a good approximation. We didn't need boards. Checking wasn't part of our game, although an occasional hard collision was inevitable. We officiated ourselves.

The thing is, I don't think we were geniuses. Nor did we spend much time trying to decide what would be the best way to structure our play for maximum satisfaction. We simply started with what was at hand and played within our environment using our imaginations. We weren't trying to be athletes. We weren't training for something else. We were playing.

On the ice it was like this. With a push against a blade, I could glide tens of feet. Several pushes and then a push-glide, push-glide, push-glide, and I sped over the ice. Leaning one way or the other, I skated into graceful sweeping curves. Crossing one skate over the other, I would accelerate as I turned. Then with a little hop, I would turn the blades perpendicular and scrape to a stop, ice crystals flying.

I, myself, made this happen. But it was also physics. This was how the laws of nature interacted with my efforts. And then, when my friends and I added sticks, chasing the puck and each other, we became a blur. Every moment was the one we were in. Shoulder to shoulder, we raced down the ice, one trying to maintain control of the puck, the other trying to steal it. A pass to your teammate just in time. A shot. Score. Of course, the sensations seem magical to me looking back. Certainly we reveled in them when we lived them.

But what I am now trying to recall is the habitat in which our imaginations flourished. Hockey was heaven—sometimes. On the ice, pure speed and agility became part of our beings for moments, extended moments.

But when there was no ice, we still had our imaginations, and we made other kinds of paradises. Vogt's pond was, after all, an ordinary pond, the drainage of the streets of a small, rural Kansas town. It was not picturesque. Start with water. Cold weather, sometimes biting. You get ice. Add sticks, raw or refined. Something for a puck. What made it possible for us to turn that pond into the only place on earth I wanted to be—for a time, at least? Imagination.

Growing up in Hillsboro, my town was a playground. Technology hadn't progressed as far as it has today. I watched some TV. I read quite a bit. But I was drawn outside to play. Again, it's not that I personally made good choices, the world out of doors was fundamentally interesting to me. Outside was the space in which I could exercise my imagination. The nature of the space was undefined; they weren't designed to be a playground—we imagined them to become one.

On Wilson Street, the houses were newer, one-story ranch-style houses with plenty of yard. Over a block, on Adams Street, the houses were older and of a corresponding older style. And so it went. To get to school we took one path or another, sometimes through alleys. I hardly remember ever not walking or riding a bicycle. I didn't lock my bicycle once I got to school. Traffic on the streets was light. And the word pedophile was unspoken. In the summer, we dropped our bikes on the grass outside the pool and swam some. Mostly we played in the water or competed in splashing exhibitions. But never was there an adult waiting in an idling car.

Our town was a kind of old-growth habitat. Almost everywhere we turned, there were niches of wildness. Somewhat raw spaces were waiting for our inquiring nature to find a fit. They were unregulated and unsupervised spaces between the places we were going, with the pace and intervening choices of direction left up to us.

And in a purely political sense, I suppose, we were libertarians and communitarians at the same time. These were the rules I lived by: Go to school. Listen to your teachers. Be home for supper. Usually, when I walked out the front door, my mother would add one more: "Be good." Space. Safety. Structure, but not too much. We were expected to do well and have good times.

Let's go back to my backyard. When people speak of The Good Old Days, games like Kick The Can and Hide And Seek get mentioned as if everyone knows what they were. But those names are mere pegs, just as "ice hockey" is a peg. In my world, a hockey goal was a pair of shoes. We had no Zamboni. If the ice was rough because the wind had been blowing or there was snow at the moment of freezing, the ice was rough. We adapted.

"Spotted Owl" is also a peg. In the study of ecology we talk of species and genus and so on. But you always come back to individuals. My friends and I played a version of Hide And Seek we called

"Midnight Ghost" or sometimes "Gray Wolf." I assume variations of this species of the genre 'children's hiding and chasing games' exist around the world—maybe even in today's United States as well.

This is how we played our particular game. Everyone played. I can only now guess who that included—Mark and Steve from across the street, and my best friend in those days, Dave, and his brother Nate, and possibly Joe, who lived on Adams Street, my younger brother, James, maybe my sister, sometimes. Whoever was there stood on our front porch counting, "One o'clock, two o'clock, …, and on to twelve o'clock—Midnight Ghost," while I—let's say in this iteration I was "it" —went around to the backyard to hide somewhere in the many shadows of our neighborhood night.

Then everyone else would venture out, looking for me. If I spotted them first, I would jump out from behind a bush or from under the bridge over that same dry creek bed that drains into Vogt's pond and tag them before they could get away. But when someone spotted me, they would shout "Midnight Ghost" or "Gray Wolf." Frequent discussions about which terminology should be used were never resolved. But whichever alarm was sounded, everyone would sprint, dodging me as needed, back to base. Those caught came back to hide with me, becoming the next round's ghosts or wolves—according to their denominational affiliation.

It is not necessary to go into details of the game to consider some elements from that time which are considerably rarer today. There was nothing digital or virtual about it. Where did the game come from? I don't remember learning it from some elder in the neighborhood. Who decided there would be a game on a particular night? There was no photocopied schedule on the refrigerators around town. Our play didn't just happen as if by magic, our games were simply a product of our habitat—our cultural as well as physical environment.

Consider another of our diversions. Long before Facebook and Farmville, my brother and I played farm on the driveway in front of our house. Each square of cement, I'm guessing about eight by eight feet, was our section, the road system in Kansas which laid out a grid of square-mile sections. Using pieces of limestone gravel, we drew our farms on the driveway sections: the roads, the fields, and so on.

And yet another game played in our yard as well as one we entirely invented we called "Gestapo." After running a long extension cord out to the bridge, one guard with a spotlight would defend 360 degrees of darkness while the rest of us tried to creep up to the bridge from behind the back hedge or the Pampas grass or maybe just a shadowy depression before being spotted.

Again, that creek running through our backyard made for a more interesting game. Had the specific lay of the land been different, however, we would likely have played our hiding and chasing games in other yards. We always managed to find ways to play, that is, to channel our energy into activities that were interesting and fun.

We roamed the town—sometimes outside it. A favorite activity was hiking the railroad tracks. That's all it was. We hiked out of town along the railroad tracks. As we walked, we discussed whether we would go to the first trestle or the next and so on. If someone had assigned that task to us it would have been grinding work, the awkwardness of adjusting your gait to land your feet on the ties, not on the sharp stones in between, trying to balance on the rails themselves to avoid the ties and the stones. But in our imagination, it was all play.

These games were a conscious deployment of imagination of a kind that seemed to occur naturally when I was growing up. I remember that our games in my youth tended to include everyone. In winter hockey games, sometimes we included the much younger brothers of my best friend, who we sometimes skated circles around, urging them off the ice after an awkward fall so they wouldn't get cold. Sometimes their dad, Doc, joined us. He had grown up in Canada and couldn't resist joining us to play on the ice on occasion. I don't suppose that this was an entirely natural occurrence, and certainly particular groups of "everyone" selected themselves among our different games all the time.

And perhaps a form of the "Watch out for your brother" rule helped us achieve the level of harmony we enjoyed.

I believe we all crave the opportunity to exercise our imagination. It is not, in my opinion, only child's play. It is a natural and satisfying function of a healthy mind. But of course, there is another element from my childhood environment that I haven't yet fully mentioned— time. We had time to fill. We kids didn't have to labor in the fields. Mowing the lawn hardly cut significantly into play time. And there was time after doing dishes for a game of Midnight Ghost before bed time. If necessity is the mother of invention, then time is the mother of imagination. And space is the father. And what if imagination is a Spotted Owl? It flourished on Vogt's pond in my day. Does it still play out on other ponds? It flourished in my backyard and neighborhood. Are they gone?

These days, I see some kids in Lawrence roaming Massachusetts Street after school. Sometimes with skateboards. I'm glad to see that some measure of safety and an occasional absence of grown-up supervision still exists. But are they making up games? Are they imagining challenges and making up purposes to stimulate their minds and their perceptions of the stuff around them into more than the simple matter it is? Is there enough time and space for children (and adults) to play, and do they have opportunities to tap their imaginations to explore and create?

I would suggest that mine was not a superior generation of human kids—that the imagination we developed grew out of our habitat and opportunity. We never lacked the raw materials for imagination to flourish. We had time and space. We had security that we took for granted. And significantly, we didn't have an overabundance of things or structures that tended to define what and how we should do things. Our fun, and our development as human beings, was in many respects up to us. We made up many important parts of our own lives as we went along.

I am not opposed to playing in virtual environments, but they lack the raw, open-ended nature of real environments. I'm simply not sure how, without the kinds of physical and social characteristics of the habitat I grew up in, kids, and then adults, will manage to nurture the quality of imagination necessary to turn vacant lots and dry creeks and dirty little ponds into playgrounds and winter wonderlands.

We, me and my friends, learned to imagine our environment as a challenging place to strive and play and explore. We weren't special. We were sheltered. But we also ran wild. We grew up in a good time and place and we made the most of it. This habitat appears to be endangered. We should not be nostalgic. We should be concerned. Who is responsible for preserving the habitat of childhood?

Mr. Carson

M r. Carson lives with his father in the house across the alley from our house. They keep a garden we can see through the cracks in a tall wooden fence around their property. During the summers, one of the Carsons' trees always hangs a few big plums over their fence, and my brothers and I watch them ripen day by day, and think of ways we might get them down.

Mr. Carson is an old man, and his father is older still. We call the father Old Mr. Carson. Mr. Carson's mother died, but we don't know why she died. Now it's just Mr. Carson and Old Mr. Carson living across the alley. Old Mr. Carson wears a felt hat and walks with a cane. I see him sometimes, through the cracks in the fence, kneeling in his garden next to the okra or the squash. When we play football in our backyard, Mr. Carson peers through the fence cracks and watches us for a while. If he sees that we notice him, he will at first pull back from the fence, but soon he will be watching again.

One day, Mr. Carson walks outside the fence and across the alley to watch us play our game. He stands in the weeds just outside our backyard, near where my parents have tried a time or two to make a garden of their own. He stands with his arms folded across his chest and watches. We wave to him and he gives us a shy little wave in return. On the days that follow, when he sees us playing, Mr. Carson peeks through his fence, then crosses the alley, and then comes into our yard. He comes farther and farther into the yard as the summer drags on. Finally, he comes closer to us than ever before, and one of my brothers tosses him the football. The ball hits his hands, but his hands are stiff and the ball bounces away. He stoops and hops after it, grunting excitedly, then throws the ball back to my brother. He doesn't catch or throw very well, but he tries.

We know that Mr. Carson is much older than we—he is even older than our parents—but we soon find that he is different in other ways. When he speaks, it takes a little time for his words to come together and come out. He moves his mouth, trying hard to get the words going. And when the words finally come out, they come out pressurized, in a stuttering, stammering flow that is impossible to understand. His hands move about in stiff, jerky movements when he speaks. The top plate of his dentures is always loose, clattering behind his lips with a mind of its own. He wears slacks, dress shoes, and a short-sleeved plaid shirt. This becomes his football uniform. He comes into our yard almost every day for a while, joining my brothers and some neighborhood kids and me in our games of tackle football. We don't say much to him. You can't say, "Mr. Carson, you go long and cut right at that old tire." He wouldn't know what to do. He doesn't understand much of what is going on, but he tries.

Mr. Carson blends seamlessly into our group—as seamlessly as any 50-year-old man can blend into a group of elementary school children. He drinks from the water hose during breaks in our games, like the rest of us. Like the rest of us, he climbs over Mrs. Keen's fence to retrieve our football when it flies into her yard. He sits in the shade with us, sweating and sipping Kool-Aid our mother has brought outside. She hands him an icy glass and says, "Here, Mr. Carson."

Our mother is worried that one of us will get hurt, playing tackle football with a grown man. One night at supper she tells our father, "I'm worried someone will get hurt."

My brothers and I have fallen from trees and off the backs of horses; we have crashed our bicycles at top speed on the brick street in front of our house; we have been run over by cattle and hogs; we have pummeled one another with hard little fists and bony knees at every opportunity; and we have hit one another in the head with rocks and clods of dirt.

"I guess you're right," our father says to our mother. And then to us, "You boys take it easy on Mr. Carson."

My brothers and I do not take it easy on Mr. Carson, nor do we take it easy on one another. Many times during the summer a brother will suffer a scraped elbow or a skinned knee, and he might lie on the ground whimpering for a while. But soon he will have had enough of being called a "momma's baby" and a "little sissy boy" and he will get up, pick the grass out of the shiny patch of blood on his arm, wipe his nose, and rejoin the game. Mr. Carson will have a shirt pocket ripped off on some afternoons, and will go home with grass stains and holes at the knees of his slacks, and with some minor scrapes of his own. No one is ever seriously hurt.

One afternoon in the course of our game, I make a long throw toward Mr. Carson, who has wandered unnoticed to a corner of the yard next to the house. Brothers and neighborhood friends lift their faces to watch as the ball arcs above them toward Mr. Carson. He extends his arms, and the ball falls neatly into them and rests there. There is a moment of collective astonishment. Mr. Carson has caught a pass. He stands there, bewildered and blinking his eyes behind thick glasses. Then, his face a mask of wonder and disbelief, he looks down at the ball in his hands. All of us cheer and whoop. We run over to him and jump up to clap him on the back and shoulders. He stutters and stammers excitedly, dentures clattering, trying to express something. He clutches the ball tightly to his chest for a while.

At dusk, Old Mr. Carson opens the gate in the tall fence and yells for Mr. Carson to come home for supper. Mr. Carson gives us a little wave and runs toward the gate, elbows pumping, head tilted up, glasses bouncing on his nose. He runs flat-footed, leaning forward, like he is falling down. He doesn't run very well, but he tries.

Cecil

A s far back as I can remember, I have been fascinated by fire, from the leaping colors around the logs in a fireplace to concentrating on the flicker of a candle's flame until the fluid wax became a sculpture. I even loved staring into the old metal trash barrel to make sure it had burned down far enough to be safe to leave it. As children, sometimes we became too curious and went beyond the boundaries of safety. Once I tried to melt a plastic Indian doll on the screen over the trash barrel, and when I tried to catch it before it fell through, I burned my thumb and right forefinger. While my father held an ice cube on my huge new blister, followed by Unguentine and a Band-Aid, he talked. I tried not to cry.

Even though I was barely old enough to understand, he gave me the oft-repeated Reminder Speech about being able to learn something from every person I met, no matter how young or old, rich or poor, smart or not so much. He said that each and every person who crossed my path, and stayed, or didn't, did so for some pre-ordained reason. It was my job to discover what that reason could be. He wondered if anyone had ever told me not to play with fire. I am certain someone did, probably him. But I still loved to. Little did I know . . .

On a breathlessly hot and still July night when I was not quite seven years old, Mom shepherded us all down to the basement as the thunderstorm warnings with potential for hail and tornadoes interrupted the program on the TV. It was a Sunday evening, because we were watching "The Big Picture" when the warnings came on and the power went off. The sirens echoed through the neighborhood. Booming cracks of thunder sounded like giant trees falling down on the house; they could have split the sky. After a quick, light rain, it began to hail golf balls. My older brother ran out to gather some in an aluminum pitcher so he could make Kool-Aid.

Suddenly, the atmosphere became totally silent, and we dared not breathe. My mother Dorothy frantically tried to find a station on the transistor radio she stored in the emergency kit. She was determined to be prepared. The stairwell and the basement were lit up with candles like Christmas. Blankets and sleeping bags covered the pool table. We waited.

When the wind and hard rain that followed finally faded out at about 10:00 p.m., Dad went out to check the damage. A huge old tree had split down the middle in the side yard, falling only a few short feet from the roofline; another down the block had fallen across the street. I tip-toed behind him, aghast at the damage and the melting hail.

We looked up at the same time. The sky to the south was a bright golden yellow. Daddy noticed me and told me to go home and tell Mom to keep us all inside. But it was too late, I knew it was a fire. I snuck out and up the alley and found him again. The power was off all over town, making that golden glow the center of this dark world. I can recall the details of what happened next as vividly as if it happened yesterday. They are forever melted into my memory.

Cecil's house had been the pale blue of a robin's egg. It was fairly square, and the yard was dotted with a few zinnias here and there. A big sagging vegetable garden out back took up most of the space between the house and the alley. There was no fencing, no flower boxes, no fancy bric-a-brac. It was a simple, nice little house for a nice little family.

Lighting struck the little blue house where Cecil, his wife, and three little children, all under 5 years of age, had slept peacefully before the storm. At first we watched the crackling flames leaping higher and higher from two blocks away. We moved closer. They were beautiful and grand, hypnotizing and enticing. The fire consumed the house and everything in it.

Including Cecil's wife and three children. I felt sick, nauseated, and horribly sad. At that young age and standing safely at my father's side, the knowledge that Cecil's wife and three little children were sleeping soundly before the fire was deeply haunting. Perhaps they didn't wake up, they inhaled the smoke while they were still asleep. Perhaps they never knew the pain and agony that wrenched their father's body and broke his spirit as well as the hearts of the firemen and neighbors, like my father, who came to see if they could help. They couldn't. No one could.

I remember watching Cecil try to run back in, watching the firemen hold him back harshly as he fought. They shouted in unison, "It's too late, Cecil! Cecil! It's too late!! Do you want to *die,* too?"

He tried to wrench himself away crying, "Yes! Yes!! Yes!!!"

But the firemen held him tighter, knowing full well that he would go back in if he could. They themselves would have done the same. Finally, he gave in, collapsing into a heaving pile—sobbing, pleading with God to take him, too. The blaze began to subside. In hard shock, he wiped the blackened perspiration from his face and neck and stared until there were no more embers, just the smell of wet smoke and ashes, deep like deep river of mud all over the floor of the crater that had been a basement. When the firemen turned the hoses off, a deadly quiet gradually replaced the thunder, the sirens, and the keening of Cecil, the husband and father, leaving only the echo of a few distant crickets singing a mournful song in the night.

Everything was gone—there was nothing left. Someone spoke of searching for the skeletal remains. I heard Cecil ask weakly, "What for? They were burned down, down to the ground together. Let them lie, together. Let them stay as they dreamed, when God called their spirits together."

For months afterward I replayed these images in my mind, imagining over and over the final moments of Cecil's family.

Early the next morning, people were out observing the storm damage and praying over the torched rubble of Cecil's blue house. My little brother, our neighbor Danny, and I went out to explore, too. Finding the basement open and littered with burnt beams, we climbed down to a wall of shelves full of canned goods. Most were covered in soot and some had eerie heat cracks, but not all. Some looked untouched. We debated whether to take some home to our mothers. Suddenly, an old man appeared and hollered at us, rather gruffly, "Get out'ta there right now and go home."

Dad explained it to us later like this. We had been desperate for rain. Crops were shriveling up in the fields. No watering was allowed. Everyone's lawns were golden brown. Dad said, "All it took was one electrified flash of lightning across the sky that landed right on that house with no lightning rod. In a split second, the house went up in flames."

Up in smoke—up and up and up into a golden midnight sky, I thought. In a poof, everything was gone. "Except Cecil." I added.

That's how it began. Cecil "carried on," in the sense that he dragged his bones and body in a forward motion, but he no longer had any particular direction or any specified goal. His mind and his heart had flown up with the cinders of his family. Everyone in our neighborhood knew this. He was a broken man. Gradually, from that day forward, everyone in town called him "crazy," and he fit the part.

Cecil could not work. He refused to have a home, not while his wife and little ones drifted all alone. He roamed the streets by day and night. He knew everyone in town, including me and all of my girlfriends, by name. He knew everywhere we went, the cars we rode in or drove in, too, who went with whom, and who didn't.

Most adults cautioned us, "Stay away. You don't know what he might do someday." Nevertheless, he roamed freely in and around our town for many, many years. His eyes were always watery with unspeakable tears, but at times he made people laugh and smile and giggle.

I remember finding Cecil hiding behind the giant scalloped concrete pillars that guarded the Citizens State Bank downtown. It was a cool spot in the heat of the day. He would delight in jumping out and growling at some serious-minded banking customers who smiled in awkward embarrassment and entered the bank with lighter hearts. I remember watching this with my friends from across the street and laughing until our sides ached.

Sometimes after school, a group of us would go uptown for some concocted and urgent reason. The high school kids would take up all the spaces at Smith's drugstore, so we would go to Woolworth's lunch counter, where the "hoods" hung out, according to my mother. We would buy two small Cokes and share an order of homemade fries for 26 cents with tax. We watched the older kids with leather jackets and slicked-back hair who hung around outside. They were "so cool." Cecil was often sitting on one of the iron benches that lined the sidewalk around the Courthouse.

Some of the girls would giggle and pick up their pace when they saw him. If we had to wait for the light to turn green, we might even change direction to avoid passing too close to Cecil. When they kicked it up and ran, I ran along, too—to be part of the crowd. Not because I was afraid of him. He never actually grabbed anyone I knew or heard about. But my friends would yell at me to "hurry up," so I did.

Myself, I was really only afraid of making eye contact with Cecil. We locked eyes occasionally, and I always looked away quickly because I didn't want him to see my tears welling up. He may have been a "boogeyman" to the other girls, but I saw those pools of sorrow, so deep I feared I might fall in. I can still recall those watery dark eyes, lined with eternal redness and full of sadness, as if I saw him yesterday. Unlike my friends, I remembered that night of storm and fire. Even when he grinned and laughed as we ran away, the effigy of that tragic night always caught up with me.

As we grew older, we found jobs during the summer that didn't interfere with our swimming pool rituals. Besides working at the family grocery store and babysitting, my first real job was at the Dairy Queen. This particular night I was off at 7:00 p.m., and my new guy was coming to pick me up to go riding up and down main street, as usual. Waiting with my girlfriend, I heard someone call me, loudly and gravely, "Kaa-*thi*."

My friend heard it, too. We knew it was Cecil again. We looked everywhere, but we couldn't find him. We concluded that he must be hiding among the many trees on the back side of the block. From then on, I walked home from work with the eerie feeling of being watched. I didn't say anything to anyone else for fear they'd call me crazy.

I don't know if Cecil was aware of my unease, but he was aware of other things. One day, Cecil went into the bank and walked up to my mother's teller window. He said he didn't have any money but he wanted to tell her something that she needed to know. He said that of all the girls in town, I was the most special. That was all. He just wanted her to know that I was the nicest one of all.

By the time she got home, Mom wanted to know from me— *immediately*—what I had done or said to provoke Cecil to say such a thing. I told her the truth—I had never spoken to Cecil in my life. Embarrassed, I reported that I thought he may have called my name a few times, but I certainly had not answered. Secretly, I was elated that he saw something special in me. I finally understood the reason he crossed my path. He gave me that great gift.

્ ્ ્

Now, decades and lifetimes later, in my own back yard, I watch the night sky and the fire, and still I think of Cecil. My chin resting on my hands, my hands resting on my rake, I stare into the fire of my "burn pile." I hear a cinder snap and watch it fly through the night, a little light, full of life, a memory of one, and others. Their energy can never be destroyed, even by the blue blazes at the center of what appears to be their destruction. In fact, it's only change—Cecil's watery eyes, finally laughing, and me, finally smiling. Thank you, Cecil. See ya' around.

Taking Cover

My healthy respect for swirling funnels of terror began to develop in 1953 when I was five. Every year our local television station would air a special viewing of *The Wizard of Oz* at Christmas time. We would eagerly anticipate its appearance, as movies were not often shown on television. I always forgot, until I started watching, that parts of this story scared me. The flying monkeys and the wicked witch and her broom didn't worry me too much, but I was traumatized by the long, snaky black funnel that dropped out of the sky, striking Dorothy's home and carrying her away. I knew that the monkeys and witches weren't real, but the tornado could be. It seemed so uncontrollable—a glimpse of a world where the adults weren't in charge and bad things could happen, even to good girls. I knew with certainty that I never wanted to live anywhere like Kansas. However, the threat of severe weather was also a regular occurrence during the warm, humid spring days of my childhood in Kalamazoo, Michigan.

WKMI, the only local radio station, was often playing in the background in our home, and severe weather announcements would send me into a tailspin of worry. Would there be a tornado? Would our house be hit and carried away in the sky like Dorothy's? I was afraid of heights. Would we have to go to the basement? Should we go there right away? These thoughts ravaged my imagination every time.

And I didn't like going into the basement either. The stairs were steep and the walls and pipes were full of cobwebs. Under the stairs was an enormous old, disconnected, rusty water heater that loomed menacingly underneath me as I cautiously descended into the dank, cramped space. No doubt about it, though, if a tornado was coming I'd fly down those steps at lightning speed, grateful for a basement to shelter me.

I envied my neighbor, Susie. Her basement had an enclosed room where her family could go if there was a tornado. It made sense to me to have a separate room with the sole purpose of protecting you from tornadoes, even though this one was small and dingy. Susie and I never went in, but its presence comforted me.

I was always planning ahead for disaster from the time I was about 6. If I heard the word "tornado" on the radio, I would gather my most cherished possessions. In one hand I carried my small Ginny doll, stuffed into her blue suitcase full of clothes, and under the other arm I stored several books, especially ones about horses. Then I sat nervously on the living room couch with my assembled treasures. It was important that I could carry everything in one trip, and as I sat, waiting apprehensively for the tornado, I calculated my speed in getting to the basement stairs.

The first of many times my mother found me in this watchful position, she said to me curiously, "Sherry, what are you doing?"

"Waiting for the tornado," I responded. She had to be nuts even to ask, and where were *her* favorite things to save? Again and again she tried to reassure me that there wasn't a tornado yet and that there might not be one at all. Gently, she explained that if one were to come we would have plenty of time to go to the basement. I wanted to believe her, but I'd seen *The Wizard of Oz* and I wasn't taking any chances.

At Parkwood Elementary School, we practiced tornado drills as if we were training for the Olympics. We all knew what to do, where to go, and how to cover our heads the second that dreaded, piercing, wailing siren went off. We never knew whether it was a drill or the real thing, so we always assumed that the tornado was almost upon us, and we frantically dashed for cover, our hearts beating hard in response to the adrenaline shooting through our bodies. The teachers all had stop watches; they timed us to see how fast we could reach our safe designations.

When I was in the fourth grade, Miss Maggie Brehms' classroom had large windows along the south wall, overlooking the playground. Our collective task, when the sirens sounded, was to shove all the chairs out of the way, push our large tables under the bank of windows, and get under them until we were reassuringly informed by an announcement over the school's PA system that it was safe to come out. One day a siren went off and, like a herd of gazelles, we sprang into action. The chairs went flying, the tables banged against the walls, and twenty-two students and our teacher, stopwatch in hand, huddled underneath. Miss Brehms praised us for accomplishing this in 20 seconds, our best recorded time ever. We all felt pretty darn proud as we remained under those tables until the gym teacher came to our classroom and said, "What are you doing? This is a fire drill!"

Several of us exchanged startled glances before catapulting out from under the tables, in as orderly a manner as possible for children who don't want to be burned alive, and running (in single file) down the hall and out the front door. We were the last to leave, and in some disgrace because we had prolonged the time it took to empty the school.

Sometimes we were let out early when severe weather threatened. In those days we didn't have Doppler radar to track storms. Predicting the direction and intensity of a tornado was more of a guessing game, and the school administration would send us home if it seemed remotely possible that a tornado could strike. We were never in imminent danger, but I did not understand this. To me, they were insane to let us out to get home on our own. I had to walk a long ways, and I was terrified by the vision of being plucked off the ground and swept off to God-knows-where if I couldn't get home fast enough. Dorothy's house swirling in the black vortex was well embedded in my head.

One such early release occurred when I was in the third grade. It was windy, and the air felt unstable, warm and humid one minute and noticeably cooler the next. We were all restless and uneasy, sensing something not quite right in our orderly world. An hour before school normally dismissed, the principal announced that we were all to go straight home as fast as possible, since a storm may be coming. At eight years old I was sure I wouldn't make it, and I ran the mile home. I was so frightened that I started singing "America the Beautiful," and moved on to "My Country Tis of Thee" at the top of my lungs to keep myself from panicking. At last I was home, ahead of any tornado. To my relief the sky was still blue and no rain drops had appeared. I burst into my house, panting from running and singing, to confront a very surprised mother, who did not know that school had been let out early.

"What are you doing here?" she asked.

Amazed that she didn't know about the tornado, I said, "They think there will be a tornado, and they told us to go straight home."

"Oh," she said, taking note of my frenzied appearance, "The tornado is about sixty miles west of here, and it probably won't come to Kalamazoo."

Hearing this I felt slightly annoyed that I had run all the way home. But she suggested that since I was out of school we could go over to the hobby store and buy a swing set for my Ginny doll.

I was shocked. "Go to a store when a tornado might be coming?" I thought. "But what if a tornado comes?" I asked.

My mother smiled wisely and said very calmly, "I think we have time, and I know you have been saving your money for a long time."

She was right, I had managed to save eight dollars to buy Ginny her much-needed swing set. It was tempting. Maybe we could beat the tornado there and back? So off we went, and gradually I calmed down. No tornado came our way. We made it home, and I was the proud owner of one doll-sized swing set. Maybe the school didn't always have the most up-to-date information about tornadoes.

That same spring a deadly tornado struck the city of Parchment, a town of some two thousand people adjacent to the city of Kalamazoo. My Aunt Mary and Uncle Larry lived there. I was spending the night with Grandma and Grandpa Van Welden, who lived some two miles from us in Kalamazoo. Once my grandparents heard about the tornado on the radio, they kept trying to phone Aunt Mary, but they were unable to get through. Grandpa thought the phone lines were down, so we all piled into their giant blue Oldsmobile and drove the ten miles to Parchment. By this time it was dark, but not raining. All the roads into town were blocked by police cars and barricades. No one could drive in. I could tell, from their hushed front-seat conversation, that Grandma and Grandpa were very worried but were trying to keep me from knowing this. Most of the street lights were out, so I could not really see much. Grandpa drove very carefully.

Finally, in frustration, Grandpa parked the car and went up to a policeman, explaining that his family lived here and that he needed to check on them. We were given permission to cross the barricade and walk into the town. Grandma held tightly to my hand. Luckily we were not far from my aunt and uncle's house.

As we walked along the street, I looked with shock at large trees uprooted everywhere, houses smashed into piles of wood, homes partially destroyed with attached carports torn off. I remember making a mental note never to live in a house with an attached garage. Those seemed to be especially vulnerable. I don't remember much of our conversation, but with every step we would exclaim over the damage. We all three stopped at one point and looked in amazement at a tiny child's playhouse miraculously intact in someone's backyard, while their house was utterly absent. I wondered what happened to the grown-ups and children that lived there. And we all wondered what we would find when we arrived at our destination.

At last we made it to my aunt and uncle's house, and we were so happy to find them safe and their home untouched. They were still a bit dazed over what had happened. They did not have a basement and had taken shelter in a hallway. I remember thinking they were really lucky, and maybe, if they had paid attention to *The Wizard of Oz,* they would have bought a house with a basement.

This was as close as I ever got to a real tornado as I was growing up, and it was close enough for me. I was very happy to get back to the safety of Grandma's house and my everyday routine, but the images of destruction remained in my memory and fueled my fear of tornadoes as well as a determination to always live in a house with a basement, away from Kansas.

Life is unpredictable, and, occasionally, ironic. The city of Kalamazoo was never hit directly by a tornado until 1980, the year after I moved to Kansas, the land of Dorothy. The deadly F3 twister struck late in the afternoon, first in the residential neighborhood of Westwood, and then followed the heavily traveled arteries of West Main Street and Michigan Avenue into the heart of downtown, remaining on the ground for some 20 minutes. Homes were destroyed, and heavy damage was sustained in the city's business center. The roof was ripped off the prominent ISB building, and its glass exterior was shattered. Windows were blown out of many buildings, cars were overturned, and Gilmore's Department Store lost its back exterior wall in one clean slice, with the bricks deposited, neatly, six feet high in an adjacent alley. Bronson Park, a beloved two-acre historical and community site, lost twenty-six of its commanding oak trees, some centuries old. Amazingly, there had been only five fatalities.

I did not know about the tornado until I was home from work that day, preparing dinner for my husband and young son. I turned on the evening news and listened in shock as Walter Cronkite calmly described the disaster that had struck my home town. The remainder of the evening was spent frantically trying to get through to my family by phone. Every time I redialed the number and heard the annoying beeping, I told myself that, of course, the phone lines were down, and my family was probably alright. I struggled against the panicky feeling that was trying to claim me. I was still that girl on the couch, waiting for the tornado, but the tornado had struck when I wasn't looking, and I didn't know where anyone was.

Finally my husband, in a calmer state than I, reminded me that my father, a deputy sheriff for Kalamazoo County, would undoubtedly be at work, and I should try calling there. I got through to him, and his voice over the phone filled me with relief, as he told me that all the family was safe. But his voice also conveyed shock as he described roofs ripped from downtown buildings and the damage to Bronson Park that would forever alter this visual historical marker of Kalamazoo's pride. He was busy and couldn't talk long. I sensed that I had caught him in a brief moment between running from urgent thing to urgent thing. The overwhelming reality of what had happened seemed to catch up with him as he spoke a few words. They didn't yet know the extent of fatalities. I knew my father to be a calm, reassuring person trained to handle emergencies. I felt uneasy as I realized that this disaster was not one he was prepared for. Maybe no one could be.

Surprisingly, missing the big storm in my hometown was a little disappointing. I had been preparing for this tornado all my life. It was my town. I should have been there. But no, I am in Kansas, where tornadoes are commonplace, but I have yet to experience one directly. Even so, I feel more vulnerable. I do live in a home with a basement. And when the threat of severe weather exists, I locate things important to me, such as my purse and running shoes, so they can go to the basement with me if necessary. Part of me is still waiting on the couch.

Tornado

While the wind whines overhead,
Coming down from the mountain,
Whistling between the arbors, the winding terraces;
A thin whine of wires, a rattling and flapping of leaves,
And the small street-lamp swinging and slamming against the lamp pole.
—Theodore Roethke

We are finishing the supper dishes when Grandma Carver steps back into the kitchen from the back porch where she's tossed the garbage.

"That sky looks sick," she says and wipes her hands on her apron. "I've never seen it look so green."

Mom says something about us being in for a big storm and goes outside to make sure the car windows are rolled up. My uncle Bernard pulls his Chevy into the garage to protect the finish in case there is hail. It is June 8, 1966, and I am ten and a half years old. I live with my Grandma Carver, my mother, my Uncle Bernard, and my sister Nancy, along with my mother's friend, Ronnie, and her son Pat. We live, squeezed into a small airplane bungalow that is my grandmother's house, in the heart of Topeka, Kansas.

Today is my Grandma Freel's 64th birthday. We've made her a cake, and Mom is preparing to go out and get her so we can celebrate. She works at Washburn University, five blocks south, where she is a cook in one of the women's dormitories. My Grandpa Freel is at Stormont-Vail hospital, about five blocks the other way, where he is dying of stomach cancer. The grownups say he has a tumor the size of a grapefruit. I try to picture a tumor but can't since I don't know what a tumor is. All I can conjure up is an image of a grapefruit sitting in his stomach.

The heat itself is indolent, shimmering listlessly up from the pavement. Even mornings don't bring relief. Dew doesn't even form on the grass because the temperature never cools enough to condense moisture. The air hangs like heavy drapes. On days like this, when the day heats up, the whole mass of humid air just expands. There is no bursting open of the hazy cloud cover, no clearing to reveal a crisp, blue sky. If the sun is visible at all, it hangs like an enormous blood orange suspended in the sky. In Kansas in the summer, wind feels like a blast furnace.

At about six o'clock, we sit down to dinner and it begins to cool a bit. Miniature breezes come up out of nowhere, causing leaves to skirl around on the gravel in the driveway. There is a low grumble of thunder in the way-off distance. From our tree-lined neighborhood, we can't see the enormous anvil-headed cloud formations moving in like giant ocean liners from the west. The television weatherman mentions a storm creeping our way, but we're not worried. Some storms materialize and some just dance off to the north without giving us so much as a drop of precipitation.

"We can use the rain," Grandma says. "But I'm not holding my breath," she adds.

Dinner is meatloaf and green beans and mashed potatoes. We always round out our meals with cottage cheese, sliced tomatoes, cantaloupe, and watermelon. The grownups sprinkle a generous amount of salt on everything. Tonight we're having sliced Wonder bread and margarine but, on special occasions, we get Brown and Serve dinner rolls or Pillsbury Pop 'N Fresh crescent rolls that come out of the magic exploding can. This is what qualifies as cooking in our house. My mother doesn't like to cook. Grandma Carver doesn't mind cooking, but she's not good at it. Nancy and I are especially suspicious of her meatloaf. She usually makes it in order to clear leftovers out of the refrigerator, so we inspect our servings closely to examine the contents. Tonight we see spaghetti, navy beans, and something unidentifiable. Ketchup helps.

It's too hot to talk, so we eat in silence. The predominant sounds come from the fans that blow dense air around the room without seeming to cool anything, producing more vibration than breeze. These fans terrify me. They are round, gunmetal gray contraptions with spaces large enough to stick a small pet in. Grandma told us a while back that one of our relatives fell asleep and her hand had dropped into the fan near her bed and it sliced off a couple of her fingers. I don't know if this is true, but I keep my distance.

I finish putting away the dishes and go outside to look at the sky. Grandma is right—the sky is sick; it's yellow-green, like an old bruise. Now the air is close, thick and motionless and damp, like the dishcloth Grandma has just hung on the holder by the sink. It's hard to inhale this kind of air. The screen door slams behind me and the sound is flat—just a thwack. The tree leaves are motionless and jungle green. The cool that had materialized before dinner is gone and it's baking hot again. Perspiration beads drip from my face onto my shirt.

Mom comes out and gets in her car, a cobalt blue 1955 Buick Special. She rolls down the window to tell me she's going to get Grandma Freel. "Set out the ice cream so it can soften," she says.

I watch her put on her lipstick as she rolls out of the driveway. I go back into the house and set the ice cream container on the table and then plop down in front of the television. Like every good American in 1966, we keep our black-and-white television turned on most evenings. Mom says someday we can have a color TV like Grandma's friends Helen and Wayne. When we're rich, she says. Now we have to go to Helen and Wayne's house to watch the Miss America pageant and *The Wizard of Oz* every year. I like it when Dorothy opens that door from her gray and sepia-toned Kansas farmhouse into the colorful world of Oz.

Our local CBS affiliate is Channel 13, with the call letters WIBW. Years later, a high school friend asks me what "WIBW" stands for.

When I say what, he hums through his lips while using two fingers to flip his lips up and down—W-B-W-B-W-B-W. Hah-hah. We get four or five channels, but the other stations we get are generated in Kansas City, fifty miles away. Getting the Kansas City stations requires rather specific weather conditions as well as a peculiar set of contortions to adjust what are called "rabbit ears," the dual-pole antennae that sit on top of the television console. They always seem to need adjusting, a task that usually belongs to me or Nancy or Pat. We stand at the set, adjusting the poles to various angles, while the grownups sit on the couch and provide feedback. Sometimes we get a good picture only when someone is touching the rabbit ears, and then whoever is engineering the reception that night gets to stand there for the entire show.

Tonight, on WIBW, a young anchorman named Bill Kurtis is keeping us informed. At 7:00 p.m., right after Mom leaves to get Grandma Freel, the sirens start to sound. We all look outside at the motionless green sky. We still aren't especially worried; sirens are common this time of year and, more often than not, yield little more than an occasional funnel-like cloud sighted somewhere outside the city. Besides, Topeka has special protection. Grandma Carver always reminds us about Burnett's Mound—a hill at the southwestern corner of the city that is known for deflecting any tornado that comes at it. It is named for the Indian Chief, Burnett, which, come to think of it, isn't much of an Indian name. The legend is that any tornado heading for Topeka will bounce off the mound, become airborne, and dissipate high above the city.

Mom gets back home as the first giant drops of rain start to fall. Grandma Freel remembers she's left her purse in her locker and they go out to the car to go get it. The sky is now almost black. The thunder that was a distant rumble a few minutes ago cracks and splinters and the sky opens. Rain starts to beat hard and furious with cold water pellets that slice down from the sky, a gazillion a minute. There is a real wind now, strong enough to shake the trees. Mom and Grandma Freel come back in the house. They are both drenched. Mom says we should probably get to the basement and I hear her tell Grandma Carver that it's too windy to get out of the driveway. I see the look on her face. The sirens sound again and this time they don't stop.

Bill Kurtis tells us that a tornado is headed for the city. "Take cover," he says. "For God's sake, take cover!"

Then I am huddled under the basement stairs with Nancy and Pat and Grandma Freel. The other grownups are standing around watching while Bernard tries to get reception on a transistor radio. Mom keeps running up and down the stairs to see if she can get a glimpse of the storm. She props open one of the basement windows so we can hear it. Grandma's cake is upstairs in a pan next to the box of ice cream now melting on the table. Our cat, a tortoise-shell named Samantha, minces down the steps and sits down next to us. Her ears are back.

The radio only brings in static. The television is miraculously working, and Mom brings us an update after one of her expeditions upstairs. "It's hitting Washburn," she says.

We can hear the tornado now, a deafening roar caused by the vortex of wind and negative pressure. Things feel like they might explode. The roar is constant, and we actually feel the pressure shift like the sky is breathing in and out and it feels like the house might explode. There is an invisible but unrelenting force pulling everything upward.

Years later I learn about vortices and wind currents and barometric pressure and become fascinated by weather and the forces of nature. Today I am shaking and I can't tell if I'm cold or scared or both. During these long minutes cowering under the stairs, I am pretty sure we are all doomed. When you are the oldest child, as I am, you are still a child, but you are a child who has responsibilities. I eavesdrop on grownup conversations and learn many things. I know that life isn't all fun and games. I know that people get sick and die, that cars crash, and that people get hurt. I know that things change, that good times don't last, and that bad people sometimes win no matter what the storybooks say. I know that Grandpa Freel has a tumor the size of a grapefruit. I know that he's not expected to last out the month.

It seems like forever before the worst thunder, lightning, and winds finally pass, and all that's left is the rain. Now we hear other sirens as emergency vehicles head out to deal with the storm's aftermath. The tornado, we learn later, is a record-breaking F-5 storm, the strongest kind, and its half-mile path of destruction nearly obliterates Topeka during its thirty-four-minute rampage from the southwestern corner to the northeastern reaches of the city. It touches down on Burnett's Mound and, ignoring the legend, barrels down the mound and plows through the heart of the city. Washburn University is demolished. Our house is intact, but our yard is full of debris.

Miraculously, only sixteen people die, although more than five hundred are injured. Mom and Ronnie, both nurses, put on their lipstick and go to the hospital to help with the wounded. We don't see them until late the next day.

A week after the tornado, one evening after dinner and before our dessert of homemade apple pie from Bobo's Drive In, Bernard takes us out for a drive to inspect the damage in the hardest hit neighborhoods. Washburn's campus is a mess of downed trees and twisted buildings and piles of limestone rubble. The neighborhood at the foot of Burnett's Mound is flattened entirely. Trees throughout the city look like distorted, petrified versions of the trees in *The Wizard of Oz*, stripped of their leaves. Everywhere, there are piles of mangled automobiles, bathroom fixtures, furniture, and other household effects. There are bizarre things as well, such as apartment buildings with an outside wall ripped away, revealing perfectly intact rooms. They look like giant versions of the doll houses I've played with. A china cabinet in my Grandma Freel's kitchen at Washburn is untouched with every dish intact, while the pots and pans are destroyed. The destruction is too much. I feel shaky and sick and go to bed without apple pie, but I can't sleep.

So I'm not surprised when, later this summer, after the tornado has struck and the cleanup has begun, my grandpa dies. I have learned that this is part of life. But this is only the beginning. Two weeks later, while on a family vacation in Washington, D.C., my mother, who never swears, who never loses her cool, never seems to get frustrated, slams her fists onto the steering wheel of her cobalt blue 1955 Buick Special and says, "Dang it!" when we run out of gas in front of the White House. In the front seat with her are Grandma Carver and Ronnie. I am in the back seat with Nancy and Pat and we push ourselves as far back into the seat as we can get, with our eyes wide open when we hear her cuss. Life as we know it is over.

PART III

The Tomcat and the Tomboy

THE ANIMAL DIARIES

1. Meow

When I was a kid, my closest companion was a big, battle-scarred Tomcat. I'd tell people that he was the smartest cat in the world, because he could say his own name. To call my cat "Meow," and then tout his intellect, was my idea of humor at the age of ten. He patiently endured my hoisting him over my thin shoulders, and he nuzzled me as I carried him draped around my neck like a sumptuous boa. I was a loner with a cat, and I was content.

He's just an alley cat, people used to say. I don't know where he came from, or when—he just showed up one day and stayed, and he was mine. His short gray fur was thick except for missing patches from his cat fights: battle scars dotted his landscape, and one tattered ear topped off the terrain. He was huge. To me he was a puma who had wandered in from the West, and he moved as if he were one generation away from a forest. When roaming through the fields, his big shoulders alternated as they protruded above his wide neck. His elbows jutted out and his tail stretched motionless behind him, with only the tip twitching. He walked with the tight muscular grace of a male ballet dancer, and he sat with his front legs in third position. We were together constantly—he explored the land with me, and he slept up against me at night. He was my family.

I had another family, but I saw little of them. This was the usual nuclear family of post-World War II, the traditional unit that I would not be able to replicate later in my own adult life. In those days my mother did not vacuum in high heels the way June Cleaver did; she was a small redhead who was both affectionate and bad-tempered. She was too educated to enjoy her role as traditional housewife, and she lay on the couch reading most of the time, and smoking. My dad traveled a lot as a newspaper reporter. He worked long hours when he was in town, though when he came home from work we shot baskets together or threw catch with a baseball in the dusk. My red-headed sister was five years older than I and was very grown up; she spent much of her time with her high-school friends. Three houses were visible from our house, and they were a long way away, and they contained no kids my age. But I had my cat.

I was a total, unabashed Tomboy. I had a collection of Storybook dolls that people had given me, clothed in elaborate, lovely dresses, but they stayed on their shelves. I didn't like dolls and didn't want to play house as other girls my age did. While the two redheads were inside the house most of the time, I was usually outside. I spent a lot of time up in trees, just as Meow did. I liked to climb the American elms at the side of our house, which wasn't easy, as I had to shinny up a rope to get to the lowest branches. Once I climbed high into one of these elms and got level with the second-floor bedroom, where my mother was lying on the bed reading. I waved to her. She levitated straight up above the bed, and when her feet hit the floor, she yelled at me: "Mary Margaret!! Get down from there right now, before you break your damned neck!" This was how she expressed her love for me.

Meow and I hung out together as I practiced basketball shots or gardened, and I talked to him. He lay nearby in the summer grass as I drew the plants and animals in our backyard with pencil or pastels. I wonder who this loner Tomboy might have become without Meow's warm purring presence in my life: perhaps a tough, aloof biology professor feared by her students, rather than the somewhat eccentric one who rescued worms from wet campus sidewalks.

Today, this place where I grew up is a densely populated bedroom community south of Kansas City. Back then, in the late forties, it was

160

country. Our house was on two and a half acres. To the north of our property was a cornfield, and I wandered through the tall corn rows with tassels dangling over me and green light filtering through the roof of leaves, presaging the tropical rainforests which would become so crucial to me later in life. The corn-leaf light formed mosaics on the squash plants that sprawled between the corn rows, bearing long green-striped squash. South of our land was a pasture, and in the early mornings an old man in an old Model A Ford herded a pack of cows down our dirt road—from where I don't know—and nudged them into the pasture. Sometimes the cows angled off and wandered around in back of our house, and the old guy just followed right along through our backyard and drove them on to their pasture. To the east was a farm pond, where my sister Dee Dee and I went fishing with safety pins tied to a stick and worms to impale on the pins. To the north beyond the cornfield was a wooded area I often explored. One fall day I discovered there a tree festooned with hundreds of monarch butterflies preparing for their long flight to Mexico. Much later I saw them, at that Mexican site, by the hundreds of thousands.

Our backyard was long and deep and culminated in a chicken house with its fenced chicken yard. This wooden structure had a Dutch door, racks for nests, and cans to hold the chicken feed. It was musty and a little mysterious and forbidding, and I think of it fondly.

One evening my dad said to me, "Come on, Kid, let's go get the rats in the chicken house."

My mother and sister looked horrified and I looked excited. He got my half-sized baseball bat, which had *Kansas City Blues* emblazoned on it, and we moved stealthily in the dusk to our target. My job was to shine a flashlight just outside the chicken-sized trap door, and his job was to bang on the wall and hit the rats with the bat as they flushed out of the little door. The rats obediently streamed out, and we soon got our limit. We returned to the lighted house giggling and triumphant, like hunters arriving home with the elk for the winter provisions, brandishing our trophies amid screams from the women folk who had remained behind.

I think my mother reacted to the dangling rats with something like, "Alvin and Mary Margaret, what in the HELL are you doing? Get those damned things away from here!"

We giggled more. We were so bad. She was such a foil, but I suspect she enjoyed this role, and I also suspect that her squeamishness endeared her to my father.

In time we no longer had chickens; I think they got old, and we ate them. Eating chickens in those days was no small feat—we didn't go to the grocery store and buy them in plastic-wrapped packages, cut into anatomically unrecognizable parts, the way we do now. On Sundays Dad did the hard part: he caught a chicken, stretched its neck over a block of wood, and chopped its head off with one whack of a hatchet. What fascinated me was how long the chicken body then ran around the yard without its head, and I used to note the time it took before the body finally toppled over. Then we had to pluck it and clean it before we could cook it and eat it.

Dad and I worked side by side in the summer evenings, like the proverbial peas in a pod that I grew in my garden. He had created a small orchard near the chicken house, with cherry and peach and apple trees. He taught me how to garden. I grew vegetables in the now chickenless chicken yard. I loved the chicken yard, for its exuberance of nitrogenous wastes produced giant radishes and carrots, and the pea vines draped over everything. The squash plants surged sideways and crawled up the side of the chicken house. Best, though, were the gourd plants. Most produced the usual little green and yellow fruits in the usual shapes. One day though I parted some large leaves and was stunned to discover, lying beneath, an enormous, long, pale green gourd. Produced furtively by night-blooming white flowers which attracted moths, more of these huge, alien-looking gourds soon littered the ground. They seemed to materialize overnight, and they thrilled me.

Meow roamed the bordering cornfields and pastures and gardens. This was a *real* cat, not like those overweight, indoor, fake cats who sprawl about inertly like so many chicken feed bags. He was a predator. He caught gophers and sought out my father in the yard to present them to him. Dad, who spent his rare free moments pushing a heavy roller around the yard, trying to flatten the gopher hills, was really pleased by these gifts. "Good cat, Meow, good boy," he'd say.

But if my sister or I witnessed this offering, we would beg Daddy to rescue the gopher. "No, no, you can't let him eat it! Make him let it go! Let it go. Please?!"

He would sigh and, being a good father, take the hapless thing from Meow and toss it over the fence into the cornfield—and continue to roll his gopher mounds, while Meow disappeared through the fence at the same spot.

We had a dog named Brick, a sweet cocker spaniel with soft rust-colored fur and a constant crop of cockle burrs dangling from the tips of his long ears. His dog bed was in my parents' room, and whenever I walked by their door, I automatically checked above Brick's bed at the junction of the wall with the ceiling—because engorged ticks occasionally dropped off him and climbed up the wall, only to be flummoxed when reaching the ceiling, where they stopped and waited, patiently. They hung there like fat little grapes, and they fascinated me.

Brick liked to run after rabbits, and bounced after them, barking loudly, panting. Meow of course hunted rabbits, and sat, watching disdainfully, as Brick futilely chased them about. Once, with feline cleverness, the cat leapt from a weedy lair and pounced on a rabbit when the dog chased it near him. Brick hung back, confused. One afternoon Brick died doing what he loved, for an infrequent car hit him as he chased a rabbit across a road a block away. The woman who ran over him spotted our house and brought his body to us, and we sadly received him.

One day Meow caught a rabbit and generously presented it to my mother—perhaps it was the same rabbit which led Brick across his final road to his end. The cat dragged the rabbit through the pet door, a little cat-sized hinged door in our human-sized kitchen door. He leaped up onto the linoleum counter with his prey and deposited the body in the kitchen sink.

Ambling into the kitchen to start dinner, Mother screamed when she saw the bloody carcass draped in the enamel basin. She sounded like this: "Eeeeeek! Eeeeeek! Eeeeeek!!" He was waiting to be praised, but she definitely was not pleased by his gift, so he turned on his paw, annoyed, and exited back out the pet door. The body probably went over the fence into the cornfield.

At Christmas my parents gave me a box with muffled mewing sounds escaping from it. Inside was a Siamese kitten, a little white thing except for her darker face, feet, and tail. Recently weaned, she cried plaintively for her mother and litter-mates.

"There, there. It's okay," I said, holding her against my chest. When Meow discovered my new cat, Amber, he just took over. Here was the predator, the tough guy exuding masculinity, licking Amber and comforting her. Though I wouldn't play dolls with my friends, some nurturing streak bloomed in him, and they slept intertwined in my bed at night. We were a threesome now, and I had a little family of my own.

One cold day Meow showed up at the house bleeding from a wound on his neck. Distraught, I carried him to Mother.

"What happened? What's wrong with him?" I wailed.

"I think some idiot shot him with a BB gun," she said, disgusted and angry.

"We've got to help him! We've got to!!" I was shrieking by now.

"I know, Honey, I know. We will."

It was late in the day, and the nearest veterinarian was far away. My sister, Mother, and I piled into the old Ford, and I held Meow pressed against me. I desperately needed him to be made whole. Eventually we got to Kansas City, Missouri, north of the Plaza. It was crowded and loud, and exhaust fumes permeated the air and trolley cars clanked along their iron rails. We pulled into the parking lot of the veterinary clinic. Surrounding it were rows of large, dark, brick apartment buildings, with small balconies facing Main Street.

As I climbed from the car carrying Meow in my arms, worrying and hopeful, he heard a dog bark inside the clinic, and he jumped from my grasp. He leaped suddenly, powerfully, and gracefully, like the barely domesticated creature that he was, and he blended into the encroaching darkness of the early evening like any wild being would. He left me standing alone.

I was stunned, and then started calling him, again and again. I knew he would come back to me. We all looked and looked—under cars, in alleys, in the street. The rough pavement blurred, and my rising panicked voice echoed back at me from the brick walls: "Meow, Meow, Meow." He was lost. Finally, we got in the car and headed out of the city. I didn't want to leave. This was my fault.

Though we all felt the loss, my parents and sister tried hard to console me. "It was only a small wound," someone said. "He is a great hunter, and he is very smart," someone said. "Maybe he will find his way home. That happens, you know," someone said. "Maybe some nice person in one of those apartment buildings will take him in and take care of him," someone said. And I thought, "Maybe he will be crushed under a truck, or slowly starve, or die of his wound, or freeze to death."

I mourned. My brain churned with the many possible fates awaiting Meow, and I had to decide which image to own. I settled on the possibility that he would find his way home. For months I waited and watched, scanning the yard, imagining him emerging from the cornfield, healthy and sleek, and loping toward me, purring. I knew he was strong and tough enough to make it. He was a survivor. When he failed to appear, I didn't give up on him. I decided then that he was sitting on the balcony of one of those apartments near the veterinary clinic. His eyes were closed and his chin was tilted up, soaking in the warmth of the sun. An old woman was sitting by him, stroking his fur.

2. Amber

We lost more than Meow during this time—we also lost most of our land. Post-war suburban sprawl encroached, and Dad had to sell two of our original two and one-half acres because of rising property taxes. The bordering cornfield and pasture and pond and most of the woods were soon gone. Our long backyard was compressed to a short strip. The orchard Dad had nurtured and my cherished chicken yard were lost. Ranch-style houses on small lots pressed against our remaining yard. These seemed to appear overnight, like the giant green gourds in my garden and, like them, they seemed alien, but in a menacing way. The wood thrushes and brown thrashers and meadowlarks were replaced by house sparrows and starlings, and the evening songs of crickets and cicadas were contaminated by mowing noises and barking dogs.

The Siamese cat I had received that Christmas, Amber, filled some of the empty space left by the loss of Meow. She was a beautiful cat, with the rounded face that Siamese cats had in those days, and jet-black points. She materialized, by some undefined internal clock, inside the front door every day at 4:00, waiting my arrival home on the school bus from grade school, and then high school. I took her with me to Kansas University where, as a senior, I married Jack. She was with us there for two more years of graduate school, then traveled with us to Albuquerque, where our daughter Laura was born, and then on to Portales, New Mexico.

Amber died in Portales of kidney failure at the age of eighteen. I did not recognize—while I myself was recovering from a bad car accident—that she was declining. We couldn't prolong her life. Jack and I buried her ancient and still beautiful body outside of town, in a desolate, flat New Mexico field. I woke that night, inconsolable with the realization that the farmer might plow her up the next spring. Jack and I drove back to her grave the next day, and he kindly dug her up and reburied her beneath a nearby tree, where she could return to the earth gradually and simply.

3. Bella

My early experiences with Meow and our land, followed by the loss of them both, shaped me irrevocably—for the soil is fertile at that stage of life. Back then, the natural world lured me outside. Later, as a biologist, I was drawn to the tropical rainforests of the New World, and I immersed myself in them whole-heartedly. One night, deep in a forest in Belize, I saw a truly wild cat—an ocelot—and it astonished and awed me. During one six-week period in a rainforest in Ecuador, where I was alone most of the time, I grew: from an older Kansas woman, who was uneasy and occasionally got lost in the jungle, to one who was completely at home there. I became an integral part of the forest, and it became a part of me. Such opulence, beauty, and rampant diversity touched my soul. A deep passion for protecting these places now flows within me, and I long to preserve them for later generations.

I go often into my backyard these days. I realized recently that I have tried to recreate, here in my suburban neighborhood in Lawrence, the country yard that was lost in my childhood. The prevalent shade and clay soil prevent my growing gourds, but I have packed the yard with berry-laden bushes and flowering trees. The rest of the space is filled with life: finches flash gold on the coneflowers, hummingbirds hover at the mimosa, and monarchs seek nectar at the butterfly bushes. I saw my first brown thrasher there only recently, flicking soil over its shoulder in search of food.

It has been six decades since I lost Meow, and many cats have padded through my life. These later cats left small paw-prints compared to those of Meow and Amber, for single parenthood and long work hours obscure other memories. My daughter Laura and I formed a tiny, loving family. Then, when she left for college at eighteen—and later moved to the West Coast—cats arrived again to fill the new gaps. Right now I live with two cats: a giant twenty-pound male who just appeared at the door one Thanksgiving, and a delicate Siamese, whose elderly owner died.

Bella, the Siamese, and I keep a ritual every morning: we go together to the deck in my little backyard wildlife sanctuary. I sit on the floor of the deck, just above the ground, with my feet planted on the earth, to which I am so connected. I sip a cup of coffee, and drink in the sights and sounds of the living creatures there. Bella stretches out beside me. At fourteen years and eight pounds, she is slender and lithe. Her blue irises resemble ice covering an azure volcanic lake. Her black face and legs and tail glow in the sun. Her cream-colored belly, with its café-au-lait center streak, beckons my hand. She rolls, longly, from side to side, luxuriating in the warmth of the sun.

We sit together, in the sun. We are both content. It just doesn't get much better than this.

4. Epilogue

Recently, I was in the area of Kansas City where Meow disappeared some sixty years ago. I studied those apartment buildings pressed up against the veterinary clinic. They are ancient and far past their prime, but they are survivors and still there—pretty much like me. Each three-story, weathered brick building has six small balconies facing the street. I scanned the balconies. Somewhere in my head I half expected—hoped even—to see Meow stretched out on one of those railings up there, looking down at me.

Perhaps someday I will live in an urban place like this—you never know where you'll end up. If so, I will have a battle-scarred Tomcat, whom I salvaged from the street below. And we will sit on the balcony, together, in the sun. I will stroke his fur as he purrs. I will name him Meow.

Jen's Addiction

I hear the familiar thunk, then a low rumble. I shiver with anticipation as I realize what is about to happen. I must decide quickly, before it's too late—Where will I get my next fix? This time it comes in the middle of our family dinner. I can't escape to one of my many sources. But next time... next time.

When the sound comes again, dinner has ended and I'm in my room, curled up on my waterbed, doing my homework. It feels like it's been hours since my last hit, and I know I can't miss out again. I fly out of my bedroom, the door slams into the brown-paneled wall behind, and I head down the dark hallway for the best heat vent in the house, in the small entryway by the back door. That's right—I'm a heat junkie.

When I was a kid my parents would often find me crouched over that 12×5" metal vent, my knees red from kneeling on the hard, mustard-yellow linoleum in our 1970s ranch-style house. It didn't matter that the cold air seeped in around the edges of the back door, or that I could feel the outside cold pressing against my back when I leaned against the door. In a way it made the thrill of warming up on those cold Iowa winter evenings all the more satisfying. I could almost feel the snow drifting around the house as the wind whistled across the dormant cornfield out back, threatening to envelop me, but the roar of the heat helped me forget. As I sat there securely, warm air blowing up the back of my shirt, I would listen to my family going about their business. The kitchen was just on the other side of a short wall. To see them I could lean forward about three feet and peer to my left. They might know I was there, or they might not. But even when I chose to remain hidden I could clearly hear the clank of dishes in the stainless steel sink, or the opening and closing of the avocado green oven door before dinner. The smell of Mom's cooking—lasagna, meatloaf, or the Sunday chicken, would waft over me, and I would feel safe and, well, warm.

I don't recall exactly when or how my heat-vent addiction began, but I suspect it had something to do with my Dad's close attention to the family's finances. The thermostat was kept at 67 degrees during the day to keep the bill in check, and God only knows how cold he let it get at night. It didn't seem to matter how thick my sweater or how many blankets I piled on my bed, I could not get warm. During the day, turtlenecks were just the first layer. I owned them in white, black, red, and purple. Over that went a coordinating sweatshirt—University of Northern Iowa Panthers to go with the purple, a grey number with the JCPenney logo covered the red, and so on. When that wasn't enough, I would grab my favorite blanket from my room—a large maroon fleece with a unicorn woven in. My mom even had the predecessor to the Snuggie—a quilt you could actually snap around you to make a wearable sleeping bag. If you unsnapped the bottom you could walk around, which came in handy when we had to let our Miniature Schnauzer, Dusty, out the back door in the dead of winter. I remember one such incident when, wrapped in a blanket and only able to find one boot, I hopped on one foot and shivered while I clipped his collar to his chain. I ended up slipping on a patch of ice and cutting my wrist and ankle on the door jamb. I have the scars to prove it.

At night I would change into a long nightgown before taking one last hit. The air would blow inside, making me look more like a pregnant teen than Marilyn Monroe. Then, I would burrow under a sheet, a thermal blanket, a fleece blanket, and finally quilt or comforter to insulate myself. Inevitably the whole stack would tip off in the middle of the night, and I'd awaken shivering, forced to climb out of bed and retrieve them from the floor. The cold was difficult to bear during autumn, but once the mountains of snow came to stand watch outside our house from November to April, I was doomed to constant shivering.

No one else in my family seemed to notice the chill like I did, nor did they comment on my attachment to the vent. This was good news on two fronts. First, I didn't have to compete for resources. And second, I had plenty of time to perfect my habit uninterrupted. If I took my unicorn blanket to the vent with me, I could create an oven effect. Suddenly it wasn't just my back that was warm—it was my whole body! I could even put my whole head under when I was really cold. This also helped me avoid burning my rear end on the metal register because I could sit next to the vent rather than directly on it. It was like being wrapped in a blanket of sunshine or standing under the stream of a steaming hot shower. Comforting. Necessary.

I began to sneak in extra fixes when no one was looking. As soon as the air in the current heat cycle grew cool, I'd make my move. Knowing my dad would be angry if he caught me, I would tiptoe across the linoleum, relaxing as my footsteps grew quieter on the green shag carpet. Just around the corner, hidden by a tall stereo stand, was the thermostat. I would hide behind it and peek around to make sure my dad, stretched out in the brown leather recliner, was fully engrossed in his TV program, or better yet, dozing in front of a football game.

When the coast was clear, I'd carefully approach that little cream-colored plastic box with the small silver knob—long before the programmable thermostat came into existence. All I had to do for another round of warm air was turn that knob to the right until I heard the quietest of clicks, usually around 70 degrees. I could find the exact angle without even looking. The cycle would start anew, and I'd quickly turn it back down again, in case a commercial might motivate Dad to leave the comfort of his chair and head to the kitchen, or worse, straight toward me on his way to the bathroom. If I made the adjustment just right I'd have another 10 or 15 minutes of heat-sitting. But my addiction spurred my caution. I was careful not to overdo this trick so Dad didn't catch on.

Most of the time, my movements were undetected. From time to time though, my timing was off and Dad would catch me in the act. "What are you doing?" he'd bellow.

Red-faced, I'd mutter, "Nothing," my voice trailing off as I moved away, trying to look like I'd only stopped to stare at the humidifier that sat to the left of the stereo. (That humidifier, by the way, blew out cold, musty air—the enemy!)

Dad would start to lecture, "When you pay the bills you can turn the heat up as high as you want. . . "

I wanted to retort, "You bet I will!" But instead I would keep quiet as he continued down the hall. To this day I wonder whether the heating bill ever indicated to him that I had more success than failure in my efforts to keep warm.

When I left home for Kansas University, I took my little addiction with me. Kansas may be warmer than northeast Iowa, but winters still have a bite. Hashinger and Oliver Halls were wonderful places to experience the joy of heat. Here, I *wasn't* paying the bill, directly anyway, so I could make it as toasty as I wanted (as long as my roommate wasn't there). And I could turn it on *full blast*!

The bliss of adulthood! What a lovely thing. Although it was hard to make this room cozy, with its cinderblock walls painted Pepto pink, my roommate (another) Jen and I did our best to cover as much of that God-awful color as possible. But the decor paled compared to that wonderful little heating unit—my key to heaven. The unit was hotel-like: the heat blew out the top and a knob allowed a flow adjustment to low, medium, or high. It was not as comfortable as the floor vent of my childhood; nevertheless, I learned to sit directly on it, as if it were a window seat. The blanket technique didn't work quite as well either. But because I could turn it on full blast, I could actually keep the room itself incredibly warm. Fortunately, my roommate accepted this quirk with all of my others and didn't comment. After we parted ways for rooms of our own, I would often fall asleep with the heater running full blast, my body buried under the comforter. The heat not only helped me beat winter's chill but also staved off bouts of homesickness.

I graduated in 1997 and married in 1998. The ground-floor apartment Dave and I moved into didn't have floor vents, and I was forced into withdrawal from my addiction. A couple of years later we moved to a little house on Rhode Island Street, where circumstances were slightly more conducive to my latent condition. There was no central air, but the house had a large wall heater in the kitchen. My husband found it more than adequate during a bad bout with the flu, and our black Lab-Chow mix, Phoebe, often sat in front of it. But my inner heat junkie discovered that I could only get my front OR my back warm at any given moment, and that simply wasn't good enough for me.

Then we bought our current house. Glory be! The floor vents were back! Its split-level design, I would soon learn, meant a cold downstairs and a toasty upstairs. I gravitated toward the upstairs and quickly learned which vents were closest to the main. The living room vents had the "nook" feeling of my vent back home, but they lacked air pressure, as did those in the dining room and kitchen. Besides, these rooms were much too bright for my cover-up. The air flow in the guest bathroom was pretty good, but the toilet was just a little too close. And the rooms that would someday belong to the kids didn't even come close to meeting the criteria.

I finally settled on the master bedroom. It had two vents—one right next to Dave's side of the bed, the other just outside the master bath. This configuration was a bit open compared to my childhood home, but I could achieve that cozy feeling by replacing the overhead light with bedside lamps instead. If I wanted to read while I warmed myself, I'd just turn on the bathroom light. Good air pressure wasn't the only advantage here: The carpet was plush white, and there was no freezing exterior door. Not only was there room enough to create my blanket oven, I could grab a pillow and actually take a little nap in it!

That first winter I was back on that metal register, blanket wrapped around me, happy and warm. Dave must have thought I was nuts. I'd painstakingly hidden the severity of my addiction from him for eight full years, after all. But he just shook his head and accepted my winter bedtime ritual of reading on the heat vent until it kicks off and I can climb into bed, toasty warm. Of course, he tries to tempt me away with promises like "I'll warm you up." But it never fails—when I finally crawl into bed and snuggle into him, he jumps back. "All that time on the heat, and your feet are still cold!" he complains.

Sadly, or maybe not, I have passed my addiction on to our children. One cold winter weekend day my sons Charlie and Ben and I were hanging out while Dave was at work. Charlie was probably six or seven, Ben three or four. I was cold, sleepy, and a little grumpy—desperate for a nap. But the kids were too young to leave to their own devices while I snoozed. So I grabbed a stack of picture books and did what any freezing cold mother would do—I invited them to sit with me, on the heat vent, wrapped in a blanket, for story time. Even five years later, any time the boys catch me on a heat vent, they quickly cuddle up at my side and vie for a piece of blanket.

Although Dave never joins us, the dog is always intrigued. Riley, our Greyhound–English Pointer mix, is always cold, too. Once she senses warm air blowing under my vent tent, she can't resist. She noses the edge of the afghan until I lift it and let her in. Our Bluepoint Siamese, Luna, soon follows. But just when the five of us are cozy and warm, the inevitable happens. The warm air begins to cool; the flow weakens, and the cycle ends altogether. We sigh and disband, but we're always listening for those signs that our next fix is on the way.

Van Welden's Drugstore

M y father, Walter Van Welden, Jr., was a pharmacist. He owned a neighborhood drugstore in Kalamazoo, Michigan, during a time when a drugstore was the only place to fill a prescription or sit at a soda fountain and enjoy a hand-made malted, and it was the choice of many for picking up the local newspaper, a pack of Lucky Strikes, or some Pepto-Bismol. The customers were regulars. Everyone knew each other's names and kept up with families, life events, local politics, and the weather. It was a hangout, a place to take your date on a Saturday night, and a safe haven to linger over a cup of coffee during the day.

The small, modest store, built from cinder blocks, was located in a short business district between Harts Grocery Store and Hoekstra's Meat Market. Large plate-glass windows across the front faced a busy South Westnedge Avenue, right by a dip in the road that caused severe flooding every time it rained. The store, without a pharmacy, originally belonged to Grandpa Van Welden. He was proud of his liquor license and could sell packaged liquor Monday through Saturday, maintaining a brisk trade as weeks neared week-ends. My father grew up working in the store, and was groomed, as the oldest of three children to take over the business someday.

Dad enrolled in the pharmacy program at Ferris State University in Big Rapids after serving in the Army during World War II. He came from a family of pharmacists, with an uncle (Frank Beattie) already practicing, and an aunt (Marie Beattie) who was one of the first female pharmacists in southwestern Michigan. After graduation, he moved with his wife and new baby (me) back to Kalamazoo, where he joined his father in the family business, proudly adding a new pharmacy to the existing amenities for sale.

The drug store was located just a few short blocks from our home. I grew up taking for granted its presence in our lives. I loved going there with my mom, brother Larry, and sister Wendy. We would drop in frequently to say hi to Dad and to pick up something needed at home. We almost always got to have a small treat.

The soda fountain was the heart of the store. Seven worn, red-leather-covered chrome stools sat in front of the long counter, which was decorated underneath by hundreds of wads of used chewing gum left behind by customers long tired of chewing. While sitting at the counter, you could see yourself in the long mirror that hung on the opposite wall, and you could make yourself dizzy spinning around and around on a stool, if your parents were not paying attention.

The red Coke machine behind the counter dispensed carbonated water and Coke syrup (in two separate streams) into a waiting glass bearing the Coca Cola label. A large area was set aside for washing and rinsing the glasses in scalding hot water, and they drip-dried on the drain board before being reshelved.

We served the best vanilla ice cream in the world (Sealtest). A malted was made with the big, green, industrial-quality, Hamilton Beach mixer. Chocolate sodas, root beer floats, and phosphates were also tempting choices. Ice cream sundaes were made with one or two scoops placed in a small metal cup with a crisp white paper liner and were completed with choice of chocolate, butterscotch, pineapple or strawberry topping, nuts, and a cherry.

Something about the ice cream made it special. I never knew exactly what it was, but it was colder than the ice cream we had at home, and I always thought that contributed to its superior taste. The metal refrigerated unit, recessed into the countertop, held two large tubs of vanilla, packed in so hard that it took a lot of effort to scoop it out. You had to have strong wrists to make a sundae. But they were the best, and I became an ice cream snob at an early age.

Racks of greeting cards, magazines and comic books took up space at the front of the store. Close by stood a tall, green scale that, for a penny, would display your weight and predict your future, as though the two were connected.

Throughout the store were several wooden display cases for things anyone might need, like rhinestone jewelry, baby bottles, vaporizers, alarm clocks, heating pads, thermometers, Chanel No. 5, lipstick, and pressed face powder. Shelves along the walls held items like pencils, notebooks, lined paper, shampoo, packaged home permanents, toothpaste, vitamins, cough syrup, aspirin, band aids, Caladryl, dye, mouse traps, coloring books, paper dolls, toys, and Silly Putty. One long display section was devoted to candy. Before my time, the store had offered books to borrow through a lending library. A free-standing metal unit offered a tempting choice of salty, warm, roasted cashews, pistachios, almonds, or peanuts, on a revolving tray; these were sold by the pound and scooped into red-and-white-striped paper sacks.

The pharmacy counter was located on the north side of the store. My dad worked there, on a raised platform, behind the pharmacy counter, where he could keep an eye on everything. White shelving units lined the wall behind the counter stacked pills and medicines waiting to be dispensed. A typewriter was used to type the names and dosages of medicines on the Van Welden's Drugs labels that were then pasted on each brown medicine bottle. I was never allowed behind this counter; I only knew that serious stuff happened there.

The packaged bottles of Jim Beam, gin, vodka, rum, scotch, and cognac lined the wall behind the checkout counter at the back of the store, conveniently out of reach of underage customers. The cash register located there was an ornate, old-fashioned, gold metal behemoth, and required more muscle to operate than a young girl possessed.

A large, refrigerated cooler was located at the very back of the store, behind a solid metal door. Chilled bottles of beer and pop sold by the six pack were kept here. The heavy door always swung shut with a resounding clunk, and I never went in that cooler without worrying that I would get locked in. Even so, I liked the smell of the air—chilled, and slightly sweet.

The bottles of Coke, Pepsi, root beer, orange and grape Nehi were returned by customers, when empty, so they could be taken back to the bottling plant where they would be sterilized and refilled. All the returns were carried to the basement (a dank and cramped space at the bottom of a steep flight of stairs), where they were placed in wooden crates and awaited a weekly pick-up. I disliked the basement and seldom went down there.

I especially liked the store at Christmas. Shelves were filled with inexpensive packages of glass tree ornaments, ropes of beads, tinsel, wreaths, Christmas cards, and wrapping paper. When I was in the first grade, Santa visited our room while we were at gym and left something on each of our desks. Included were small, beaded Christmas trees that I recognized. Dad sold these in his store. I couldn't wait to get home and tell my parents. I burst in the door after school that afternoon shouting out "Guess what! Santa came to our class today and we each got a little Christmas tree that comes from the drugstore!"

My parents, thinking that I suspected the truth about Santa, didn't seem excited by this news. I realized they didn't get the significance of what I was saying, and I patiently explained to them what was so crystal clear to me, "Don't you see, that means Santa has been in our drug store!" They smiled and nodded their heads in relief.

I was always proud of being part of a family that owned a drugstore. Where else could you, as a seven-year-old, sell your hand-made potholders or spend the afternoon crafting a witch's cauldron out of soda fountain supplies to decorate the front window for Halloween? When I was in the third grade, my Dad provided all the orange pop for our class picnic, and I was the envy of all that day. Life was good.

Every January, Dad would need to do an inventory of everything in the store. We all helped. The whole family, including Taffy, our cocker spaniel, would go to the store on a Sunday, when we were closed, and count the stock. It always started out as an adventure. Dad always took care of the bottles of liquor and beer and everything in the cooler. Mom always counted the greeting cards. I usually got to count things like the candy bars, school supplies, and vitamins, as did my brother and sister, when they became old enough to do this.

It didn't take long for the fun to wear off, though—counting became tedious. We each had a pad of ruled paper, and we made lists of each item, noting the quantity and price of each. Sometimes I had no idea what the item was, and usually just dutifully wrote it down. One day I was just plain tired of not knowing what things were. I went to my Dad and asked, in frustration, "What in the world is this?

Dad looked up at the box of prophylactics I was holding and said, "Don't worry about those, I'll count them."

My first job, apart from babysitting, was working for my dad in the store. At the age of fifteen, I wanted to earn some money for Christmas, and Dad agreed to let me work a few hours once school was out. I labored behind the soda fountain, proudly and carefully pouring cups of hot coffee and serving Cokes. I did the dishes, too, and kept the glasses sparkling. A shy girl, I never said much to the customers, but they knew my dad and tolerated his daughter behind the soda fountain with patience and humor. I could serve ice cream once I perfected the strong wrist movement needed to scoop it, but a request for a malted meant I had to go to the pharmacy counter and get my dad.

I also spent a lot of time sweeping the floor with a long-handled broom and red sweeping compound, sprinkled about liberally to keep the dust under control. I liked doing this because I liked the smell of the compound, which, I am sure, was not something that we should have been inhaling.

I felt grown up and proud that my dad trusted me to work in the store. Most days my feet hurt, and I discovered early that when business is slow it can get boring. But I made $10.00 that first Christmas season, and I thought I was rich.

The drug store formed a backdrop to my childhood. It was a part of my life that I never expected to go away. However, times were changing, and my father was quite concerned about the chain pharmacies, like Walgreen's, that were springing up all over. They could sell things for lower prices. What could be done? We were incensed. We were worried. We regarded Walgreen's as the enemy.

When I turned seventeen my father decided to sell the store. He received a fair price for the business, largely due to the liquor license

179

that went with it. I didn't know he was going to do this until he told us, one spring day, that he had made the sale. I was very disappointed, though I did not tell him this. I felt betrayed. I had worked in that store too. In my mind, the drugstore was an integral part of our identity. Who would we be if we were not Van Welden Drugs?

We adapted. I came to think, wistfully, of the drug store in those days, too preoccupied with finishing high school and starting college to give it much space in my head. My father continued to work part-time as a pharmacist while pursuing a career in law enforcement—something he had always wanted to do. I don't think he ever regretted selling the store. As an adult, I came to respect his decision to start a new career in mid-life, something that could not have been easy, with three growing children. It took courage to change jobs, to start over again, knowing that you would probably make less money. I never told him that I admired him for making this tough decision. I wish I had.

When my father died in 1982, seventeen years after selling the store, many former customers came to pay their respects. Van Welden's, it seemed, lived on in many people's memories.

Dad got it right. Today the small neighborhood drugstore has been replaced by chain pharmacies often located in super discount stores like Walmart and Target. Our small store would not have survived the competition. He was right to sell. The building occupied by Van Welden Drugs is no longer standing. Ironically, a Walgreen's now sits on the same spot.

The Red Velvet Fish

THE ANIMAL DIARIES

W hen I was twelve, I learned about love from tropical fish. And I discovered my passion for the natural world because of two snails, which I followed along a sinuous trail for the rest of my life.

ঙ ঙ ঙ

I found two snails in a wooded creek near our house, which was in an outlying part of Kansas City. I put them in a small fish bowl and sat at the dining room table, watching them for hours. Something fascinating occurred in their mouths, which opened and produced a mysterious moving thing, and then closed again. Later I learned that the mouth thing was a radula, a chitinous strap covered with teeth, which scraped off algae for food. But then it was just a mysterious mouth thing.

My parents were standing outside the dining room doorway, watching me. "Do you think there is something wrong with her?" my mother asked.

"I want fish. Can I have fish, huh? Please?"

"No, of course you can't have fish. The cats will eat them." This was, again, my mother, demonstrating her total lack of understanding of the staggering interest developing in my brain.

Despite the presence of the voracious, predatory cats in the house, my father soon arrived home after work carrying a small Chinese carry-out carton. In it were two guppies. My father was a dignified, urbane

181

man who was a reporter for the city newspaper. But he had a contrarian streak which caused him to pose probing questions to politicians and then write about them with witty insight. He enjoyed shaking things up in an understated manner. This streak also allowed him to circumnavigate my red-haired mother's strong opinions. She moved forcefully and heavily, like a B-29 bomber in the War that shaped their lives together, and he moved like a resistance fighter on the ground. He understood me.

The two guppies soon died because of my ignorance. I begged my Great Aunt Marnie for Imm's *Aquarium Fishes* book, and she generously sent it to me for my birthday. I read and read. My parents humored me and, though they had little extra money, they kindly supported my intense interest. In time I had several aquaria, filled with thriving plants, giant snails, and a variety of fresh-water tropical fish of flashing colors. The cats never ate the fish.

I started a fish club in the seventh grade and induced several friends to come to a meeting. As the self-appointed president, I read to them out of my *Aquarium Fishes* book. They would not return for a second meeting.

Haunting the little library in our grade school, I asked the librarian almost daily if she had any books on fish. Each time she told me no, they did not have any books on fish. For two years, up through the eighth grade of our school, the library never acquired any books about fish.

I joined the Heart of America Aquarium Society. My mother drove me to a meeting one evening at the Kansas City Museum. This must have been a difficult drive for her. We had a 1949 Ford by that time, which had recently replaced our bulbous beetle-shaped 1939 Ford (the War car). She didn't drive much, and the museum was in an old part of northeastern Kansas City, Missouri, far from our outlying house in Kansas. But the arduous trip was well worth it for her. The club was discussing a hunt for *Daphnia*, tiny crustaceans which inhabit roadside ditches and are a favorite live food for fish. A woman stood up and said,

"Well, I ain't never saw it did, but I think it'd be fun." My mother, who taught high-school English briefly before marrying and becoming a "housewife," whipped out a notebook and feverishly wrote this down. "My God!" she would say many times later. "There wasn't a single correct word in that sentence!"

My sister, Marion, was in high school during this year. She was a glamorous redhead with blue eyes, perfect teeth, and a "good figure." I was a skinny kid with wild brown hair, brown eyes, and braces on my teeth. If we were indeed from the same gene pool, her genes had been skimmed off the top, and mine had been siphoned off the bottom. One night she had a party, and our house was filled with older high school kids. The girls wore bobby socks with black-and-white saddle shoes, full skirts, and short-sleeved sweaters. They had pony tails.

I stood on the bottom step of the stairwell wearing some kind of a dress, which was unusual for me, and sporting a giant bandage on my elbow from some unsuccessful adventure. Henry, an old family friend, came over and said, "Hey, Mary Margaret, you look kind of glum tonight. What's up?"

"Well, my sister made me promise that I wouldn't mention my fish during her party."

"Oh, yeah, right, you have fish. Hey guys, let's go see Mary Margaret's fish!" And every male there trouped upstairs to my room and spent most of the evening watching my fish, abandoning the girls below.

One evening, at a sleepover at a friend's house, a phone call came from my father. "Mary Margaret, I think your bettas are reproducing."

"What? They are? Really? Are you sure?

There was a pause. "Do you want me to come and get you?"

"Oh, yes, please, please! Thank you!" I don't even remember which friend I was visiting, but my abrupt departure couldn't have helped our friendship. I recall vividly, though, what happened in my aquarium.

I saw reproduction on a lyrical, ethereal scale that evening. *Betta splendans*, also known as Siamese fighting fish, are strikingly beautiful.

The males have very long fins, and their tails are longer than their bodies. Mine had a pink body and deep red fins, and he looked like a piece of floating red velvet. He was curling around the female, who had a turquoise-colored body and shorter red fins. They swayed and circled together, and as she shed her eggs, he caught them in his mouth and swam up to a bubble nest, which he had built earlier at the surface of the water. He placed the eggs gently in the nest, near the air, where they needed to be. Their reproductive dance continued for some time, and I watched, mesmerized. Later, tiny fish hatched from the eggs, and when they drifted down out of the nest, he gathered them into his mouth and carried them back up to the nest. He was a good father, though not as good as mine, for, whether through stress or inexperience, he eventually ate his offspring. This was devastating, but at least I witnessed their balletic lovemaking.

This all happened during my twelfth year. It was 1951. When my friends were asked what they wanted to be when they grew up, they said they wanted to be mommies, or, if they were career-oriented, they wanted to be secretaries. I told everyone I wanted to be an ichthyologist.

Twelve was the year that my migration pattern through life was being locked in. I became a part of the natural world: my passion for nature flourished, and I recognized my connectedness with every animal and plant in my small surrounding universe.

Twelve was when I also became fascinated by the interaction of light and color: this was the role the fish played. The eye-shocking green glow of the neon tetras, the velvety red of the bettas' fins, and the light catching the bubbles rising from the aquatic plants intrigued me. I often drew the many living things in my life with charcoal or pastels. These creatures, the light, and the color were my art.

At twelve I was adventurous and fearless. I often climbed high up into trees, and sure, I wanted to fly. I aspired to be Mary Marvel, my favorite hero in my vast comic book collection. Wonder Woman was too adult and too daunting. But Mary Marvel had a name like Mary

Margaret, and she was younger, had great powers, and could fly. Somewhat earlier, my mother had sewn a Mary Marvel costume for me on her primitive treadle Singer. It was a red dress with a full short skirt, a yellow lightning bolt down the front, and a white cape edged in yellow. When she gave me the dress, I was ecstatic. I ran upstairs, put it on, and then, from the top of the stairs, excitedly called, "Here I come!"

My parents and sister were sitting below, but my father jumped to his feet and ran up the stairs. Understanding me well, he explained that, despite the dress, and even though I wanted to, I couldn't really fly. But my mother, who often terrified me with her terrible temper, also did things like creating for me a costume which allowed me to soar.

Twelve was a very powerful year: I didn't care what anyone else thought about me. Everything seemed possible. I could do anything, and I could be anything I wanted to be.

ಜು ಜು ಜು

Then puberty occurred. Abruptly, we moved from the eighth grade of our elementary school, filled with children, into our four-year high school, filled with adult-like students. It was 1953, a time of enormous conformance. On some mystical day during the fall, everyone suddenly appeared at school wearing wool instead of cotton. The same thing happened in the spring, in reverse. How did everybody know the specific day? Was it like the minute shifts in day length that drive the life-cycle changes in plants and animals? I lived in morbid fear of selecting the wrong day to make my sartorial change. My attitude of not caring what other people thought of me had drifted off to some other place.

I was absurdly thin, and, indeed, most of us were thin at a time when processed foods did not exist, television was just appearing, and we spent all of our free time outside. In this era, Marilyn Monroe and Jayne Mansfield were idolized; this was how real women looked. Many of us didn't feel very glamorous. Lots of us weren't popular. Most of us studied a lot.

In college I studied zoology. The idea of a double major, in which I might study art, too, was unheard of. The prevalent attitude of that time was this: If you are going to study science, by God, you are going to study science. I married in college and later produced my sweet daughter Laura. Before long though, I ended up on my own, with a two-year-old child to raise and support. Despite all the cocky talk at twelve of becoming an ichthyologist, the fifties had not prepared me to be, in the sixties, a single parent with a decent career. I just kept working and going to school and getting more degrees, not knowing what else to do. But finding a good job eluded me. I trudged on, stubbornly.

Finally, I got a decent job teaching. I loved teaching and learned a lot more about what makes animals tick. I had to work hard, though, to finish a Ph.D., get tenure, and keep that job. I needed promotions to increase my modest salary. The working hours were very long. I was frightened that I would fail myself and, especially, my daughter. Through a long struggle of two decades, my passions and vivid interests sank to some deep place and lay there inertly, without light or oxygen. I allowed myself to lose what Rachael Carson aptly called, "a sense of wonder."

ରେ ରେ ରେ

Eventually, my tides started turning. A friend altered my course by inviting me to join a group going to Trinidad and Tobago. It had never occurred to me to go to Trinidad and Tobago, but I had tenure, and Laura had graduated from college. So I went. On that trip I discovered tropical oceans and tropical rainforests.

Floating on the warm deep water between Tobago and Goat Island I saw, through my snorkel mask, a school of giant manta rays far below me. Then, in a mind-blinding moment, one of the manta rays rose up and started swimming just a few feet beneath me. They get to be 20 feet across, and it wasn't that big, but it was huge. Two lobe-like fins on the front of the head funneled water into the mouth, and great, pointed side fins undulated hypnotically. Her ancient eyes regarded me. We recognized each other on some level. We swam a good distance together, and I would have followed her to oblivion, had my guide not grabbed my ankle to keep me from being swept away in a strong cross-current.

Later, on a sabbatical and alone in a rainforest in Ecuador, I saw a damselfly floating through the hazy forest. It was enormous—much bigger than my outstretched hand—with a long wire-thin body and long transparent wings. The only part that was visible on that humid, shadowy forest floor was a vivid white-blue iridescent disc glowing at the tip of each wing. I followed this ghost creature as long as I could, with only its wing tips revealing it, until it disappeared.

Later, in the jungle of Belize, I left my thatch-roofed hut one afternoon and, as I emerged into the hot sunlight, swirling around me were thousands of inch-long insect wings. These had just been shed, *en masse*, by a great swarm of termites. Their searching colony had settled to earth somewhere nearby, where they pulled their wings off, to dig and begin anew. Each floating wing reflected shards of colored lights from its iridescent surface as I stood, transfixed, in some bizarre, just-shaken, jungle snow globe.

Later, in the ocean off Belize, I floated above a coral reef, watching the many jeweled fish swimming below me and hearing only my breath passing through my snorkel. I did not move at all—I just drifted, like birds buoyed on thermals. Unlike other times I had snorkeled in tropical waters, this time I noticed the tides causing the water to rise and drop. I too rose and dropped above the reef, a small fragmental part of the earth's inhalation and exhalation.

ಬ ಬ ಬ

It is now 60 years after that pivotal, light-drenched twelfth year. As life's obstacles gave way and I could embrace nature more, my early passions and connectedness resurfaced from the depths—first as a small column of bubbles, and then in a great stream. I draw now with pleasure and write with contentment; and I long to go again, soon, to the tropics. The staccato call of a cicada and the flash of a monarch's wing bring joy. My sense of wonder pervades me.

Before long, some of my atoms will be bonded with those of other creatures. This will be *my* life after death. Perhaps some carbon atoms will be linked to others in the eye of a giant manta ray, gliding through a tropical sea. Maybe they will be part of a glowing iridescent disc on the wing of a ghost damselfly in a rainforest. They might be in the radula of a snail, gliding over its field of algae. Or perhaps they will be part of the red velvet fins of a male betta, curving in synchrony around his mate, rapturously.

Tales from a Teacher's Daughter

S trawberry Point, Iowa: Home of the World's Largest Fiberglass Strawberry, Backbone State Park, the Wilder Doll Museum, and just over 1,300 people—including my family. My parents moved there shortly after they married in the early 1970s for Dad's teaching job at Starmont High School. The town stretches only about two miles in each direction, but it supports a half-dozen churches and probably more bars and taverns than that. When I was growing up, Union Bank and Trust Co. sat on the southeast corner of Mission and Commercial, also known as Highways 3 and 13. The Franklin Hotel anchored the intersection on the northeast, Rosella's Beauty Shop on the northwest, and The Mustard Seed, a Christian book store, on the southwest. Not that this is a major intersection, but it was the town's single stop light. It hung from wires stretched across the intersection and flashed red in one direction and yellow in the other, until one day when a semi-truck came through and accidentally tore it down, forcing the city to replace it with a four-way stop.

Before it was paved, my parents bought a ranch-style house on Westwood Avenue, the last street on the west side of town. After the street was paved, the bottom of the driveway, a city easement, remained gravel throughout my childhood.

The three-bedroom, one-bath house was medium-yellow with decorative brown shutters on the windows and a white storm door. A kitchen, dining room, and living room all connected; only a long wall separated the kitchen and living room. We ran laps around and around, traveling across yellow linoleum and green shag carpet until we drove our mother crazy. The house was modest, but both the front and back yards were huge. In front, a white birch towered over the roof, shading the front window from the summer sun. Under this tree was a large rock, perfect for sitting, until Dusty, the Miniature Schnauzer we got when I was in fifth grade, made it his peeing rock. Out back there was plenty of room to play ball and swing on the dark blue and white swing set without disturbing Mom's vegetable garden. The property backed up to a corn field until my teenage years when Community Bible Church bought the land and built behind us. In the summer we loved to watch it rain from under the single-car carport. The swimming pool was a five-minute bike ride south; the grocery store, post office and drug store (complete with old-fashioned soda fountain) were about the same distance east. I was born in 1975 and lived in that house until I left for the University of Kansas in 1993. My brother came along in 1978, and he, too, spent his entire childhood there.

In a town the size of Strawberry Point, everybody knows everybody. If you're not a preacher's kid or a teacher's kid, you're probably a farmer's kid. While Mom worked as a secretary at the Area Education Agency in the nearby town of Elkader, Dad taught Biology and Physiology at Starmont High School, six miles west of town. It was centered between the three towns that made up our district— STrawberry Point, ARlington and LaMONT—hence the name. At that time, each town had its own elementary school, so being a teacher's kid didn't mean much to me during my elementary years. But by middle school, I started to get a taste of just how tough it was going to be. I remember a day at the swimming pool with my friends. Two rather large girls approached me in the shallow end.

"We hate your dad," they said. No reason, just hate. I didn't know how to respond, and it hurt my feelings terribly. Tears burned my eyes as I tried my best not to let it show. Later I learned that many more high school students, especially the cross country runners Dad coached, had great respect for him. Most of his critics only disliked his high expectations in the classroom.

My freshman year at Starmont High School arrived before I knew it. While I had navigated new buildings before, this was different. There were four banks of narrow lockers around the main square of classrooms. Mine was about two-thirds of the way down the yellow bank. They were the super-skinny kind, with a second little door above the main cabinet. Not only did the combination have to be right, I also had to squeeze between Lance and Mike, who had the lockers on either side of me. Lance had shaggy, brownish-blonde hair and was several inches shorter than me, which made it much easier to reach over him to get to my books. Mike was about my height with dark brown hair cut short. Despite their slim builds, it was still a tight squeeze. Class changes were no longer organized duck lines moving from one room to the next; now a crush of bodies swooped past, loading up books, pens, and notebooks, socializing, and still making it to class before the small ceiling lights throughout the school blinked off—the tardy signal.

High school also brought a new proximity to my dad. We often rode the six miles to school together so I didn't have to walk the half-mile to the middle school to catch the bus. During my freshman year, when I was feeling shy, I would skip the study hall in the cafeteria before school and hang out in Dad's classroom doing homework. Clyde, the classroom skeleton, would grin at me from the glass case next to the door. (Dad often dressed him with one of his ties, to make him look more professional.) The smell of formaldehyde permeated the room, and specimens lined the cabinets: a centipede, scorpion, mollusk, sponge, and so on, in jars too numerous to count. Dad would continue his morning routine, checking papers, going to meetings, and preparing for the day. It was peaceful and quiet; he always left the back of the room dark at that time of day.

As I grew more confident and involved, I spent less and less time in Dad's classroom. Instead I was dashing off to play rehearsals or Quiz Bowl meetings before school. My friends met in the cafeteria before homeroom to study and socialize. Dad would wander through periodically, his long stride never slowing. I knew he was doing his best to remain in the background to assuage the stigma of being Mr. McCullough's daughter.

The hardest part of being a teacher's kid was putting up with the rumors that I was a cheater. I studied hard and got good grades in all subjects—including those taught by my dad. While he helped me with math over the years, we remained distant when it came to biology and physiology. He treated me like any other student, clarifying points and answering questions about concepts like mitosis and photosynthesis.

But friends would sometimes pull me aside to convey the rumors, "People think you get good grades in Biology because your dad gives you all the answers." I never did find out who or how this all started. Had I gotten the opportunity to confront them, I had my response prepared: "Of course I'm good at Biology. I'm the teacher's daughter. Don't you know we learn this stuff by *osmosis?*"

Then there were the boys—or should I say lack of boys. I considered several my friends: Pete, Paul, Kevin, Scott, Jeff and the others from the cross country team. But most steered clear of asking me out. The few—or should I say two—who did date me were exceptionally brave. It's tough to make moves on a girl when her dad is likely to pop out of the next classroom, but both Reid and Paul managed to survive Mr. McCullough's omnipresence. They were even good sports when Dad chaperoned school dances, wandering the darkened cafeteria to make sure there was plenty of space between slow-dancing bodies.

However, I also had to survive the reputation my dad built for me before I got to high school. Picture the week we started fetal pig dissection my sophomore year. Sitting in my seat in the back of Biology class, elbows propped on the black lacquer tabletop, I heard him speak the words of doom: "This is our fetal pig diagram."

At the overhead, Dad had placed an overlay on which he had used a black Vis-à-vis marker to draw the outline of a fetal pig onto the roll of acetate being projected onto a screen at the front of the room. He paused dramatically, then announced to the class, "You know, Jenny was the model for this diagram. Well, the female version at least." My cheeks flushed fiercely. "Yeah," he continued, his smile widening. "I laid her up there when she was just a baby and traced around her. Her brother is the male version."

I. Wanted. To. Die.

The entire class giggled unsympathetically. A short time later, though, Dad made up for it with another joke at the class's expense. It came on the last day of fetal pig dissection. "This is the last day of dissection," he told the class.

I smirked from the back of the room, knowing full well what was coming next.

"Did you see they're serving ham patties for lunch today?"

I think most of my classmates knew he was joking, but at least a few faces turned white at the thought that Dad might have actually donated the pigs to the lunch ladies.

But Mr. McCullough wasn't done with me yet. When our genetics unit rolled around, Dad had yet another tall tale to spin for the class, with me in the starring role. On this particular day, the subject was dominant and recessive genes.

"You know," he said, "a recessive gene causes polydactyly, a condition in which a person has six fingers or six toes. In other words, you have to get it from both parents in order to have the condition."

Oh, boy, I thought, here it comes. The big one—the story he'd been telling his Biology classes for years before I set foot in Starmont High School.

"You know, Jenny has six toes that are webbed. That's why she runs so well in the rain."

Silence shrouded the class once again as they turned to look at me. This time, I was all smiles. The questions started: "Jenny, do you really have six toes? Can I see them? Take your shoes off? Does it hurt?"

"Yes, yes I do have six toes," I would reply with a straight face, catching Dad's eye.

This was more than a joke—this was Starmont legend. I had to play along with the ruse. One of the greatest challenges of my high school career was coming up with excuse after excuse not to show my feet.

Changing after gym class became increasingly tricky. I would shower and change, then pull shoes and socks on as quickly as possible. No sooner did I have my shoes tied then one of the other girls would slam her locker shut, plop down on the wooden bench, and exclaim, "Hey, let me see your toes!"

The other girls would gather around in various states of undress, just in case the persuader was successful this time. I would always claim I didn't want to catch a chill, or that I was embarrassed. No one pushed too hard until my junior year.

After incessant questioning all season long, the girls' cross country team decided to take action. One day, Karen gave the signal. The next thing I knew, she, Chelsey, Janelle, Sherri, and a horde of other girls were running toward me. I took off, thanking my lucky stars I was the fastest on the team. But even I couldn't run forever, nor could I hold off a whole mob of girls. After a few minutes of dodging in and out of bodies like a football player, they tackled me to the ground. Sherri held my arms, Karen sat on me, and Chelsey tore off my shoes and socks.

The truth was uncovered: my feet are as normal as the next person's, though they are exceptionally large. (My dad also called me "Paddlefoot.") Interestingly, the team decided not to let the word spread. I think my plea for discretion combined with their respect for Coach McCullough stayed their tongues. The legend of his daughter's six webbed toes remained a part of Starmont lore until Dad retired in 2009.

I knew I had to be there for his retirement. I put in for time off work at Audio-Reader, left my husband Dave with our two boys (ages three and six at the time), and drove the 400 miles from Lawrence, Kansas, to Strawberry Point, Iowa, to surprise Dad at his reception. I went directly to the school, carefully parking my white Subaru Outback decked out with telltale KU stickers where he wouldn't see it if he glanced out his classroom window.

With my laptop case swung over my shoulder, I walked into the cafeteria, ready to play a video I'd spent hours making. The video featured photos from many of Dad's cross country teams over the years, notes from his students, and newspaper clippings, set to the songs we had listened to on the bus on our way to meets: *Paint it Black* by The Rolling Stones, *I Feel Good* by James Brown and *We Are the Champions* by Queen. Mom had helped me gather this material in secret while Dad was at work, and she snuck it to me via a USB drive and the U.S. Postal Service.

I scanned the room and greeted many of my former teachers, also there to honor my dad. I walked across the room to hug Mom, who was standing with Mike, a former cross country runner (and my former locker neighbor), who had driven nearly three hours from Muscatine, Iowa, for the occasion. We prepared the video, and then watched for Dad's entrance.

Soon he came striding in, wearing a light gray-checked shirt and dark gray slacks. He looked around the room, taking in the attendees—fellow teachers and coaches—before his eyes fell on Mom, Mike, and me. He stared for a minute. Was he having trouble figuring out who we were? I waved. He did a double-take, and then a sweet smile and look of disbelief spread across his face. He greeted me with a huge bear hug, then shook Mike's hand, words, for once, escaping him. We played the video, ate cake, drank punch, and congratulated Dad on a wonderful teaching career. He kept saying, "I can't believe you drove all this way, just for this." But how could I miss it? After all, he was, my favorite teacher.

Chrome Dome

For many years, the principal of the high school in Manhattan, Kansas, where I mostly grew up, was a guy named Herbert Bishop. According to student scuttlebutt, he had been a chemistry teacher when he was younger. One day, some student threw together an unauthorized combination in his lab that created a cloud of fumes. They got this concoction into the fume chamber, and Mr. Bishop stuck his head in, trying to figure out what it was. And these fumes caused his hair to fall out, never to grow back. I think this was student folklore—no chemistry teacher would do that, and as far as I can research it now, he taught math. But whatever the cause, he was undeniably bald as a cue ball. Not even a little fringe along the edge.

Mr. Bishop was more interested in athletics than anything else. He loved to stand up in an assembly in front of a line of athletes, big guys, uncomfortable in their coats and ties, unsure what to do with their hands. He liked to hang out with athletes, be their buddy. These were the same guys who were out getting drunk, getting girls pregnant, and getting arrested. (At least two out of my class have done serious jail time.)

I did some research on Herbert Bishop, to make sure my memories were fair. I found a quote from an address he gave to a group of educators in 1960. He said, "Extra activities in drama, music and speech take pupils away from their schoolwork more than athletics do." Q.E.D.

Mr. Bishop would really come into his own at pep rallies. After the band had played a couple of rousers and the cheerleaders had led the crowd through some bleacher-stomping and thinly veiled threats to our opposition, he would take the podium at center court. He would repeat this pet phrase, "We're gonna kick the slats out of 'em!" over and over, building in intensity. He'd get all sweaty, and the gym lights reflected off his bald head like sunlight glancing off a car bumper. Wherefore did a generation of students call him "Chrome Dome."

Chrome Dome didn't like me from the beginning. The hair started it.

My family spent the year before I started high school, most of 1964 and half of 1965, in Cambridge, England. By that time, the Beatles and the Rolling Stones had appeared stateside, but this country was still in the midst of what was called the British Invasion. It was part of a worldwide phenomenon—Britain was the epicenter of huge changes in youth pop culture everywhere.

The Who released their first record while we were in Cambridge. The Animals appeared, as well as a band called Them, whose lead singer was Van Morrison. The Yardbirds hit, a band that graduated Eric Clapton, Jimmy Page and Jeff Beck—three titans of rock guitar.

But it wasn't just music; every aspect of society seemed to be tilting. There were the button-down, skinny-tie Mods on their Vespas, who regularly scuffled with the leather-jacketed Rockers on their Triumph motorcycles. Kids wore bright, colorful clothing in wild geometric patterns, ridiculously tight or dreamily loose. Op Art and Pop Art appeared in galleries, crazed experiments in theaters. There was an electric sense in the air that the old, stiff-upper-lip order was about to fall, to be replaced by something wilder, more colorful, more free. It was very exciting. And I had gotten to spend a year living in the middle of all that, soaking it up.

When we returned to Kansas, my friends told me people said I had a certain aura, and they said I had picked up an accent. I didn't hear it. I knew about music that hadn't made its way here yet. I knew what was soon to be cool. I knew what was coming.

I enrolled at Manhattan High School.

I showed up with a standard British kid's haircut. Think early Beatles—full, down a bit onto the forehead, lapping over the tops of the ears, sneaking down over the collar. Even for those of us who lived through the arrival of the Beatles in our culture, it is difficult now to remember how revolutionary their haircuts were, how scandalous. They look so unremarkable now, but some people were literally frightened by them.

Apparently, it was so with Chrome Dome. On the first day of school, before second hour, he called me into his office, having heard reports. My hair barely touched my ears, but it seemed that was the trigger point. He sent me home to get a decent haircut.

My parents were sympathetic but made clear it was my battle. I had no leverage, so by noon I had a standard Midwestern American kid's haircut—short on top and nearly shaved on back and sides—and the seed kernel of an abiding resentment of Herbert H. Bishop.

Then there were the pants incidents. I took apart an old pair of Levis and used them as a pattern to make a pair of pants. I used a single kind of fabric, but I made the legs different colors. One was harvest gold, the other olive green, so I looked like a couple of 1960s refrigerators standing next to each other. I knew this style was just around the corner. I wore them to school, and halfway through second hour I was back in Chrome Dome's office. He sent me home to change; the festering coals of my resentment glowed brighter.

Not long after that, in a store in Manhattan, I found a wonderful pair of pants. They were black and white hound's-tooth check, big, each square spanning more than an inch. I knew this, too, was a coming thing. I had seen it on the streets of Soho in London. But the same thing happened, and by second hour I was on the way home to change. I didn't plead with him; I wouldn't give him the satisfaction. I had no realistic choice but to comply and privately detest his pettiness.

I didn't give him much to work with after that. My cultural foreknowledge inevitably ran out, and before long other people took over pushing the envelope. Nonetheless, I stayed on his shit list all three years. I think he saw me as a wedge, cracking into his comfortable world. I know I saw him as a desperate guardian of doomed crew-cut conformity. He shook my hand when he handed over my diploma, but he didn't smile, and the glint in his eye made it obvious he was glad to see me gone. The feeling was mutual.

I never saw him again. He died in 1983.

Decades later, my grandmother was living in a nursing home in Manhattan. My mother had died, and I had become my grandmother's guardian, so I drove over once a week or more to keep tabs. One night, walking down the dimly lit corridor toward her room, I noticed a new nameplate by a door: Mrs. Herbert Bishop. I was surprised by how strongly I reacted. My ears got hot. The tan linoleum seemed to shift. I stopped in my tracks and had to catch my breath. I went on.

Over the next few months as I passed that door, I thought about doing … something. I considered getting a replacement nameplate, Mrs. Chrome Dome, and seeing how long it took someone to notice. I rehearsed a speech about how bitter, petty, and small-minded her husband was. I wanted to tell her that, whatever crack I might have made in his world, he was better for it. One night as I was leaving, tired, anticipating a 90-minute drive home, and down because my grandmother was fading, I actually took a few steps into Mrs. Herbert Bishop's room. I could hear her snoring. I backed out.

In the end I didn't do anything. After all, she had done me no harm. If it had been the man himself in there, it might have been different. But even so, overt expression of bitterness and anger has never been my style. I'm a Kansas boy born and bred, with a dash of British. We just don't do things like that.

It Was Early

E arly spring, early life, early '60s. It was the first of May, and we were busy enjoying how early it really was. Perhaps our parents or teachers saw the world through older eyes, remembering the hard times of the Great Depression when a five-cent head of cauliflower was the nutritional underpinning for a week of study; or the ration days of World War II, when Victory Gardens supplemented store-bought groceries but could not make up for the lack of sugar or gasoline; or, more recently, the 1950s, which had brought another bitter taste of war and the growing fears of nuclear holocaust. No, for us teenagers on the first of May 1963, the world was ours, and Lawrence was the center of that world.

Of course, some of the great events of the larger world had penetrated to us. We knew about Khrushchev's antic shoe-banging at the United Nations, we knew about the Bay of Pigs fiasco and the October Missile Crisis, we knew about the Berlin Wall and the ever-colder Cold War, and we knew about May Day parades in Red Square. Most of all, though, the first of May held the memory of our own younger days when we created May baskets out of construction paper, filled them with lilac and spirea sprigs from the yard and tiptoed to the doors of neighbors to place them there, before ringing the doorbell and hurrying away before they opened the door. This, we knew, was the proper ritual for May Day.

This particular May Day in 1963, however, found us high-schoolers somewhere between the rituals of childhood and the anxieties of the adult world. On this day we arrived at Lawrence High School to hear the principal, Mr. Wherry, announce a special assembly.

Assemblies generally were dismal affairs with someone pontificating to the submissive student body about something we were not interested in hearing. Today, especially, the prospect of the assembly was dreary. With Communists flaunting their missiles in Red Square, the local citizenry had decided to take action. We were told that the First of May was now to be celebrated as Law Day, and the schoolchildren of Lawrence were to learn about the U.S. Constitution, Democracy, and the American Way of Life. To counteract the Communist display of power in Moscow, a judge from a local court now stood before us, ready to help us understand the difference between what we were witnessing on nightly news reports and the wonders of the way of life which we assumed to be our birthright. This being 1963, we submitted quietly to the inevitable, but we were offended by the obviousness of the sermon and bored, to boot. To our minds, this was neither the proper way to celebrate May Day nor to enjoy the springtime of our own lives. We needed the old tradition, and we needed some fun.

Whose idea it was, I no longer know. But the appropriateness of our response and the potential for fun were obvious. We'd celebrate May Day the right way and simultaneously show the adults that we were not going to accept their attempts to paint Communists as the enemy or to spread political messages of inevitable world conflict. May Day was a festival of country life, a festival of the rebirth of nature, a time to rejoice in the youthful season. We'd need May baskets to deliver to our chosen recipients, and we'd need some costuming and props to help dramatize our message, and we'd need something with which to appease our audience for the unexpected performance, and we'd, well, we'd need what all teenagers need—we'd need wheels.

Surprisingly enough, the elements of this escapade came together quickly and easily. The recipients would be our favorite high school teachers, a good lot in all and quite tolerant of our creative minds. Our message would be delivered in a kind of street theater. We'd portray Russian peasants, country folk drawn, like country folk everywhere, to the rites of spring. In view of the rural celebration of the rebirth of nature, we'd carry some agricultural tools as props. The *pièce de resistance* would be the full-sized field scythe that belonged to my father and was stored in the garage at my house. As a goodwill offering, we baked some cookies and, careful to maintain our theme, we shaped them into the workers' emblem of the hammer and sickle and sprinkled them with red sugar. And finally, Steve Oldfather had a VW bus we could use. We were ready to roll!

Several of our high school teachers received unexpected knocks on the door that evening and opened to see a motley crew of peasants wearing burlap and kerchiefs and holding garden tools. It really was not possible to turn us away. In we came, boisterous and noisy and extending baskets of flowers and plates of Communist cookies. Everywhere we appeared, we were received in the spirit of the day. I do remember that one teacher was obliged to phone a girlfriend to let her know that their date would have to be cancelled since we showed no sign at that moment of vacating his apartment. No one seemed to find this situation problematic, though, as we settled in on the sofa, chairs, and floor for a longer stay.

Riding around Lawrence in the VW bus as we sought out the next house to visit added another dimension to our merrymaking. What fun to be off on adventure together, experiencing a foretaste of the open road! But driving across the top of the hill, down Jayhawk Boulevard, gave me, at least, a moment's pause. We were for the most part faculty kids. Among us were Oldfathers and Paretskys and Prices and Wrights and Baumgartels and Argersingers and more. What if campus cops did not understand the logic of a busload of costumed kids and an open sunroof with the long blade of a scythe poking out the top?

But nothing happened; no one bothered us or questioned our mission. This was the first of May, 1963, and we were celebrating the springtime of our lives. Still ahead lay the dark days of the Vietnam War, the Civil Rights campaigns, sit-ins and protest marches, assassinations of Kennedys and King, the Kent State shootings, boycotts of class, a student union in flames, a computation center bombed, and the deaths of Tiger Dowdell and Nick Rice.

It was early. But it was already later than we could ever have imagined.

Night Train

The clock struck midnight in Charleroi, Belgium. I shifted uncomfortably on the hard wooden bench in the train station. Outside, the March night was wet and cold, but inside, the station was stuffy and overly warm. My sweater and brown Chesterfield coat, damp from the incessant, gloomy rain were starting to smell unpleasant, like fermented wet wool. It was quiet in the waiting room. I was the only traveler; everything was closed up for the night. A sleepy agent sat behind a grill, ready to sell tickets in the unlikely event that someone would come in needing one. His occasional snores and the ticking of the large station clock provided the only sounds. I didn't need a ticket—I had a Eurail pass—and I was waiting for the train to take me to Paris, where I would switch to one bound for the city of Clermont-Ferrand, my temporary home.

I was not supposed to be in Belgium. I was definitely not supposed to be traveling alone. It was 1969, and I was a Kalamazoo College student spending part of my junior year abroad, studying at the University of Clermont-Ferrand.

"K College" was well known for its international program, which placed its students at various universities in France, Germany, and Spain. Some 150 of us were spread over the Continent. A French minor, I had just taken my final exams in Medieval History, French Literature, and Archaeology. In less than a week I would be back in Michigan.

I was returning home a different person. I had discovered independence, different viewpoints, Paris, French food, wine, Romanesque architecture, café au lait, the Louvre. I had learned what it was like to live somewhere where being American was not necessarily a good thing. And, oh, did I mention *Paris*?

I missed my family and friends, but I was not ready to leave the heady experience of living in France. My angst was complicated by the existence of a boyfriend at the University, an Egyptian pharmacy student named Akram. Indirectly, he was the reason I was in Belgium, traveling alone.

Like many other "K" students I planned to do some traveling before returning home. The trip was planned long before I knew Akram, and he was unable to travel with me. I was torn between wanting to spend my last few weeks with him and wanting to see more of Europe. Who knew when, if ever, I might get this chance again? I opted, reluctantly, for travel.

The college required us to travel with at least one other person and to file an itinerary with the faculty member who was our liaison. My friend, Dana, and I had planned an ambitious trip that included travel to several countries.

After filing our itinerary with our liaison, we decided to make a change because I wanted to go to Amsterdam, and Dana did not. We started out traveling together, then we split up to travel separately for a few days, with plans to reconnect in Germany. It was too late to send anyone notice of the change, but we decided to do it anyway. The pre-France Sherry would never have done this. But living in a foreign country, away from family and having more independence meant that I had become more adventurous.

We could make these last-minute changes because we both had Eurail passes. For two hundred dollars a pass provided three months of unlimited first class travel on any European train. You didn't need a reservation, you just showed up at the train station and boarded. It was a wonderful opportunity, and I made the most of it. I often traveled at night, taking advantage of the fact that I didn't have to pay for a hotel room.

As planned I left Dana in Barcelona and made my way to Amsterdam, past field after field of windmills. My father's side of the family had come from Holland (my birth name is Van Welden), and I had grown up interested in my Dutch roots. Oddly, I felt as though I was coming home, though I had never been there.

I didn't speak Dutch, but I managed to navigate my way around and to locate a hotel. I spent the first day walking around the city in the pouring rain, taking in the canals and the merchant homes built high and narrow, ducking out of the elements for coffee when it was too cold to keep going. I visited the Anne Frank Museum and Home.

The second day I spent at the Rijksmuseum. In the late afternoon I shopped in the wonderful book stores. But the onslaught of cold and rain continued, and I was lonely. A brisk wind blew the wet air right through me. I couldn't get warm. I kept thinking about my boyfriend who wasn't that far away, after all.

Around dinnertime it occurred to me that I could get on a train, travel to France through the night, and be in Clermont-Ferrand late the next morning. I'd have a day with Akram before needing to leave to meet Dana. The more I thought about it, the better it seemed. I skipped dinner, impulsively checked out of my hotel, and barely made it to the station, boarding the first train leaving. It was going to Charleroi. At least I was headed in the right direction.

My train to Paris was due in at 1:30 a.m. I knew it would be on time. But the hour and a half passed slowly. A cup of coffee and a little food would have been most welcome, but the café was closed. What had seemed like a good idea in Amsterdam was beginning to feel like a poor one as I struggled to stay awake, inhaling the wet wool smell wafting from my body as the overheated air in the station wrapped me in an oppressive cocoon of heat. At last the station master announced the train's arrival over a microphone, though I was still the only person in the station, and he didn't need the amplification.

Exiting the station, I headed to the train, long and sleek, illuminated by the sporadic platform lighting, with darkened windows attesting to sleeping passengers inside. It was cold, and I could see my breath as I hurried along.

A conductor stood on a small stepstool outside an open door into one section of the train, and shouted at me, "*Allons y*" or "Let's go," in a booming and impersonal voice. The train was scheduled to be in Charleroi for only several minutes, and timetables were adhered to with precision.

I climbed the metal steps and hefted my suitcase up to the waiting car, thinking, "At last." No sooner had I stepped into the train than I heard the conductor shout out a warning and observed him lifting the step stool back into the train. Seconds later we lurched forward, moving slowly and rhythmically out of town. I began my search for a seat.

The train was organized in what I had come to think of as typical for European train travel, a long string of compartments that provided bench seats for up to six passengers, with a sliding door that opened into a hallway that led to a bathroom and to connecting cars.

I had discovered some time before that the secret to traveling by train at night was to find an unoccupied compartment, or at least one with only one other person in it. Then you could turn off the light, stretch out across the leather seats and sleep, pulling your coat over you for a blanket. Of course, if the train was full, this didn't work, and you would end up squashed in with as many as five other passengers, upright. Conductors would usually let you stay sleeping across the seat if there weren't many passengers, but if more seats were needed they would come in, turn on the light, and require you to make room for others. Keeping the light off and lying across the seat was also a good way to discourage others from coming into the compartment. It worked well at least half the time. I really wanted to sleep.

The train was not full, but I could not find an empty compartment. I finally settled on one with only one other occupant. A woman was stretched out across one side, seemingly asleep. "This looks safe," I thought as I entered.

The room was dark, and I did not turn on the light, trying to be as quiet as I could, situating my suitcase and settling onto the opposite bench seat. As I drew my legs up under me to lie down on the lumpy bench the other passenger stirred, and sat up. "Darn," I thought, "I woke her up, and I was trying to be so quiet."

She spoke to me in German.

"No sprechen zie Deutsche," I disappointedly said. I didn't speak German and we wouldn't be able to converse. Actually, one did not usually speak to other train passengers, so I was kind of surprised she had tried to talk to me. That was unusual. Maybe I had made her mad, waking her up. But she didn't sound angry.

Then it occurred to me to speak to her in French. "Parlez-vous Francais?" I queried.

"Nein," she disappointedly answered. Though I did not speak German, I knew the answer was no.

We sat in silence for several minutes. The train was picking up speed as it left Charleroi rapidly behind, the familiar clicking and clacking lulling me into a relaxed state. We might have travelled on in silence if I had not, suddenly, remembered that I also spoke English, and maybe I should see if she did too.

"Do you speak English?" I asked.

She laughed and answered perfectly, "Yes, I am an American!"

"Oh, I said, I am too!" And we began talking animatedly. About ten minutes into our conversation I had learned that she was from New York and had been studying in Germany. This was her first trip to France, and she was meeting friends there. I explained that I had been studying in France. We went on chatting about various topics for some time before I thought to ask where she studied in the United States.

"Oh," she answered, "I go to a small liberal arts college in Michigan."

I felt the hair on the back of my neck stand on end.

She said, "It's a small college, and you probably don't know it, but they have a wonderful foreign study program. I attend Kalamazoo College."

"What?" I shouted, "I go there too!"

Astonished, we both reached up to snap on the light at the same time. Could we actually know each other? We were in the same class, for Pete's sake.

As it turned out, we didn't know each other, but this fact did not take away from our amazement. We both attended the same, small, private, liberal arts college in Michigan—it was uncanny. No, it was surreal. I could have picked any number of compartments. What had led me to hers?

She was very nervous about her trip to France because she didn't speak any French. She was meeting her traveling companions in Paris, but she would need to change her money in the train station before meeting their train at a later time. And she was worried that she would not be able to do this. I told her not to worry. I would help her, since I did speak French. Much relieved, she settled down to go to sleep, and I did the same, thinking about the truly small world we live in. Really, how high was the probability of meeting a K College student in the middle of Belgium on a train in the middle of the night?

I went to sleep amazed at the serendipity of our encounter. Coincidence? Divine intervention? I certainly didn't know what to think, but for sure night train travel was a world unto itself, always interesting, and sometimes astounding.

Coincidence?

I t's July 14, 1989, in La Place St. Sulpice, Paris, one of the dozens of open spaces where bands are playing outdoors for the bicentennial of French Independence Day. I'm swaying to the music and minding my own business, when a short young woman just in front of me in the small crowd, someone I've never seen before, turns around, looks up, and asks, "Don't you teach at KU?" *Coincidence!* (It's the same word in French.)

I learned long ago, even before that Paris encounter, that wherever I am and whomever I'm not with, I should behave as if I were in my own territory. Whatever you do at the faraway and supposedly anonymous place you've gone to, *caveat traveler!* I suggest adding to your stock of wise clichés that not only is there no free lunch, there's no Hernando's Hideaway, either.

But hiding from prying eyes isn't my issue; "coincidence" is. What brought me and that young KU student to that spot on that day? Rationally speaking, it was a purely random meeting, however unlikely. Yet many people, including some scientists, are willing to entertain the idea that such conjunctions may be more than just fortuitous. If you accept that random chance governs such meetings, then you probably have to accept that life itself is random, and not purposeful. Some say that anything else is mere ego. I don't agree. Though I consider myself a rational man, I also think that we're all more linked than separated—and in more ways than we know.

We've all heard of "six degrees of separation" (and probably of the game "Six Degrees of Kevin Bacon"). This networking notion has me looking at my own life for a closely related phenomenon: my connections to others by supposed coincidence.

What has been true for me might be so for you too, no? Have you had encounters and experiences sometimes so far-fetched that they seem to strain the number of zeros available for any statistic describing them? If so, what do you make of them? Most adults can narrate at least one or two such unlikely occurrences to which the hearer says something like "Wow," or "Bizarre."

"Be reasonable," I say to myself. I learned a little about probability in college, so I know that what seem to be astonishingly unlikely encounters are usually less so, statistically. And I know that we all have at least heard of enough of them to be used to them—though still we tend to shake our heads and smile in disbelieving acceptance each time.

It's just that my life seems to be really rich in such unlikely coincidences.

Starting graduate school in Indiana, I met a naïve Hoosier and told him I had grown up in New York City [population at that time about 8 million].

"Oh," the rube says, "maybe you know ___ _____."

I *did*—he was a high school friend. Who was the rube now? "Whoa," I say: The odds were actually far better than 1:8,000,000. And in the case of the supposed Hoosier rube, he and I didn't have to go any further than a friend of a friend to connect us.

But the very fact of those connections made me think: Is the usual approach to coincidence lacking something, something beyond our ken? Studying English literature as I was, I thought of Wordsworth: "Late and soon, getting and spending, we lay waste our powers." What powers of perception or intuition might we have had as children and lost—or perhaps, more likely, never had? We have only our five puny senses, after all. Don't we feel sometimes that they're not enough, that some tantalizing perception is just beyond our reach? None of us senses the changing air pressure over Dallas that has had an effect on the approaching tornado in Kansas.

When I was about 24, still at Indiana University, my mother told me by phone that according to <u>his</u> mother, a guy named David, my

212

best friend when I was 3 years old in the Bronx and whom I hadn't seen or even heard of since, would be coming to Indiana for his graduate work. Okay, I promised her; that might be interesting. I'd try to look him up among the hundreds of other graduate teaching assistants there. Then I came to the office for the first day of class, and the guy at the desk next to mine was (you guessed it, didn't you) that same David—in the same department, seeking the same degree, teaching the same courses. This experience, again involving someone from my earlier life, again set me contemplating coincidence.

Rather farther down the road, a few years after I had a degree, a wife, two small children, and a position at Kansas University, I convinced the Brazilian-American Fulbright commission to pay me to live and teach for a year in Rio de Janeiro. Halfway into that remarkable year filled with the new and different, in March or April, my wife and I were sitting at a café table in the Brazilian city of Salvador, Bahia one evening during a Latin American conference on North American literature. With us were another American couple, several Brazilians, a Colombian, and a Paraguayan. The conversation gradually grew more and more animated as we learned that each person at that table, with the exceptions of the other two U.S. citizens, had lived (not just visited, but *lived*) in Lawrence, Kansas. Oh, the laughter that followed! The sharing of addresses, memories, hopes to return! *Que coincidencia!*

A few months ago, at the Toronto airport, I was passing through U.S. Customs. Examining my declaration form and passport, the agent questioned me about why I had been in Canada (a wedding), where I live (Lawrence, Kansas), for how long (40 years), and about what I do (retired English prof.).

Then, apparently out of nowhere he asked "Do you know ____ _____?"

"Yes I do: he was a graduate student in one of my classes and now teaches English at KU," I reply. "And—my wife, here, treated one of his sons."

"Well, he was my English teacher."

Stamping my passport and handing it back to me with a little smile he said, "Welcome back to the United States. Rock, Chalk, Jayhawk!"

What were the odds that Agent Venn (who happens to be black, by the way—a very small minority among KU students when he was there about 15 years ago) would be my Customs agent in Toronto? I don't know, but I think they're rather slim.

I've been hearing perspectives on these matters from friends. One, a churchy sort of guy, says that what we call coincidence is actually part of a grand design which we can and will never know. Another, a rationalist above all, says that I'm simply mathematically challenged. Still another, a psychologist, says that I'm making mysteries because I enjoy mysteries more than plain reason. But my Hindu friend advises me to escape the prison-house of reason and those five limited senses. "Bugger-all with that simple Western rationalism," he laughs.

Past lives or not, we're all more intimate in some ways than we think, despite all that superficially separates us. Relations, histories, families, friendships, encounters, memories, and dreams, create threads, tendrils, fibers, filaments, webs known and unknown, which all link us. Might "coincidence" be mainly a placemarker for later understanding, really a product of our current conceptual limitations and our need for what seems to be logical? I say yes, and here's one additional reason why:

During one of the two years I lived in Europe, I had a much younger artist friend, Melissa, who was a channeler and listened to spirit guides. I should have found her too flaky for my taste, but from the time we met, at a reception, we liked each other and could talk easily on many subjects. She was animated, shapely, and pretty, and I admit that I thought of her too much for my own peace of mind. One night, after not having seen her for a week or two, I dreamed about her being a cat. In a dream-logic story plot, which quickly faded from my memory, she was somehow associated with a penguin.

When I phoned the next day to tell her the remembered remnant of my dream, she let out a sort of *"Aaahhh."* Then she said, "Last night was Halloween."

"I didn't realize that," I replied. While she was living in a graduate dorm at the Cité Universitaire with other Americans, I was living alone, renting a Paris apartment, and not speaking English with anyone most days. And there's no such holiday in France. "So?"

"So we had a party. I went as Catwoman and my friend Sylvie went dressed as The Penguin."

"No! What do you make of that, Melissa?" "I think you opened a channel of some sort in that dream." More than 20 years later I think so too. In this case saying "coincidence" just won't hack it.

My dear audience: you can stop waving your mental hands and crying silently, "But...," But...." I agree with Hamlet:

There are more things in heaven and earth,
Horatio,
Than are dreamt of in your philosophy.

I think that unseen patterns of human interrelations, physical and otherwise, exist, to be found some day, perhaps by using different sets of assumptions than we do now; let's say found by a new Benoît Mandelbrot. That genius of the future might someday reveal the substructure of our superficial separation, the substructure of what we helplessly call "coincidence": that researcher might reveal new patterns of being—new, beautiful fractals of world and of mind. Perhaps you've already guessed that I would *really* like to be here then.

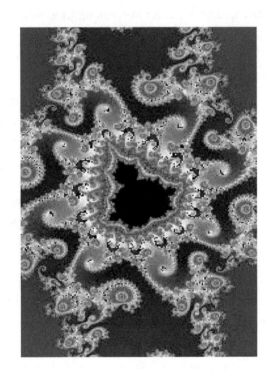

PART IV

Imagine Yourself as a Mother

By the third month of trying to get pregnant, I had restricted my husband to sex only on the days the calendar deemed super fertile, days 15, 16, and 17 of my menstrual cycle. During those days I thought of driving to his office in nothing but snow boots and a sundress and pulling down the backseat all the way, but didn't. Sex had to be in the early morning anyway—the time of day was important because a woman's body temperature fluctuated and that affected my eggs, a website said.

My husband began to roll his eyes when I mentioned babies that third month of our efforts. I had ruined it, and it didn't even take me very long.

I knew I was going about this in the wrong way—this was a special time for couples, all the books said. We were supposed to have fun trying, focus on each other and the miracle of life. But I had had brain surgeries. When I was in physical rehabilitation afterwards, I learned all sorts of ways to strengthen my body quickly, to get my weakened right side and loss of balance back to way it used to be.

I didn't let nature take its course. Rubber resistance bands, small hand weights, and heavy jump ropes were used every day. Playing jacks increased dexterity, word searches trained the eye. There was nothing better than walking in sand to help balance, and the game Connect Four helped with depth perception. Aqua aerobics, Bikram yoga, acupuncture. Zinc. Hypnosis. Meditation. Low doses of electric shocks. Whatever the doctors suggested, I did. I scoured chat rooms and message boards for ideas, too. I bought every tool, took every pill. This was no different. If I did all the right things I would get results. It was simple.

No one could know we were trying to have a baby. It had to be a secret, otherwise the pressure would stress us out, my husband and I told each other. The same week my husband and I were supposed to have sex as much as possible we had to be at a family reunion. It was at the YMCA in the Colorado Rockies, and everyone was staying together in a big lodge, all of us with metal bunk beds and dirty carpet.

We had a room to ourselves, but next door were my mother and stepfather. They left their door open all the time and kept snack foods on the bedside tables. People were always going in and out with fistfuls of chips and dried fruit. At night, my mother walked around the halls in wet hair and a sleep-shirt talking to everyone. I was glad to be with my mother, I had missed her. I always did.

On the drive out to Colorado, we stopped at a truck stop, and I, looking for a bathroom, passed doors with locks that looked like dial pads on pay phones. I could feel heat from steam and smell green, and I was very close to a naked stranger, probably a man.

Of course, I couldn't decide to have a baby without considering all of the reasons for not having one. My hearing loss in one ear, for one thing. I didn't always understand what people were saying. I had a hearing aid, but I couldn't do things like wear a hat or talk on the phone or exercise with it in, so I forgot to wear it a lot, and it sat in the bottom of my purse for weeks at a time, getting sticky with candy residue.

But mainly I thought about the physical disfigurements. There was an off-center eye, a paralyzed half of my face, problems with balance. I had answered questions about my appearance to small children before, explaining that I had a boo-boo, and I wondered how I would explain it to my own child. I wondered if he or she would feel ashamed of me.

The big kitchen in the lodge was for everybody, and so I hid my special fertility juice behind the condiments. I was supposed to drink it in the morning on an empty stomach when I took my prenatal vitamins, which I hid in an outer pocket of my suitcase. They were big yellow capsules that smelled like sardines. Alone in my room, I got online and looked at pregnancy message boards. Posts were titled:

WHY CAN'T I GET PREGNANT and WHEN CAN I PEE AFTER SEX? I learned what angel babies were. They were babies that had died.

When we were supposed to have sex, my husband and I told the rest of the family that we were going on a solo hike. Afterwards, I got into the candle position for twenty minutes. It was like a headstand, and I had learned that on the Internet, too.

My cousins and brothers got up at 3 a.m. to climb the tallest mountain in the park, which required ropes and watching for falling rocks. A rule was that they had to put used toilet paper in their backpacks and hike it down. They didn't want to leave a footprint.

Before bedtime, I checked my underwear and noticed how my breasts felt. I asked myself if I disliked certain foods I usually loved. An aversion to onions was common. My father should be the last to know, I had heard. I had heard not to tell even my husband right away. To let that secret be mine. But that was wrong, I thought. We should decide to have a baby as a couple. After all, we will be a family.

A bunch of us drove to a trailhead where there was a hike to a waterfall. In the backseat, my cousin's rich hippie boyfriend alternated between talking about how sugar was just as addictive as cocaine and his dissertation on constructing an office building out of plants. His apartment was crammed with them, he said, and so they got more oxygen and felt better than most people. His favorites were jade and bonsai, for obvious reasons.

"Do you ever think about having kids?" I asked my cousin. I couldn't help it, maybe it was the hormones, stronger during fertile days.

My cousin worked at a running shoe store, made her own almond butter and ate raw garlic. She looked at me like my question was a trick.

"Maybe someday," she said, "but we have so much we want to do. Travel, for instance. At least we got to check India off our list, right honey?"

She looked at her boyfriend, not at me.

I nodded. I wanted to travel, too, but my husband and I never had the money to go anywhere but St. Louis, where his mother lived. I wondered about taking what I had heard called a Babymoon, which was the last vacation a couple took alone before a baby was born. Maybe we would take a Babymoon to St. Louis, or if we waited, maybe we could save up to go somewhere better.

I remembered when we said that we wanted to have a baby for sure. We were in a lake, treading water. I had just lost my sunglasses, but had a spare in the car.

While some people at the reunion hiked, others went to the Crafts Room to tie-dye T-shirts. Some others went horseback riding where the horses were old and hosts for flies. Some sat in the Commons Room and drank soda. Before dinner, I stared at myself in the mirror and tried to imagine myself as a mother. I had never seen a mother like me before.

During happy hour, I watched my husband from across the room, fending for himself with three of my uncles who all stood with their short legs spread far apart, hands in their pockets, comfortable forever.

I sat next to my mother. She was wearing one of her son's college sweatshirts and her face shined with lotion. When she laughed, I noticed how much people were liking her. I reached for my mother and squeezed her hand, then received the squeeze back.

My mother didn't ask about my health often anymore. She didn't need to, which was a relief for us both. It had been five years, and for the year of the brain surgeries we talked about nothing else.

My husband and I drove back home at the end of the week, and I began buying things. Just a book, at first, *The Conception Chronicles*, a fake diary of one woman who was TTC (Trying To Conceive). It was terrible, but I read it twice—I even highlighted parts. My period came. The next month I bought the pregnancy tests, the ovulation kits, the membership to an online calendar that kept track of basal body temperature, for which I had to buy a special thermometer that I had to stick in my mouth the moment I awoke. I got a special pillow to wedge under my butt to help the sperm travel.

I looked at one website for parents with disabilities, but it seemed to be directed at women in wheelchairs, and I didn't look again. Nothing happened that month. Nothing happened the next one, either.

I accused my husband of skipping sex when he knew my fertile days were there. He came home late from work on the best day, Day 12, after I had fallen asleep in an itchy negligee, candles burning. When he got into bed I woke up and sniffed him, but he didn't smell like beer or cigarettes, but like nothing. He had breakfast meetings and lunch-hour basketball games for the rest of the week. Or maybe I was being paranoid, maybe he was being normal. Either way, I was worried.

So I scaled back. It was Christmas, and I told my husband I didn't care about babies anymore. The two of us went to the grocery store parking lot and bought a real tree. I spent too much money on his present of an electronic map and baked him his favorite, a Dump Cake. The cake was made of canned pineapple, canned cherries, a box of yellow cake mix and two sticks of butter. When the two of us pulled the wishbone off the turkey, I had no idea what he wished for with his victory. I didn't know what to ask for myself.

There were so many friends I wanted to talk about this trying thing with, but I only chose one, who already had a child. I told her about trying while in her kitchen helping decorate an Elmo cake for her son's first birthday. The icing flavor was Black Licorice for the inside of the puppet's mouth.

"Well, we may get pregnant at the same time," my friend said with a wink.

"We're going for baby number two."

In college, the two of us went to a party in a barn and my friend leaned on a standing space heater, smoking a cigarette. After a while she ran her fingers through her hair and then grabbed and took a fistful. She had burned the back of her bob off. I, for my share, wore the wrong coat home and puked all over it.

My friend called a week later and said she was pregnant.

"Sorry, I'm a Fertile Myrtle," she said.

The test finally read "pregnant" on a Tuesday morning, and all I could do was stand around in my bathrobe. I called my husband, who was driving on the highway, and started to make up a lie about the toilet overflowing to get him home so I could tell him in person, but then just screamed the news. We both cried.

That night, I wanted to call my mother, but hesitated. I was sure she was in bed, or I thought that she might be reading an interesting book or writing in her journal, or having some sort of important conversation with my stepfather, something to do with her recent knee surgery, or his high cholesterol. He also had sleep apnea, they could have been talking about that. She could be doing any number of things and not want to be disturbed.

My mother took up tennis when I was little, and one year for her birthday my father gave her a nylon warm-up suit of black and pink geometric designs. She started watching tennis on TV while she was ironing, bought a bunch of short pleated skirts, and joined the city's team. The next year she stopped playing, just like that, and started cleaning the house obsessively, wearing kneepads when she stripped and re-waxed the kitchen linoleum. The next year she started running, and did half-marathons soon after. By the time my parents got divorced my mother had earned her Master's in Library Science by driving into the city three nights a week for two years. She didn't stick with that, though, but did other things, like moving across the country and buying a business with cash.

Until I got sick, then my mother's life became me. She moved me into her house, where the two of us watched movie marathons during the day when she should have been working. She helped me shower. Read aloud by my bed every night.

I remembered the wedding reception of my mother and stepfather's a few years ago. She and I had held hands at the head table as everyone started to leave for the night. I was dating someone, my now-husband, and life was getting better. My mother looked at her new sparkling ring and said, "May you be this happy someday." Suddenly, I was.

Star Wars

J anuary 30, 1991. Spenser appeared on a Wednesday under a full
moon when all kinds of terrors were being unleashed in the
Persian Gulf.

I lay on my side in a hospital bed with silver chrome bars, my white
hospital gown tied loosely several places in the back. With my swollen
stomach, breasts engorged with milk and eyes tightly shut, I breathed in
furtive rhythm, like a hibernating animal. I could hear voices speaking
around me, and feel hands being placed on my body.

"We have to check to see how much you've dilated. An eight." A
short woman with peppery hair appeared far away at the end of my legs.
The pain of the contractions dwarfed the discomfort of her inserted
fingers.

"Margaret, we'll be in the waiting room." My mother and sister
stood with their coats on. I knew by reading my mother's facial
expression that she would not stay. She doesn't want to be around
when things get visceral. When she cared for my aunt who died of
cancer, she told the nurse, after my aunt went into a coma, not to call
her until after my aunt died.

They left, but I couldn't have used them, because I was spiraling
into a vortex deep inside.

The monotone sound of the television broadcasted news
correspondents incessantly chattering about the imminent invasion of
Kuwait. Excited by prospect of war, they stood in their trench coats and
clutched their microphones in gleeful anticipation of the slaughter.

"Turn it off, turn it off!" I yelled at the television.

I was powerless to stop the war, even though I had lugged this
unborn baby around the state capitol through a sea of voices in an anti-

war march. But it was no use. The country was whipped up in patriotic fervor, exulting in the bright lights of Star Wars, lurid over the prospect of misery, not unlike a small boy secretly crushing insects on the driveway, alone, sinful, and emotionally charged by the agony of death.

My husband Steve, a frightened onlooker, shut off the television, but his yellow paper gown and spectacles were fading away. As the drug Pitocin intensified the contractions, I let go. I just let go, and my soul floated out to the hill overlooking Lake Perry, where I rode my horse past fields of purple scurf pea, white daisies and bright orange Indian paintbrush. As the grasses bowed away from the wind, his hoofs hit the ground and bounced, bounced, bounced on our shadows. I entreated the baby, "Please come to us. You'll have a wonderful life, and a big brother."

The peppery-haired nurse came back.

"This is why they call it labor. It's the most strenuous physical thing you've ever done." She spoke loudly, as though I were deaf.

This wasn't the most physically taxing thing I had ever done. When I was twelve years old, our junior lifesaving instructor told us to jump into the lake and swim back to the shore. After I plunged in with a scissor kick, the chilly water surged through my body like electricity, and all I could see was dirty green. My arms and legs wiggled like a frilly paramecium, while the waves tossed me from side to side.

"I don't know if I can do this," I gasped.

The instructor, his wet hair flattened around his tan face, squinted at me.

"Are you chicken?" he yelled.

So there was no choice. It was preferable to drown than admit fear. I forced my aching arms into the rocking waves, and when my feet touched sand, my legs could scarcely bear my weight.

"I have to measure to see how far you've dilated," the peppery-haired nurse said. I felt like a mountain as I shifted onto my back. From between the frame of my spread legs, the sharp glint in her eyes signaled that she didn't like what she saw.

"Everything's proceeding very nicely. You're a good girl," she intoned, pulling down my gown.

"The doctor! Where's the doctor?" she yelled as she charged into the hall.

Distant voices told me that I was fully dilated, but it was too late for any pain medication.

"Push, push," the nurses cheered from the sidelines. I pushed. With my hands clasped around my knees I strained at the height of every contraction, but nothing happened. I had no urge to push. The baby would not come out.

The doctor, a small man with neatly-trimmed dark hair surveyed the situation. A profusion of chest hair sprouted from the V in the top of his green scrubs.

In the darkened delivery room, this doctor scurried around pacing from one apparatus to another. He knew things were falling apart. He had been delayed by his other surgery, and now he had walked into a mess. His hand, gloved in squeaky plastic, entered my vagina and felt the baby's head. Again I pushed. Same resistance.

As a little girl who had been bad, I beat my forearms against the door of my room in protest until they were shot full of pain. The door held fast.

Next, the doctor directed a nurse to roll a machine with a big box toward me. He pried open my vagina and attached a suction cup. They probably use this when they evacuate the contents of the uterus, or perform abortions. The machine rattled for a few futile moments, like a jackhammer on a distant construction site. Nothing.

The doctor increased his pace, traversing quickly from one point to another. With steel cold forceps, he yanked hard, turning me inside out. I howled.

The doctor stopped. He was sitting on a rolling stool at the end of the table, with his head and shoulders encircled by the white glare of the surgery lamp. He propped his arm on my leg, and I felt his head drop onto my thigh.

227

"I'm going to have to cut you open," he said quietly.

He and the nurse moved in the shadows outside the surgery lamp.

"Will she have a spinal block or general anesthesia?" the nurse asked.

"General," the doctor muttered, and crossed to get another instrument.

As the waves of contractions kept rolling inside my body, I was pushed on a squeaky gurney past doors that opened and shut behind me.

They talked quietly around me when the intravenous injection dripped into my vein. The fluid in a plastic bag swung from the metal contraption overhead. The anesthesia would knock me out, but after pushing for three hours, I wanted the darkness,

When I regained consciousness, on a gurney in a darkened enclosure with sheets as walls, a dark-haired nurse felt my pulse, and asked small, simple questions. I wanted to slip back into the oblivion because I was bottomed out, and lacked even the energy to feel excited about the baby who had just been born.

The gurney rolled me down the hospital hallway, emitting long squeaks. I didn't know where they were taking me because nobody told me anything, but I assumed it was to see the baby. The elevator dinged, thrust open its doors, and buzzed again after a descent. Other people passed by, a moving kaleidoscope of white jackets, stethoscopes, light green scrubs and pastel pictures. We rolled past proud parents and relatives making little motions through the window at the healthy newborns on display. Why weren't we stopping?

The gurney paused before the automatic doors of the neonatal intensive care unit.

We shouldn't be in here. Something was not right. When I was wheeled beside the isolette containing my baby, I saw a tiny, thin figure, eyes tightly shut and cheeks bruised from the forceps, that shuddered slightly in grief and pain.

Is that the baby?

I would always feel guilty about my first impression, but with his little wizened face and slightly slanted eyes, he did look strange. There was something foreign about him, unnatural. That couldn't be my child.

My sister told me that after his birth, the medical personnel viewed him from one angle and then another. No, they decided, this was not a happy outcome, so they consigned him to the neonatal intensive care unit, where the lights shine all night against struggling odds, and gleaming memorial plaques mirror tears.

I was finally rolled into a deathly still wing of the maternity ward. Although I could hear noisy throngs of relatives with flowers and balloons walking down the hallways of the ward, my room was quiet. A photograph adorned my door of a modern sculpture in the hospital courtyard titled "The Tear."

"Why is that picture next to my name?" I asked the nurse on rounds.

"That's for mothers who are sad because of miscarriage or stillbirth. It serves as a warning for the staff who enter the room."

I didn't want that thing on my door, or to be labeled a tragedy case. I expected a healthy baby, and flowers from smiling people offering congratulations. That thin wasted body with the agonized face, a prickly memory, stung me.

The birth certificate read 2:39 p.m. Steve drifted in and out of my room. He was shocked by the turn of events, ineffectual, a shade who spoke a few garbled words I couldn't comprehend. Even though I fully intended to answer him and could formulate a response in my mind, the drugs prevented the words from coming out, so the emotional attachment between us pooled up and died in the long pauses.

The afternoon passed that way. No nurse brought a fat baby swaddled in a blanket, wearing a pastel knit cap. Nobody talked to me. Nobody told me anything. It was cold outside, dark, January.

The end of January is anti-climactic, a letdown, something to be survived. Despite the fluorescent lights in the hallway, the window

229

panes bespoke a dull blackness. I slept through low talking outside in the hallway, the sound of people passing, some shuffling, some with sharply clicking heels. Nobody came into the room. I was barricaded by the tear.

I sat up in my hospital bed, alone. Because the anesthesia was lifting I clicked into focus. On the television, a Marine, one of the first casualties of Desert Storm, was being interviewed. He stared into the camera, dressed in fatigues and mouthing words, but not seeing, and not believing.

"The bullet entered my leg and I started bleeding, but that's not what got to me. What really got to me was knowing that," he paused and stared blankly at something that wasn't there, "was knowing that I'd been hit."

Ben's Boots

"**S**hoes off! Boots on!" exclaimed our youngest son Ben, age two, upon meeting his first pair of cowboy boots. We had been dining at the T-Rex restaurant at The Legends shopping center in Kansas City, Kansas. The restaurant was a favorite of big brother Charlie's, age five. Charlie was all about dinosaurs; he could rattle off names and statistics with no effort. As we headed back to the car, we passed Cavender's Western Store and spotted some John Deere toys in the window. Ben was infatuated with anything on four wheels, especially John Deere. In fact, every time we passed the tractor sales lots on our way to Kansas City, he would scream with delight, "Tractor! Tractor!" We couldn't resist stopping in to take a look.

We opened the glass door and entered a western wonderland. The front counter was built to resemble a horse stall, complete with saddles, tack and other equipment nailed to its border. We passed rack upon rack of western wear, women's to the left, men's to the right, as we made our way to the back of the store and the small toy section. The boys dashed ahead as Dave and I sauntered behind, hand-in-hand, smiles spreading over our faces.

Dave has always been a big fan of cowboy boots, so while the boys oohed and ahhed over the toy tractors, he and I headed for the footwear. Dave wore boots almost exclusively the entire time we dated. I, on the other hand, was not a big fan. As a child I had played dress-up with Grandma Doris's shoes, her cowboy boots included. When I grew into them in fourth grade, she gave them to me. I truly wanted to love them, just because they were hers, but they pinched my toes and gave me blisters. I outgrew them quickly and never desired another pair. So while Dave eyed the men's boots, I browsed the little boys' boots in all colors—blue, red, green, brown, black. Then I saw something glorious! In the back corner of the boot section they stood out like a green thumb: John Deere cowboy boots complete with bright green and yellow uppers.

I called out, "Dave, come here! You have to see these!"

He appeared at my side and quickly agreed with my assessment. "Ben would love these," he said. Being the family budgeter, I quickly checked the price tag. No point in getting a two-year-old's hopes up if we couldn't afford them. It said $25—more than I would normally spend on kids' shoes. "If we buy them big, maybe he could wear them for a couple of years," I said to Dave, justifying the purchase. He agreed.

"Hey Ben, come here!" Dave called out. We watched as Ben's blonde head, hair styled into a bowl cut, bobbed toward us.

Charlie followed along, starting to complain. "Can we go now? How long is it going to be?" he whined. "Not long," I told Charlie as Dave presented the boots to Ben. His blue eyes widened immediately as he said in his best 'Back off 'cuz I'm calling the shots now' voice: "Shoes off! Boots on!" His Pull-Up-padded bottom hit the sales floor and his shoes were off in a flash. We quickly fitted them with the John Deere boots, feeling very much like Cinderella's footmen, smiling as he leapt to his feet and strutted about the store admiring his newly shod feet.

I picked up the box and headed for the check-out stand, continuing to assure Charlie, whose feet were beginning to drag, that we were almost finished. Halfway there, the price tag once again caught my eye. They weren't $25—they were $75! A pit began to form in my stomach. Ben was obviously already attached, but we couldn't afford $75 boots, especially for a kid whose feet were sure to continue to grow quickly. I showed Dave, and we headed back to the shelves hoping for a mistake. There was a mistake alright: the price tag I had seen was for the baby-sized boots. The toddler boots took a steep price jump. Dave and I immediately discussed our options.

"We can't afford this," I said.

"But he's already attached," Dave countered.

"He's going to outgrow them too fast."

"We'll buy them a full size too big instead of a half-size. He can wear them longer."

"But won't we have to do something equal for Charlie?"

"Charlie doesn't seem to care that Ben's getting something and he's not."

"What if we got them for Ben's birthday?"

"Yeah, we could do that."

"But that's still six months away. Maybe we shouldn't." I've always been indecisive.

"He's two, he won't know the difference. Besides, he'll get plenty of presents from other people."

"Okay," I finally relented, the pit growing bigger as I made my way back to the cash register.

The cashier rang us up, smiling obliviously as she swiped the credit card. I smiled back weakly. "He sure looks cute in those boots," she said. "Yes, he does," I agreed. Ben was busy charming every female in the place. I signed the receipt and took the box, his tennis shoes tucked neatly inside. Ben was the proud owner of his first pair of cowboy boots.

Ben and his boots were inseparable. He wore them every day—rain or shine, hot or cold, blue jeans or shorts. It didn't matter. His boots were part of his personality. His style. When they began to grow too snug about six months later, the discussion of a new pair began.

"I think Ben needs new boots," I said to Dave. It was September, and Ben's birthday was approaching. "Maybe your mom would buy them?"

"Maybe," Dave said.

"Or maybe we should. He's already gotten boots once. Maybe he won't be as excited this time. She would be disappointed."

"Maybe," Dave said. His turn for indecision. We tabled the issue.

As Christmas approached Ben outgrew his John Deere boots completely, and we couldn't deny it any longer. Ben REALLY needed new boots. We decided to buy them ourselves, but this time I searched for and ordered them online. I found the exact same pair, one size larger, at a slightly better price. They were still expensive, but they were worth it. His eyes glowed that Christmas. I quietly spirited his first pair away to the cubby in my nightstand to save them as a keepsake.

The second pair of boots lasted until Ben was nearly six. By then, his baby face had grown slimmer, his baby talk less pronounced, and he now chose to wear his hair in either a buzz cut or a Mohawk. As he grew, his feet grew, and soon he started to avoid wearing his John Deere boots.

"Ben, why aren't you wearing your boots?" I'd ask.

"I just don't feel like it," he'd say. Only once in a while would he admit the truth: "They make my feet hurt." It wasn't that he didn't want to wear them—he couldn't wear them.

Again, Dave and I discussed, or should I say negotiated. "Ben needs new boots," Dave said.

"I know, but it's just not in the budget," I countered. We were in the throes of our journey to freedom from credit cards, and there was no room for splurging. Dave couldn't argue.

When it came time to buy new shoes for kindergarten, Ben asked, "When can I get another pair of boots?"

I had to explain to him that we could only afford one kind of footwear. "You need tennis shoes for gym class, so that's what we have to buy first," I said.

"Okay," he replied. I was surprised and proud of his response. A few years before, having to wait would have reduced him to tears.

But it was only a matter of months before a solution emerged. Dave wanted to use his birthday money to buy a pair of boots for himself. He headed to Nigro's Western Store (where else?) to check out a pair he had seen online. I was hanging out at home with the kids when I received his text.

"My boots came in under budget," it said. "What do you think about getting a pair for Ben?" The negotiation began.

"How much?"

"Probably $25 more than I have."

"I think so, let me check." I did some quick figuring. "Okay."

"Which ones?" He texted me pictures of boots with green, black and blue tops.

"I like the blue."

"I like the green."

"They're for Ben. Should I ask him?"

"Yes."

I called Ben upstairs. "Hey Ben, which pair of boots do you like best?"

I say.

"Is Daddy getting me boots?" he asks.

"Maybe," I replied.

"Hmmm . . . ," he said, looking at the pictures. "I like those." He pointed to the ones with the blue tops.

I texted the answer back to Dave, instructing, "Put it on the debit card."

An hour later Dave returned home with two boxes of boots tucked under his arm—one large, one small. "Hey Ben, come here," he called, and Ben came running up the stairs.

Dave handed him the smaller of the two boxes, and Ben threw the lid open. He gently pulled back the tissue paper, and his grin stretched from ear to ear as he gazed upon his new infatuation: brown boots with Jayhawk blue uppers laced with red and white stitching. Big boy boots. His shoes were already off, his bottom (no longer padded) hit the carpet and once again he had them on in a flash.

We hadn't gotten anything equal for Charlie. Thankfully, Charlie didn't care. When he came in to check out his brother's new prize I asked, "Are you upset your brother got boots and you didn't?"

"Nah," he replied. "They're just clothes."

But they were more than that to Ben. I was surprised later that night when I went to check on him in bed and he wasn't sleeping with them.

Like the first two pairs, these were worn whenever and wherever Ben wanted. They became constant partners for bike riding, swinging, visiting friends, going to church and school. The first day Ben wore them to school, the teacher called me to bring extra shoes. "They're just a little too big and they keep falling off," she explained. We sent Ben with shoes for back-up every day after that, but he insisted on wearing the boots. Eventually he learned to keep them on his feet, and the shoes were no longer necessary.

On the first day he could wear shorts with them, Charlie, nine, snickered, "You look ridiculous."

"I don't care," Ben replied. "It's my style."

One day, Ben got angry and kicked his boots off into the air, almost hitting me with one. I took them away for a week. He begged and pleaded, "Please, can I have my boots back? I won't do it again!" I held firm, promising he could have them back the following Thursday night. On Tuesday morning, he approached me as I got ready for work.

"Can I have my boots back today?"

"Nope—you lost them for a week."

"Tomorrow?"

"You lost them on a Friday. Is tomorrow a week?"

"No. So I get them back Friday then?"

"I'll give them to you Thursday night."

As promised, after he was asleep that night, I placed them in his room by his bed so he would see them first thing in the morning. When he awoke, he was thrilled to get them back, hugging them to his chest like a long lost friend.

As with the first two pairs, the blue boots have been put out to pasture—holes in the bottoms of both heels from dragging on the ground. Now Ben is sporting a pair with bright orange uppers, flames stitched into the sides. Dave and I didn't think twice about buying them. It only took four pairs to realize that boots aren't footwear to Ben; they're his best buddies.

Ben's first John Deere boots, age 2, compared to his new boots, age 6.

On the Trail

I t was so hot that we didn't know whether it was worth it, but Tad hoisted our bikes onto the bike rack anyway. With the intoxicating freedom of a day off stretching before us, we took off for the Flint Hills Nature Trail, an abandoned rail corridor now converted to a bike path. Rails to trails are spreading like capillaries all over this nation, stirring up controversy with every mile that is laid. Despite the inconvenient truth that the railroad land was never theirs, the local land owners, with their yapping hounds and gun racks on their pickup trucks, stand their territory, red-faced with their blustering threats. Over in Missouri, a local landowner even hauled his hog barn over the bike path to obstruct the Katy Trail some years back. Now the hog barn has vanished and many cyclists stream by, but the resentment still seethes, worming its way through the breeding bacteria in the soil.

We didn't calculate how stifling it might get. We would handle the heat somehow, or maybe, magically, despite the forecast, it wouldn't get to be over one hundred degrees.

After winding through side streets at the edge of Ottawa, past trailer courts and restaurants closed until noon, we found the bike path. The sun was at its zenith, but we never can get organized enough to start out early. We parked just off the road in brome grass that had recently been mowed. The landscape was dotted with farm houses surrounded by pastures and plowed fields. A hundred and fifty years ago, buffalo would have waded through lush bluestem as they slowly wended their way to the creek.

"Here, take your water bottle," Tad said. I jammed it into the holder. He wriggled his grey Trek bike off the rack. We fastened our helmets under our chins, clicking the clasps which sometimes pinch the skin. When he started off, he did a little jump and catapulted into his bike seat. I pushed off with a few long strides, as though I were propelling a scooter.

The wheels churned through the grey dust. No puddles nor black muddy stretches lay in the path before us. The sun had sucked them up. When was the last rain? The chorus frogs, the trilling toads camped out in low marshes have it all calculated, but we bury ourselves in the daily grind and forget.

We pedaled along at a good clip. Because the sun was straight overhead, my shadow stayed just under my pedals. Beads of perspiration ran down the crevice between my breasts. The helmet squeezed my head as if it were in a vise. There was no breeze, no headwind or tailwind. The air hung around us like a heavy, rich pound cake. How could we have imagined that this might have been fun? Still we thrust our legs in circular motions, again and again, even though we were now out of the shade and no trees flanked the path in front of us. We kept going. Just kept going. We had left the woods for open fields that stretched far and wide.

Covered wagons traversed this prairie with pioneers staking their claims to land promised by the Homestead Act of 1862. Slowly, surely, with the measured step of every hoof, the oxen helped carve the wilderness into parcels of one-fourth of a section. Courthouses sprouted in cities, where settlers would file deeds for ownership of the land. The land remembers. It is even written in the wind. But who owns the land? The indigo bunting, warbling with his head cocked to a blue sky, or a ghostly pack of coyotes howling at the moon?

After sizzling for about an hour, we spied an intriguing patch of land on the side of the bike path, with tall trees casting shade, flanked by the creek. We laid our bikes on the grass and approached the edge. A tufted titmouse flitted through a shrub growing from the erosion of the banks. The creek gurgled as it coursed over red and orange pebbles, as water bugs did their lazy gymnastics on the surface of the water. We lowered ourselves onto the grass, slightly stiff from so much riding, the black spandex of our shorts cutting off the circulation to our legs.

Facing the bike path was a gate, and farther down a gravel lane curving behind the gate we could see the partial outline of a house. A wooden post by the gate bore a black and white sign: "No Trespassing."

No trespassing. No littering the property with beer bottles, or interrupting the quiet with a raucous boom box blaring heavy metal music. No building a fire, or pitching a tent to overstay your welcome, or amputating limbs from the trees. If you alight to be soothed by the breeze, do so softly, without leaving a trace, like the feathery down that floats from the pod of a milkweed. If I owned this land, as if anyone truly does, I would suffer the weary traveler. It's charity, and the right thing to do.

There were shouting sounds coming from the house in the distance, and the monotonous drone of a gas-powered machine, that stopped occasionally, only to start up again. Behind our shoulders another road detoured around the trees into a field of corn silage stubble. We imbibed long draws from our water bottles. In the shade on this triangular piece of land, the wind whirled around in the upper tree branches as we rested, beside our bikes laid flat on the ground.

A motor vehicle whizzed down the road behind us. Two men in an off-white pick-up truck came around the bend. The driver idled his motor and stared at us, his arm resting on the ledge of the open window of his truck. The four of us paused, sizing each other up. The man had dark curly hair, and perhaps a mustache. His companion in the passenger seat was wearing a ball cap.

"Get off my property," the man said.

I don't react well to authority. I bargained for time. "We're just resting her for a moment. It's horribly hot, and we're enjoying the shade," I answered.

"There's shade up there on the trail," he said, jerking his head to the left to indicate the bike path from which we'd come.

I searched for words, my mind at a loss of how to get through to him. I looked at his face, but couldn't penetrate it. The man stared back, refusing to budge.

"If you don't leave, I'll call the law."

Saying nothing, Tad stood up, and in slow motion obediently started walking toward the road.

I stood my ground. How could I transform his glare into generosity? How could I undo years of harshness, poverty, maybe hard scrabble living, with well-crafted words? I took one step toward him, then stopped. This stranger might blast me away with a gun.

We biked farther south. We had long since lost the shade that formerly arched over the trail, so the sun beat down on us hotter than ever. No matter how hard I pedaled, I couldn't leave the man's words behind, couldn't shake off his cold, sterile hatred. His obsession that he owned a particular piece of land because of a real estate transaction, during which grey bank notes slid across a Formica desk top in an air-conditioned room, clung to me like a weight that I couldn't shed.

We kept pedaling down the path, perhaps out of stubbornness, with no particular destination. We rode over the same territory where the bison were all but exterminated by 1884. They were slaughtered by the white man for their skins, who left their bodies to rot in the waving grass. Because their herds could damage locomotives that failed to stop in time, the railroads encouraged the massacre of the buffalo. The land still remembers. It always will. The railroad kept chugging smoke into blue skies and ripping a path though the land until it was stopped by the vast wondrous Pacific Ocean. This was destiny.

I plotted my return to that spot in the future. I would remember the junction, about ten miles from the start of the trail, the park-like setting of tall trees and lush grass that is circled at the top with the deep ravines of a creek. I would act. I would bring a sheet of lined notebook paper, and I would write the message in black pen. I would tape the message to the solid pole of the gate leading to that man's driveway. The note would stay there, simple in its block lettering, in stark contrast to the green and brown of the surrounding vegetation. If it did not rain, if the wind did not blow it away, that man would rip the note off from his gate and read it. The note would say, "I bring you peace. The peace that passeth all understanding."

The purple gayfeather, the darting house wrens, the spirits of the buffalo, and the heavenly bodies overhead will bear witness. All of these innocents will testify, these captives to those who hold title.

Lane, Margaret, Tad, and Tristan Kramar on a bicycle trail.

Roadmaster

T his story has three main characters. The first is my daughter Brooke, a headstrong and determined person. The second is me—I just happen to know a fair amount about cars. The third is a Buick Roadmaster station wagon, big enough to come with its own ZIP code.

If you have children who have reached a certain age, you know that, as time passes, you occupy different spots on a spectrum of attitudes. You begin as the Fount of All Wisdom. As your kids come to realize you're fallible, but usually on the mark, you become a Person Worth Listening To. And then, for a while you become the Idiot Oppressor. With luck, after several of those magic years, you slowly move back in the other direction.

As our daughter prepared to head back to coastal Washington state for her second year at Evergreen State College, she decided she should drive. At that time, her mother and I were still pretty much in Idiot Oppressor status, and I didn't want to make that any worse. Plus, I remembered the road-trip impulse. So, despite deep misgivings, we decided *not* to say "No." We figured if we let things take their course, the idea would die its own natural death. First, we said she could not make this trip by herself. No problem, she came up with a fellow road-tripper within two days, a girl who went to the same school. We remained confident she would abandon the plan, which lacked a critical element: Neither of them had a car.

Little Miss Headstrong and Determined solved that problem by borrowing a car from another friend from the same school. He didn't want to drive the car across country himself, but he would be happy to have it there.

"What is this car?" I asked.

It was a 1991 Buick Roadmaster station wagon, about 15 years old. Whatever else those monsters were, they were the ultimate road-trip car. Seeing our parental position weakening, we tacked and set some requirements.

I told them they had to get the car checked out thoroughly, insisting they take it to a certain mechanic I trusted completely. It had to have decent brakes, steering, and tires. All the brake and signal lights had to work—just the basics required for safety. I figured this car would never pass muster, and the little scheme would evaporate without need for a fatherly fiat of refusal.

About a week later, they brought me the mechanic's report, and amazingly, the car checked out. Nothing about it was in great shape, but nothing really put it in the danger zone, either. Finally, we had no choice. We folded, and plans proceeded for the Great West Coast Road Trip.

The day came for loading and leaving, and the Roadmaster creaked and rumbled up in front of our house bright and early. Despite the mechanic's report, its hood was held closed by a Bungee cord. It was mostly dark blue with highlights of other colors, some not entirely harmonious. As the girls loaded their considerable cargo into the back, I undid the cord, popped the hood, and had a look at the power plant. In this car, the term was not hyperbole.

I was torn. In seconds it was obvious that I could run to the auto parts store, pick up about $150 worth of wire, hoses, tubing, belts, and the like, and spend two hours making a real difference in this car's condition. But I resisted. It wasn't my car.

I let the hood slam. As I refastened the Bungee cord, I said to my daughter, "It'll be a miracle if this thing makes it past Hays."

"Oh, Dad!" she said gaily.

They finished loading, all smiles, bouncing on the balls of their feet and squeaking. We said our goodbyes, and they drove off. We watched the behemoth car until we couldn't see it anymore. They had three solid days of driving ahead of them. We went into the house and tried to catch our breath.

About six hours later, the phone rang. They had made it to Hays.

By the time they called us, they had broken down, called a AAA wrecker—we had enrolled Brooke just a week before—and had ridden with him around Hays until they found a motel that would let them park the Roadmaster indefinitely at the back of its lot. That wrecker driver had treated those two cute young women really well. But the car had been declared dead, and we had no alternatives. I set out for Hays in our minivan, by myself.

About five hours later, as I approached the eastern edge of Hays, I could see the Roadmaster from the highway, with two little figures sitting next to it. Brooke and her friend were camped in the parking lot, sweaty, listless, and subdued. Briefly, I wondered what they had talked about since calling us. We loaded their stuff into our van and headed home. Brooke was deflated. No matter how headstrong and determined you are, you cannot will a dead Roadmaster down the highway.

Both girls promptly fell asleep. They had had a big day. My second five-hour drive of the day began much the same as the first, essentially by myself. Near Salina, maybe three hours along, Brooke rolled over toward me and said, "Dad, how did you know?"

"How did I know what?"

"That we would only make it to Hays."

I thought fleetingly about admitting that Hays was simply a metaphor, and that I could not believe life had worked out to make it literally true. But I didn't. Instead, I said, "Well, Brooke, your old Dad knows a thing or two about cars."

She said, "Thanks, Dad. You're awesome." And she rolled over and fell back to sleep.

And I could wax sentimental about how that moment made it all worthwhile. But honestly, it didn't, not considering all the negotiation and fuss and time it took to get us to that moment. However, I admit I enjoyed feeling my status shift a little, away from Idiot Oppressor toward Person Worth Listening To.

Irises

With an overcast sky and hours of work before us, we planted the irises on a cold, grey afternoon in March before Spenser died. Spenser, my son, looking as wan and lifeless as the grey sky, could barely lift his trowel.

"Spenser, why can't you help?" I implored. Spenser said nothing, his profile framed by the bare branches that laced the sky. He was dying, and never told us. When a few weeks later he was diagnosed with terminal cancer that had metastasized all over his body and the doctors looked at us in amazement, we met their gazes with blank stares. No one had had any warning. We did take him to the doctor, the Tuesday before he died. The nurse practitioner diagnosed a sinus infection, wrote out a prescription, and sent us home.

My other son, thirteen-year-old Benjamin, is a hard worker, a toiler of the soil, who throws himself at impossible projects with all his youthful energy. Benjamin relished the arduous job of transplanting all the irises. He thrust his trowel into the gravelly soil again and again, spreading the roots of the irises that fanned out like the tentacles of a deep-sea creature. When the light drizzle turned into an insistent rain, we stopped.

The irises did bloom in mid-May, a few weeks after Spenser's funeral, and every year they shower our entire hillside with mostly purple flowers, but some yellow and white. In photographs of ourselves, a mass of irises floods the foreground. I wish more of the irises could have been royal purple, instead of a dirty-looking brownish purple. I also wish that Spenser could have lived longer, but he didn't.

The day after Spenser died, Benjamin, nestled under the moose and bears of his North Woods comforter, never left his bed.

"Benjamin won't be in school today, and I don't know how long it will be until he comes back," I telephoned the middle school principal.

"I totally understand. You let him take all the time he needs," the principal stated. I rested in the honey tone of his words.

The very next day, Benjamin dressed, hoisted his arms through the straps of his back pack, and hiked up the driveway to catch the school bus at 6:30 a.m.

If Benjamin ever cried, we never knew it.

After Spenser's death, we filled our house with foreign exchange students, one right after another, from Japan, Germany, and Norway. Brothers for Benjamin. Sisters for Benjamin. Replacing the cavernous silence with the cacophony of laughter by carving a pumpkin for Halloween, or baking red and green pinwheel cookies at Christmas, might deflect our attention from the framed portrait of our blond boy on the fireplace mantel, always smiling, always ten years old. Benjamin camped out in his own bedroom, hovering over his books on the round oak table.

Several months later, home from school, Benjamin found me sobbing softly, with a vegetable peeler in one hand, and the skins of potatoes, carrots, and onions piled in the sink. They smelled of damp springtime earth. His face hardened as he retreated toward his bedroom, dumping his backpack outside his door. I pursued him.

"Benjamin, don't you ever miss Spenser?" I entreated. I grieve for Spenser, but I'm lifted like a feather, lightly from the earth, because I believe in God, in angels, in heaven, in the resurrection.

"He had a funeral, a grave and a headstone. You're making a big deal out of this. I don't agree." Benjamin crossed his arms, standing his ground.

"Do you even believe in God?"

"How can I answer that? That's like asking why the sky is blue. I guess that if I'm forced to answer yes or no, I would answer yes."

What about the afterlife?

"It's comforting to know that there's a place where there's no suffering," he stared not at me but the wall, "a place where we will know the answers." He turned and walked away.

With prompting, Benjamin visits the grave. His face contorts at the sight of the inscribed bronze plaque, but he has told me that Spenser visits him in dreams. He can hear Spenser making noises while playing with his toys in the adjacent bedroom.

Every fall I plant bulbs in memory of Spenser at his elementary school: crocuses, grape hyacinths, tulips, and daffodils. The dry skin wrappers flake off to reveal a cadaverous white bulb. I plunge the trowel into the ground, tucking the bulb into a moist brown hole, and then rake the dirt over. In the spring the yellow and red tulips, their colors as bold as neon, sway slightly under the lavender buds of the redbud tree. In the clamor of children playing at recess I can hear Spenser. I catch a glimpse of him as he files onto the school bus. He is there, and always will be. Every word of this is true.

The winter solstice comes right before Christmas. The darkest day of the year. Christmas ornaments, with little school pictures of Spenser glued onto a paper doily snowflake, or a reindeer face, hang all over the tree. A huge red and green wooden nutcracker stands sentinel under Spenser's picture on the fireplace mantel.

Spenser attended *The Nutcracker Ballet* almost every year of his short life. He marveled at the ballerinas twirling around in the snowflake scene, the enchanted Christmas tree expanding at midnight, and the spell that mysterious Godfather Drosselmeyer cast transforming the wooden toy nutcracker into a breathing, dancing prince. In the magical season of Christmas, these things really happen. The light comes after the darkness. The holy birth. The candles held high in the darkened cathedral during Christmas Eve services, the parishioners droning "Silent Night," the colored lights that twinkle on conifers in the silent snow, the blazing yule log in the hearth. The light, the light of the world.

Spenser is still in the house, larger than his picture framed on the fireplace mantel. There are ghostly occurrences and unexplained crashes in the basement. I'm not making this up. For example, several years ago I couldn't find my Christmas wreaths, encircled with wooden candy canes and gingerbread men. I store them at the end of a long hallway in a cupboard, stashed away in a cardboard box. Nobody ever goes there. Well, we venture in occasionally for aluminum tins, wrapping paper, or documents stuffed into boxes lined against the concrete wall, but rarely.

"Where are my wreaths? I labeled the box! Why isn't it where it belongs?" I screamed in frustration. Nobody answered.

The next day, after turning the key in the front door, I nearly stumbled over a Christmas wreath laid neatly on the terra cotta tiles of the foyer. It was so unexpected that I gasped. People try to find logical explanations, and blame cats, but how could a cat extract that wreath from a high box in the storage room and carry it all the way down the hall? I swear it wasn't Spider, nor any other cat.

"Benjamin! Come here now." Of course he didn't do it, didn't even know of my fruitless search. He examined the wreath, lying on the stone cold floor, his face registering no recognition. Spider, the Siamese whose clear blue eyes peered out from a fat chocolate brown face, sniffed the wreath and continued on his way with silent mincing steps, his tail held aloft.

When I was a teenager, I read about a widow mired in her late husband's financial affairs. She answered the phone, and through the static, an unknown voice told her what to do. It made perfect sense to me. Christianity is brimming with prophets and angels. Scientific reasoning pales in comparison. The umbilical cord is never broken. Death cannot sever it.

The irises multiplied every growing season, so last spring Benjamin divided the rhizomes, his boot pressing the rim of the shovel into the soil. With his right hand, he yanked them out and shook off the clinging clods so they could bloom in another garden in another spring.

We planted the originals when Spenser was still alive, and now, ten years later, they had increased tenfold.

"Mom, what are we going to do with all these irises? Even though I'm transplanting them, there's a whole bunch left over." For his Boy Scout Eagle project, he hauled out rubber tires sunk into the dirt and choked with brush that violated the pristine woods. He really did this. Now he's twenty-four, but when I look at him, I see the baby, the toddler, and the child, all collapsed into one. Dark gorgeous lashes frame his grey eyes. His face is basically my face; the same periorbital bones set our eyes in their sockets. My feet, my legs, moles in the same places on our bodies. From my body and of my body. The same DNA, the same specks of stardust. The strongest human link is between mother and child.

"Maybe we can sell them at the farmers' market," I suggested.

So we bagged them up in brown paper lunch bags, ten for ten dollars. A bargain, because in the seed catalogues the rare and exotic iris varieties, the pinks, oranges and unusual bi-colors, sell for ten to fifteen dollars apiece.

They didn't sell, so we stashed the bags of irises under the wooden bench on our front porch. Lined up in row after row were hundreds of irises. Dumped in the compost heap they would never get a chance to blossom.

But sometimes we're forced into doing things we don't like. We buried Spenser under two sycamore trees by a pond thick with rushes housing red-wing blackbirds. I had hoped that Spenser's body could return to the earth, but the cemetery rules required us to put his white wooden casket in a concrete vault so there wouldn't be an indentation in their perfect lawn. I stayed until the gravedigger, dressed in a plaid work shirt and laced work boots, mounted his backhoe and shoveled the last scoop over Spenser's body. Kneeling beneath majestic trees arching overhead, I stretched out my hand, and cupped it over the mounded coolness of the clay.

What to do with the irises? Benjamin finally got an idea. We put a want ad in the paper: "Irises: Ten for five dollars." Having resolved the matter, I set about getting everything else into the ground, now that it was the beginning of June, and temporarily forgot about the irises, until the day I grabbed the phone from its cradle to stop its loud, insistent jangling.

"I'm calling about the irises." Her voice was circumspect, matter-of-fact.

"Yes, how many would you like?" I gushed, sinking down into the plaid couch.

"How much you want for 'em?" Her voice wavered.

"We're charging five dollars for ten, or maybe, I don't know, we could throw in some more." I could see the rows and rows of iris bags sitting outside the window.

"Well, I can afford thirty dollars' worth. Thirty dollars sound like a deal?" The inflection in her voice rose. I could calculate the amount of irises we would deliver later, probably about six bags of them.

"Sure, sounds like a deal. So what's your name?" She shut down, froze into a silence.

"I mean, when will you pick them up?"

"I work two shifts, get off at 11 p.m.," she continued in a monotone, talking about late-night shifts and transportation problems. "My son don't work tomorrow. Maybe he could pick them up. His name's Randall."

"Maybe we could meet at the public library," I suggested.

The next day I put six bags of irises in the car, and yelled at Benjamin that we were leaving. All the other irises stayed behind on the front porch.

"But Mom, is that all you're taking her? What about the rest of them?"

"We'll sell the rest in the fall."

I glanced back at all the bags lining the front porch. The heat would penetrate them, and the irises would shrink, eventually turning to dust. Maybe we could get busy and plant them somewhere else. But where, and when?

"Benjamin, we're loading all these iris bags into the car." He didn't ask for any explanation. I grabbed as many bags as I could, and after we got them all, I turned the key in the ignition and we headed up the hill.

I fumbled for my cell phone a few blocks away from the public library, to tell Randall that I was on my way. Spenser's name is in the library, inscribed on a blue leaf plaque attached to a vine with leaves commemorating other people. We live so as to honor them. They are dead, so through our hands, our voices, our labor, they can do their work on earth, as in heaven.

"Benjamin, do you see an old gray Dodge Dart anywhere?" We scanned the parking lot. "Maybe he'll see us if we get out of the car and stand in plain view on the sidewalk."

My cell phone rang. His young voice sounded upbeat, yet cautious. "Do you have on pink shorts and a white blouse? Yeah, I see you. I'm right over here in the first lane."

Randall was about the same age as Benjamin, and the same height. We piled the irises into his car. The paint was a faded blue-gray and there was rust edging the wheel walls.

"If we gave your mother all these irises, would she even want them?" I asked, as we thrust even more brown paper bags into his back seat.

"My mother loves irises. She plants them all over. Then whenever we have to move, I get the job of digging every last one of them up." Wearing jeans, with a gray hoodie slung over the shoulder of his t-shirt, he smiled as he lifted the cardboard boxes into his car. More and more bags, stashed on top of each other, on the floor between the front and back seats. Hundreds of irises. We never counted them all.

Spenser would have done the same thing. Whenever he danced, or played soccer, or acted out a part, he always gave more than one hundred percent.

With the irises loaded, he took one step out of the car and pulled three crumpled bills out of his pocket, exposing the white lining of his jeans pocket. He smoothed the creases from the face of Alexander Hamilton before he placed the three tens in my hand. Not that I would haggle with him.

"Thanks so much." He was frozen there a moment with his smile, and one leg resting on the lower frame of the car. Then he revved up the motor and drove away. All these details will verify my story.

I do fidgety things late at night because I hate to go to bed. From about ten at night until two in the morning is the best time of the day, especially in the summer. The house is quiet, and I can read to the solitary sound of the ticking clock, or leisurely leaf through correspondence. Plus, there's always one more thing to do before tomorrow. Around midnight I checked to make sure the cat was safe inside.

I never carry cash, a habit formed when I was a single mother. If you don't have it, you can't spend it. The thirty dollars we earned from the irises, still inside my otherwise empty coin purse, needed to go into the farmers' market envelope.

I pulled out the three green bills from my worn leather coin purse. Andrew Jackson's flowing mane flashed at me not once, but twice. Three twenty-dollar bills jumped out at me, bold and emblazoned with truth, just as the wreath had done on the floor of the foyer.

I stepped back, puzzled over what my eyes were telling me. I had not taken out nor added any cash to that purse since we met Randall. Absolutely none. I replayed mental tapes of the exchange at the library. He gave me three tens.

I gripped the bills firmly in my hand, and slid one wrinkled green twenty away from the other, like a bank teller dealing cash in deft motions so that the bills don't stick. Three twenties, three twenties, no matter how I stacked them. I wouldn't lie about this.

"Benjamin! Benjamin! How much did I charge that guy for the irises?"

I heard him open his bedroom door. Even while leaning barefoot against the door frame, he's slightly taller than I am. I noticed his tousled hair, and knew that it was time to cut it again, his thick brown hair, probably even thicker than mine.

"Wasn't it thirty dollars?" He started to turn away.

"But did you see the money? When he handed it to me? The three bills?" I couldn't stop interrogating him. This defied scientific logic.

"I don't know, Mom. You took it. I didn't." He closed his door.

Spider's smooth, silky fur brushed against the calf of my leg. When I stooped to stroke him between the ears, his purr intensified. Just like with the wreath, there's no need to explain.

Roaches in Heaven

THE ANIMAL DIARIES

L aura and I are cooking dinner together. We have learned to do Chinese stir-fry and have discovered the wok, fish sauce, and bok choy. Led Zeppelin is playing on a 33$^1/_3$ record on the old Webcore player that used to belong to my parents. It's summer in Kansas, it's hot, and it's 1980. Laura is sixteen years old and growing up fast.

I'm working on a Ph.D. dissertation in entomology, which involves, for some reason, studying the antennal movement patterns of cockroaches. Laura notices a *Parcoblatta* woodroach sitting on the door-jam over the kitchen door, the flying, outdoor-kind of roach we have around here.

She grabs my arm as I'm scraping onions into the wok, and says, "Mom, look! That cockroach is moving its antennae in beat with the music!"

Suddenly we're both standing on chairs, noses close to the creature, watching, studying, and laughing. It is, indeed, doing just that: flinging its long antennae up and down in synchrony to Led Zepellin's *Stairway to Heaven*. A line in the song goes like this:

> And a new day will dawn for those who stand long
> And the forests will echo with laughter.

I don't believe in heaven and hell after death. Adolescence is hell. Fearing I will lose my job because I can't get my Ph.D. finished in time is hell. But standing on a chair, that first step in the stairway, with my teenage daughter, watching a cockroach keeping antennal time to Led Zeppelin—that is heaven.

Turtle U-Boats

THE ANIMAL DIARIES

I am driving south, by myself, in Lawrence, Kansas. It's Memorial Day weekend, 2012. A black garbage can is wedged into the front passenger seat, upright, barely fitting. Clawing, scraping noises ooze out from inside. There was no way that the can could fall over, or that the lid could get loose, but I have lost ninety degrees of visual field because of the garbage can, and I begin to fantasize about what would happen if I had an accident and that can became untrapped.

୫୬ ୫୬ ୫୬

We had just recently moved into our first house in Lawrence after living ten years in a run-down, crappy, squalid apartment. There were four new houses on our side of the street, all cookie-cutter places where one style alternated with the other style, but the vaulted ceiling in the living room tantalized me and was so different from the little ranchers I had looked at in my house search. The street in front ended with a "T" to the west, and beyond the T was a little ravine with a small creek at the bottom. Young couples occupied the other three new houses, but ours, besides being the farthest from the creek and ravine, was also the outlier with its single mother and child.

It was July Fourth, 1978, and Laura woke me from a late, deep sleep. At fourteen she was long and lean and already taller than I, with deep brown eyes, long wavy hair, and amazing dimples. I was teaching full-time thirty miles away in Topeka, and had started a daunting

Ph.D. program in order to keep that teaching job. I slept whenever I could.

She shook me awake. "Mom, Mom, you've got to look outside—there's something really weird in our yard."

I stumbled outside. The grass was tall in our front yard—way too tall compared to our neighbors' manicured yards—and something was cruising covertly through it, like some German U-Boat from World War II, with only its periscope showing. The periscope rotated, scanning, looking for destroyers, aircraft carriers, maybe a slow squirrel or a little kid. The snapping turtle stopped its excursion, and its periscope head swiveled, zeroed in on us, and stared at us. It had probably left the little creek in the ravine, looking for food, and was hungry. It was bigger than a dinner plate, and its shell was covered with a small mountain range of pointed elevations. It looked prehistoric with its enormous scaled feet, huge claws, dinosaur-ridged tail, sharp beak, and very, very long neck. I don't think it was sizing us up as prey, but I wasn't sure.

This was just too damned much. I knew I couldn't ignore this situation, but I had no idea of what to do with the thing and was not in a let's-discover-science mood. Laura was excited and happy though—she had the inspired idea to trap the beast in a garbage can. So we hauled out the battered, brown plastic can and placed it on its side, gingerly, near the turtle. Somehow we herded the turtle into the can with the lid and were ready to go—somewhere.

We hoisted the garbage can into our Datsun B-210. This was a little, medium-blue, used car made before the Japanese learned how to manufacture good cars. If I rolled my window down too enthusiastically, the handle kept circling around and came off in my hand. Its two-door style was sporty, but the back roof sloped down so much that my tall daughter, when sitting in the back seat, had to sit with her head bent to the side.

We headed south on Iowa Street toward the Wakarusa River. The turtle can was in the front seat. Laura was in the back seat, head angled, arms thrust forward, pressing down hard on the lid. The turtle was clawing and banging around inside, and I imagined the sharp beak chewing and shooting through the plastic and biting off some important appendage, or perhaps the monstrous periscope head popping the lid off and swiveling about. I drove faster.

Meanwhile, the turtle's reptilian brain (for that was all it had) was no doubt filled with fear, as it was imprisoned in a dark, hot, plastic-smelling cage and was hearing, for the first time, The Rolling Stones. Maybe they were singing *Emotional Rescue*. I pulled off near the bridge crossing the river, though the river was more like a stream, and we dragged the can down the steep bank, pushing down on the lid at the same time. Near the water, we carefully laid the can on its side and opened it up.

The turtle emerged, blinking in the light. It swiveled its giant head toward us, then toward the stream, and then ran—yes, ran—to the water. It disappeared into a little pool in the stream and sank, U-boat-like, and turned its periscope on us. It semaphored a coded turtle signal to us, and then the periscope disappeared too.

Laura and I climbed the bank, our arms around each other's waists. We had just driven the marauding saber-toothed tiger away from the entrance to our cave, we had just invented fire to keep the wolves at bay, we had almost, almost, brought down the wooly mammoth for our winter's food—just the two of us.

೮೮ ೮೮ ೮೮

It's the morning of May 26, 2012, and I stumble downstairs in my robe in the same house, no longer new and tantalizing, to answer a sharp knock on the door. The nice young guy who lives across the street is at the door, and he tells me not let my cats outside. He likes cats, and warns that a giant snapping turtle is in my yard. He, his girlfriend, and I all stand at a respectful distance, staring down at another plate-sized, prehistoric-looking snapping turtle. I know just what to do.

"Well, we need a garbage can." I say, with authority.

They look at me, and blink.

So again I am driving south with a giant snapping turtle in a garbage can wedged into my front seat. This time I'm driving a burgundy-colored Toyota, and the Japanese have built an exquisite machine. The windows raise and lower at the touch of a button. N.P.R. is on the radio. Laura is half a continent away and has her own teenaged daughters with which to share "let's-discover-science" experiences.

This trip isn't nearly as adventurous or exciting or scary or fun as the earlier one. But I do know exactly what to do. And one more specimen of a maligned species has been rescued. I drive the creature to Prairie Park Nature Center, where an earnest young man receives it gladly. He will release it in their local lake, Mary's Lake, and that is good.

Less Alone

Knowing the birds around one's home
generates mindfulness about the environment
. . . and . . . makes us less alone.
—Robert Antonio, in an e-mail

1

A city kid, I squirmed in nature of the woodsy, buggy, dusty Midwestern kind. It oozed with discomforts. I startled when branches thwacked my thighs, screamed when I was scaled by a daddy longlegs, dreaded snakes. (When Cousin Marshall chased me with sticks that looked like snakes, I ran, hysterical, in the opposite direction, giving rise to a lifelong resentment of old Marsh.) I became conscious of the menace of ticks because of the strenuous measures my father took to pry them loose from my tender flesh: He brought the glowing tip of a cigarette near their bodies (and mine) to loosen their hold.

Ever since then, the natural world has been a problem for me. Decades of Earth Day celebrations, You Tube videos of love affairs between tortoises and hippos—none of this has dented my tendency to favor *Homo sapiens*— though not uniformly. My prejudices against the most common social scapegoats, the ones based on skin color or ethnicity, are absent, but I am a confirmed morphist; as a child, I hid my fascinated loathing with the sheets of skin that hung, like a bloodhound's sagging jowls, from Grandma Martin's arms.

When newborns arrive in my vicinity, courtesy of a proud parent, I smile, it smiles; I *kootchey-koo* and hope it gurgles rather than wails, all the time feeling a little shame for feeling so little. Of course, some are more comely or appealing than others, but in general I'm not so interested in human life at the stages when automaticity overrules whatever small degree of freedom we manage to eke out in our best years.

I prefer pets to babies and to be truthful, baby kittens to their human counterparts. They may squirm away from my unschooled touches, but even if they evade me, they don't squall.

Very early in life, pets weren't all that easy either. I had to reach my mid-50s before I acquired an animal that I would deem *mine*—that I could be foolish about, whose endearing habits I would describe to strangers: *She comes to me when I call . . . and this is a cat! MY cat!*

I count this bond a real comeback. I mean Fletcher, the family cocker spaniel who growled at me because, spazzing around, I stepped on his foot so often, was my folks' choice. This wasn't a doggy-in-the-window choice, it was an endowment laid on my father by a co-worker. So was Mikey, the cat whose throat was opened by something nasty and who was trailing blood around the house when we got back from vacation and who had to be put down. Yes, the goldfish from Woolworth's were mine. But they're hard to warm to, as was the half-dollar-sized pet turtle confined to a spiraling plastic ramp topped by a tiny palm tree. A creature you're not inclined to name Ronnie or Louise is a creature apart.

2

My first wife did have cats, and through her, I began to warm to them. Still, I retained a certain patriarchal aloofness toward one, named Alice, until the day she died. We were both there, hovering, hands on her body, when this cat, who'd suffered from feline leukemia, opened her mouth wide and gave a loud, eerie cry just before she breathed no more. Then *we* wailed.

My second wife connected me to dogs. Fred, her wire-hair terrier, ever eager for society, amused us by dry-humping a pillow, sometimes dragging it onto our bed when we were lying there, reading, as if he wanted us to witness his thrustings. On the day Fred had to be put down, we knew the time had come because this most social of animals began to hide, as if going off to finish life alone. We sat on a patch of grass outside the vet's office. We wanted the vet to deliver the fatal injection in the open air. As with Alice, there were four hands on Fred at the end.

Then came Sabrina, *my* cat. She was born on a farm near Everest, Kansas, a town named not for its mountains but a railroad attorney. Beth and Jim, my wife's sister and husband, and their kids live there. It is a place where unfixed cats whelp gobs of kittens, many succumbing to the cruelties of outdoor life in northeastern Kansas, which, besides natural predators like coyotes and owls, include trucks traveling down the gravel road that runs by their house, driven by people who sometimes deliberately steer their vehicles so as to turn cats into road kill. The final threat to the farm cats comes from the farm dogs. When I took Sabrina back home to Lawrence, Kansas, she bore punctures in her neck inflicted by one of the dogs. Unable to compete for food against the other kitties, she was skin and bones. Even my nieces and nephew were happy to see Sabrina go. (They didn't like her farts.)

I adopted her because my third wife, Barbara, was then living in Nashville, working for an art museum. A cat lover, she thought it was time I become one, too. She lobbied for my taking on Sabrina who, it turned out, was pregnant.

Mark Twain said, "The person who hoists a cat by the tail learns things that can be learned in no other way." The same is true of a person who goes through a cat's giving birth to a litter beneath his futon, as Sabrina did in our first months together.

I won't enumerate the many endearing traits of Sabrina except to mention her coming to me when I call to her and her following me as I go about yard work—behaviors I think of as canine, not feline. I could mention many more endearments, but who wants to hear a parent rave about a child? Just one more, then: She would sidle up to me in bed then drape her paws across my shoulder and rest her head there. Until Sabrina, I had no idea I could get so schmaltzy about a creature that lacked an opposable thumb.

3

If pets had been difficult to love, wildlife, except for such obviously striking critters as deer, were certainly Other.

Then came the wrens.

A pair had for years built a nest, one twig, feather, and leaf scrap at a time, in our mailbox. Then, in the fourth year, they laid eggs in it. Unlike the lilies of the field, wrens spin, toil, and a whole lot more. It is a wren compulsion, I've learned, to build several nests and then settle on one for the nursery. Having witnessed the time and energy it takes to craft just one, I get tuckered out thinking about their making several.

Our mailbox is mounted four feet above the concrete porch that bridges our driveway to the front door. Why would birds lay eggs in a nest at such a busy (and perilous) intersection? The books say that wrens are "tolerant" of people, i.e., unafraid. I also suspect they'd eyeballed Barbara and me tiptoeing around them and heard our whispered apologies when we stepped out of the house and accidentally caught them in the act of nest-building. Maybe they'd calculated that we'd treat them like pets, even if they weren't. They were right.

The Wren Drama that unfolded evoked strong feelings, and not just because I admired their fierce industry in nest building and tireless catering to the hatchlings. And not just because of the thorough surveillance they made of the area, heads ratcheting in every direction, multiple times, before entering the mailbox. And not just because they scolded creatures with bodies much larger than theirs who came too near.

Those habits generated admiration, but the stronger feeling in me was a dull dread. Consider the potential for mayhem during their hundreds of trips back and forth to the nest. They were, after all, in the territory of our cats, our beloved—I hate to say the word, but it's true—*predators*. And our cats weren't the only menace. Everything's food for something.

Another part of the dread was the question of whether the parents would find enough food to sustain the peeping machines that finally hatched. The emotional charge built day after day. The vulnerabilities of the babies were clear from the start, evidenced by their small cheeps from the mailbox. Wrens are born blind. They made the tiniest squeaks, a whole chorus of which accompanied the arrival of every humble parcel of food. They're supposed to leave the nest in a couple of weeks, but I couldn't imagine anything making such tiny creatures grow fast enough to fly the coop that quickly.

One might think that the distance between the porch and the mailbox would give me some assurance of their safety, and it did, until an event shortly before the peepers hatched.

One day, sitting at my computer, I heard a lot of squawking and hurried out to investigate. I saw that Sabrina had leaped upward, mightily, toward the wren nest/mailbox and was hanging there by her claws, very precariously. I suppose that even if I make peace with the natural world, that doesn't stop the war, does it?

After the babies were born, we kept the cats indoors for hours each day. They became sullen, torpid. There was random peeing. An underfed cat skulking over from a neighbor's house worried me. Yet through it all, the feeding of those chicks went on… and on… and on. I was so smitten I would sit in the shadows of my garage silently, camera poised, trying to get a decent picture of mother (or father?) bird delivering food to the mailbox. Then one day, a parent flew away from the box with something white in its bill. What's that, we wondered? Was she taking the chicks to safer quarters—our hope?

We called a birder. He said, "She's probably taking stuff out of the nest to make room for the growing chicks."

Then they were gone.

There had been a gathering at our house, a salon at which we discussed the topic of books and reading. Bodies trooped in and then out, past the domicile. I fretted. On the way out, I told one of our guests about the fear I had and the magic of this visitation.

She remembered a time when, in Mexico, a bird had flown down and landed on her, then flown away. For her, she said, it was a waking dream.

The morning after the salon, the wren parents stopped coming. We heard no peeps from the nest. We waited two days. On the third, after taking a couple of pictures by pointing the camera into the nest and shooting (I was afraid of scaring the chicks to death with my big face if they were in there) and seeing nothing, I rapped on the box. Silence. I picked at the nest with a straightened coat-hanger. Nothing.

The chicks had fledged. The drama was over, almost.

A few mornings later, Barbara heard cheeping. On the front porch. Sabrina was somewhere in the yard. We hurried to look. There was a small bird on the concrete. A Carolina wren. Was it injured? We saw nothing obvious, though I noted the tail feathers seemed diminutive. Had Sabrina de-feathered the bird to toy with it? She wasn't around. Had the bird dropped from a branch, trying to fly, and failed? It wasn't very talkative—in fact, it was trembling in much the same fashion as humans when they go into shock. It spread its wings, slightly, a few times, but besides that and the trembling, it moved little.

We called our birder friend, a sociology professor. He said that wrens will, in their first attempts to fly, manage only to glide. Then the parents have to come along and put the fledgling in a bush or into some other confinement where predators can't find it. How they managed this wasn't at all clear to me. So Barbara put on her gloves (she didn't want the poor thing smelling like a top primate) and tried to nestle the chick in a bush.

Where it remained for an hour—quiet. I would walk out toward the bush, hoping to find it gone, but there it would be: once with its eyes closed, which scared me. Our friend told us that we had to position the chick in a place where the parents could find it, so we moved it again, this time beneath a shrub.

I tried to stay away, failing after 15 or 20 minutes. I was disappointed to find it still there.

We kept the cats in. I worried.

Another fretful hour passed, and when I went out this time, the little wren was gone.

4

How could I have been so numb, all those years, to the lives of other species?

Perhaps it was something in the fabric of the times I grew up in. Americans in the 1950s loved their dogs and cats, but they weren't yet *companion animals*. Even to hippies, who tended to favor large flea-ridden dogs, human beings were the crown of creation, as Grace Slick put it in a Jefferson Airplane song. Did 87 percent of pet owners, back then, include pets in holiday celebrations or did 65 percent sing or dance for a pet, both findings of an American Pet Products Manufacturers Association survey from 2007–2008? Huh-uh.

Perhaps in the 1950s we were too close to our rural roots. Rural society is, at least in some places, less hospitable to pets for any number of reasons. Maybe "companion animals" are a luxury for the well-heeled. And perhaps their coddling—the amount of money spent on pets doubled between 1999 and 2009—isn't morally defensible.

Neither were there YouTube videos bringing frolicking animals to our desktops. Cats weren't doing such zany things or, if they were, they were still a family secret. Owl families were hidden from view, not the subject of 24/7 Web cam revelations; elephants did not use their trunks to paint self-portraits; there were no gnu–lion buddies or tortoise–hippo pals.

Nor were pets included in therapeutic approaches like those described by Froma Walsh, of the Chicago Center for Family Health, in 2009, when she published an article in the journal *Family Process* that referenced "pet-facilitated therapy or pet co-therapy." (It should be noted, however, that Freud did keep his Chinese chow, Jofi, around during some counseling sessions.)

The animals of my childhood were, if less cherished, also threatened on far fewer fronts than the animals of 2010. Rachel Carson hadn't written "Silent Spring," frogs hadn't become the victims of the ozone layer's destruction, honeybees weren't vanishing, pelicans weren't slimed by oil spills, the slaughter of dolphins that turned a cove crimson wasn't the subject of Academy Award-winning documentaries.

The disappearance of species has made some humans warm to creatures more than they otherwise might have. It has also led to flashes of political rage and intraspecies jousting among humans who think such concern misplaced, foolish or half-nuts.

Let me be clear. I dislike the fundamentalism of those who would never sacrifice a laboratory animal for the sake of our species. And though the worldview of Jainists is fine in theory, I don't hold every living thing sacred. Moles, for example, may have their admirers, but I'm not one. Yet this is also true: When I hear a biologist speaking through sobs on NPR about trying to clean up pelicans slimed with crude oil, a tear runs down my cheek, too. That wasn't always so.

And my sympathies seem to be enlarging. Some invertebrates have even won me over. When it was rainy in northeastern Kansas one recent spring, the snails were out and about.

It's just a slug in a shell! my wife groused.

Hmmm, slugs. I wonder. . .

Things Come Inside

THE ANIMAL DIARIES

In the hot and humid summers we have here in Kansas, I have casually meandered into my kitchen in the evening when something catches my eye: a giant slug crawling up the kitchen wall near the back door. It is moist and long and brown with black spots, and it may later leave a pearly, glistening trail on the ceiling. Sometimes, when it rains really hard, I have nearly stepped on an earthworm working its way across the carpet, seeking dry earth. I guess I should try to make the doors fit better, but my house has become lopsided. When I was an adolescent, something went wrong with my spine—differential growth, perhaps—and I started listing to one side, too. Like the Tower of Pisa and my own body, the house continues to lean, a little more all the time. And the creatures come inside.

Once a strange flower-like thing on my kitchen counter caught my eye as I casually wandered through the small, narrow room. The flower-like thing had a large brown center and was completely encompassed by many tiny, shiny black petals. My brain did a double-take, trying to process this: "What IS that?"

Close examination revealed many small ants encircling a fat drop of Kahlua, which had spilled on the counter, somehow. They stood thorax pressed against thorax, mandibles drinking deeply. The Kahlua drop was turgid and bulging, and I thought, "What a nice example of hydrogen bonds holding those water molecules together, and I could use that in my Biology 100 class, except that my students might be confused by such an example."

The convex dome of Kahlua gradually sank to a flat disk, and then disappeared. The ants then moved about slowly and randomly, trying in their stupor to find their pheromone trail and return safely to their nest, where all their sober sisters waited, front legs folded across their thoraxes. I guess I should spray poisons into all the recesses and watch for little bodies curled up on their backs, legs in the air, but I don't want to. They're okay.

I bought this house—my first and only—at the age of 37, after living ten years in a small duplex apartment which suffered from non-benign neglect. In that apartment, raw sewage occasionally moved up into the bathtub, and ice coated the inside of the windows in winter. This was a brand new house when I purchased it, and everything was so crisp and clean and pretty, and my twelve-year-old daughter Laura and I were ecstatic. After we lived in the house for a while though, the slab foundation started to crack. They built these houses fast and carelessly. The house started listing then, and the rectangular doors no longer fit into their trapezoidal frames. So things come inside.

One evening I reached for my favorite ceramic cup—a nice hand-thrown piece of mottled blues and browns—and poured some merlot into it. I'd had a hard day, teaching those biology students. Savoring the wine's bouquet and hints of tannins, I drank it slowly and prepared my dinner. By the time my meal was ready, I drained the last sip of wine from my cup and, again, something caught my eye. Peering into the bottom of the cup, I saw eight shiny, besotted eyes staring back at me. Hovering within a tiny nest of webbing, and clinging to it heroically, was a jumping spider—sure, Phidippus audax, dark and hairy and spotted. These are small, very furry spiders with big eyes and giant fangs and, when sober, a finely honed ability to pounce on prey or to hop around on your hand. We were both in a state of shock. The spider was fine, though, if a little inebriated. I was fine, if very sober. I released it outside and it stumbled away. Maybe I should have written a grant to study the effect of alcohol on insects and spiders.

A friend recently reminded me that I had told her, "If you have a jumping spider in your bathroom, you can never feel alone." Yes, I greet and talk to the one who lives in my bathroom. I know that, later, others will follow in her tarsal footprints and will come inside, too. They are good company.

Sometimes things come inside even more so, though they are already inside. Once, arriving home late one night, I noticed the lid on one of my tarantula cages ajar, revealing a two-inch gap. Sighing at seeing the cage empty, I began a cursory, unsuccessful search. Hell, I should just go to bed and find it tomorrow. The probability of the tarantula climbing upstairs, crawling into my bed, and biting me seemed statistically low. My other two tarantulas were laid-back Chilean rose-hairs, and I could carry them around on my palm or on my shoulder. But the escapee, a nice orange-kneed variety, was less domesticated than my other two; she might cause problems with the cats during the night. So I got a flashlight and finally spotted it behind a big bookcase. Sighing again, I took all the books out, got the dolly, leveraged the bookcase away from the wall, and caught the sucker in the usual lid-slid-under-overturned-jar technique. I slept better that way.

Recently, this happened: I was brushing my teeth before going to bed. I was tired and my brainwaves were pretty flat. I took several sips from my water glass and spit out the remaining toothpaste, and swallowed several more sips. Then, lowering the glass from my mouth, something caught my eye. Floating on the water remaining in the glass was a spider. This spider, like the jumping spider, had no doubt frantically tried to avoid the huge dark maw opening repeatedly as the water rushed into it.

Staring hard at the spider still floating in the glass, I noted that it was a recluse spider, possessor of toxic venom which destroys skin. Yes, *Loxoceles reclusa*. Now, as an entomologist, I'm not quite as bothered by these recluse spiders as everyone else is, but nevertheless I uttered a word of limited imagination: "S---!"

I slowly analyzed. If the spider had been in my mouth and I rinsed it out, it would be in the basin, right? If I had swallowed the spider, it wouldn't still be in the glass, right? Then I wondered: Would the spider release its venom while being violently sloshed up and down in a glass? Had the venom swirled around in my mouth? What denatures spider venom protein? All I could think of was papayas. Yeah, we always have those in our kitchens in Kansas. This particular spider was not fine after its ordeal was over; it went into a vial of alcohol. I survived just fine.

So the recluse spiders come inside, and the jumping spiders, and the slugs, and sometimes even an earthworm. And time just keeps moving on, inexorably. The discs get squeezed, and so do the nerves. I list more. The sheetrock develops cracks, and sometimes the front door won't open. The house shifts more. Energy input decreases. Entropy increases. Things come inside. And they're all welcome.

A Memoir in Birds

1. Husband

One early weekday evening in late October, we sat quietly at the kitchen table in the fading warmth of the sun as it splashed soft peach echoes across the living room into our eyes.

"Wanna know a secret?" he asked.

"Sure," I smiled, meeting his eyes.

"I wouldn't tell just anyone this," he said, as if our twenty years together might in some measure have fallen short of my earning this confidence. I waited silently and he began.

"I was having lunch at The Merc today, you know, in that cafe dining room. I was sitting there by the windows in the southwest corner next to the liquor store, eating my sandwich. On the sidewalk outside was this little junco. He was sick, you know, kind of lolling around struggling there. Then this young man kicked him as he was walking into the liquor store."

"On purpose?" I asked.

"No," he continued. "He didn't even notice him. Anyway, he was bobbing around there gathering himself up. He was really sick, and I watched him the whole time I was eating. I could tell he was going to die there on the concrete and asphalt."

A cloud crossed the horizon in that moment—the sunlight changed from peach to strontium red, setting the dining room aglow.

"So after I got done eating, I took a paper towel and scooped him up. I thought about what someone would say if they saw me doing this, how I might look if someone I knew from work saw me holding this little bird in my hand, but I did it anyway."

As he paused, the light softened into a dull and dark gold, and I mused at his gruff, thick hands on the table.

"So I took him across the street to that park, you know, the one where we used to play when I was a kid."

"Centennial Park?"

"Yeah. That one. I found these bushes on a little hill by the playground and put him under there in a safe place. You know, so he could die in peace. And as I stood up to go I looked back at him, and— don't believe me if you want—he looked at me right in the eye, and I could tell that he was saying, 'Thanks.' "

2. Mother

"Go quickly, it's wet out there," my mother's aging voice cracked as I departed for my car through the late May rain. "Drive safe, it's dark."

But suddenly I stumbled across an obstacle on the cobblestone walkway and screeched as I caught my balance, "Ahhh! What's this?"

The porch light came on immediately. Strangely, a straggly decorated grapevine wreath lay on the ground in front of me, soaked.

"Just leave it there," she called, "I'm getting the birds out of it."

"The what?" I replied. Then I remembered watching the pair of house finches making trip after trip to the summer wreath covered with silk flowers and ribbon as we had sipping iced tea on the patio the week before.

"They were driving me crazy with the peeping and noise all the time. So I took the wreath down and put it out there. I was going to put the nest in the trash after they were gone."

With horror I realized that the small black sopping lumps on the sidewalk reflected in the hollow glow of the light were, indeed, dead baby birds.

"Oh, Mom! How could you do that? That's horrible."

"Well, they were bothering me, so I got rid of them," she retorted from the doorway unapologetically.

Inspecting the scene, I noticed something wiggling in the rain-soaked nest.

"Get me a shoebox and a towel," I commanded disdainfully. "Honestly. And heat up the towel in the microwave. It's a long drive home."

With my tiny charge gently deposited in a fold of perfect temperature, securely engaged in a much brighter future, we made it, albeit soaking wet, to the car. I began to laugh quietly as I carefully tucked the towel in the box for the trip home. She waved from the shadowy shelter of the doorway. Lightning flashed as it began to pour harder, and I drove away.

3. Father

"Where is that new centerpiece?" my grandmother muttered as she paced. "I need it for the table. It's the one with the angels on it I saved from last year. It must be out in the Quonset hut."

"Can I go?" I pleaded immediately. The Quonset hut was a treasure house usually reserved for summer exploration. "*Pleeeease?*"

"Okay," she said, "But you bundle up warm and wear your boots—it's COLD outside."

We headed across the South Dakota barnyard in the winter morning sun, icy crusts of shallow snow crunching underfoot, our breath suspended in hard, white clouds that outlasted our passing steps. Around the back of the freestanding garage, next to the huge wood pile under the winter skeleton of an ancient elm tree, two semi-cylindrical huts waited silently, about 7 feet high, 10 feet wide, and 20 feet long, painted Pepto pink, the same as the small farmhouse we'd left 40 yards behind.

"Let's see, it wasn't in the west one with the decorations, I already looked there."

Good, I thought. I love the east one the best. It has all the good stuff in it. As she pressed the door into the piles inside the overstuffed little building, a narrow path revealed itself. "So Gramma, what was this building for?" I asked the same question, one of the rituals we repeated every visit.

"Well, this was the building your dad and Uncle Bud used to live in during the summer. Your dad had this side," her thickly gloved hand swept to the right, "and Bud had this side." The door swung closed behind us as our eyes adjusted to the dimmer sunlight now filtered through dusty window panes. She pointed, "The dresser sat over there, and the bookshelves are still right there. You know, they read books all the time, just like you."

My eyes locked onto the sacred geometry of familiar quilts, the carved bed rails poking through stacks of memorabilia, and the stark spacey patterns on the open drapes that had been sewn and hung in the fifties.

"Where did I put that thing? It is so pretty." She pulled back more sheets that covered piles of magazines, letters, knickknacks, and picture frames.

"Gramma, what's this?" I said, eyeing what might have been a large shirt box on the top of a familiar stack on the overfilled bed.

"Oh, yes. That old thing. Let's see now." Indulgently ignoring the cold and her task at hand for a moment, we pulled off our respective gloves and mittens, and she lowered the box to me and carefully removed the lid. "This is that collection the boys did one summer when they were kids."

I knew she meant my dad and uncle, but it was impossible to imagine either of them ever having been my age, much less having assembled what lay before us. Wonderful and confusing as always, this artifact captured me every time I saw it. The box held a perfectly spaced grid of six horizontal rows and five vertical columns; each square was precisely labeled with perfectly cut paper slips, typed and curling and yellow. Centered in each square, each in its pristine natural color and distinct size and shape, were 30 tiny eggs.

My grandmother continued, "Oh, one summer they got an idea, from a *Boy's Life* magazine or contest or something, to collect bird eggs. They went around climbing trees and raiding nests all summer long. They learned all of the bird names and nests and eggs. We ordered bird books from the library. It was quite something."

She gently handed me the box and continued her search. Chimney swift, chickadee, several warblers, Baltimore oriole, blue jay, grackle—speckled, tan, green, blue, rounder, more pointed, arranged smallest to largest—the tiny time capsules stared up from their cardboard archive as I conjured visions of nest raiding, tree climbing, onerous identification and labeling tasks, the library miles away. All of these romantic ingredients of boyhood were far different from the hardened tales of primitive farm work my dad and his brother told over and often—raking hay with draft horses, picking corn by hand, making lye soap, trooping to the outhouse in winter. The repetition of these eye-witness details made the evidence at hand as seemingly unlikely as it was well-worn. The sheer number of species, much less their genuine whole eggs, implied dizzying dedication and knowledge—not to mention gentleness and care. *My* father? *My* uncle? *Really?*

After several frozen moments the cold overtook us. My grandmother carefully replaced the lid on the box, then the box on its pile, then the cover on the pile, and tucked the angel centerpiece under her arm.

"I guess we'd better get back inside. It's getting cold out here."

4. Daughter

Painfully unzipping my sweaty legs from the leather seats of our little Subaru station wagon, I parked on the street in front of 905 Maine beneath a monumental pin oak in the sizzling summer heat and opened the car door. "Oh, dear."

"What, Mommy?" chirped the voice from the car seat in back.

In a near miss I had almost squashed it with my sandal. "It's a baby bird."

"Oh Mommy, let me *seeee.*" And in that moment the rituals that would consume the next several weeks began to unfold. "Can we *keeeeep* it?"

"Oh, honey, it fell out of the tree a long way up, and this pavement is so hot. It probably won't live."

"But Mommy, we have to try!" Indeed. Who could refuse a precocious five-year-old girl?

"What kind is it? What are we going to name it? Can we keep it?" she prattled on.

Rare is the ugliness God gives a baby bird. But in those first skeptical hours of negligible motion, closed bulging orbital protrusions, bare bumpy flesh thinner than tissue, and scant fuzz, little Ashleigh vigilantly watched over the struggling bundle, following precisely every instruction we gave.

"Don't touch him. Keep him covered up and warm. Stay quiet." I was sure it wouldn't live the night. Life's lessons.

"Oh, he might make it," my husband had said that evening, taking a turn at preparing the Exact baby parrot food just the right temperature and painstakingly plunging a small glob of the gooey mixture into its tiny crop.

And make it he did. "Peeper" occupied us steadily through the rest of that hot July. We settled into the gradually progression of answering to an incessantly regular peck and call that filled our already overflowing days. The growing fledgling downed dozen after dozen gargantuan bait-shop nightcrawlers cut into four or five squirming sections. Ashleigh learned to meticulously insert them with special black plastic tweezers into the angular yellow mouth that magically evolved day by day into a healthy black beak. She never lost interest and never missed a feeding. Each day brought enough growth and change to keep her fascinated.

"Mommy, what are those pokey things coming out everywhere?"

"Well, honey, those are the beginnings of feathers. You'll see. He will be a beautiful robin soon."

When the old canary cage no longer held our speckle-breasted friend comfortably, the ultimate time approached. Even with days of warning and preparation, the moment began bittersweetly.

"Mommy, why do we have to let him go?"

"Because there is nothing more we can do. He belongs outside now."

"But Mommy, I want to keep Peeper!"

"Whenever you are ready, honey. You'll have to open the door and let him go."

Summoning great strength and courage, she finally did it. And in a beautiful twist, Peeper jumped squarely onto her head. Ashleigh stood stock still as the tears rolled down her cheeks.

"See Mommy, he doesn't want to leave!" she whispered, her mood brightening.

"That's because you are such a good friend, Ashleigh."

She started to smile, rolling her eyes toward her forehead trying to see. Then she started to giggle at the funny face she was making and the thought of a bird on her head. On cue, Peeper hopped onto the porch railing, flapped his ready wings a few times, and disappeared into the neighborhood.

Nature's Beauty Lingers

T he winding river of life is a theme captured in some of the memorial windows of stained glass created by my great-grandfather Louis Comfort Tiffany. His leaded Favrile glass window titled "Magnolias and Irises" depicts such a river running down from a mountain into a lake, with the irises and magnolias in the foreground. Symbolic of the passage of life, the winding river lingers in my mind as a metaphor for the cherished places of beauty that inspired me and gave me solace in my youth, and for the three vital people connected to these places who are now gone.

In 2007, the U.S. Postal Service honored Louis with a commemorative stamp. Amazed at the happenstance that had made me the Tiffany family member standing on the platform next to philatelic dignitaries, I shared my thoughts. "I believe Tiffany's legacy leaves all of his descendants this gift of a discerning eye in their appreciation of beauty inherent in natural colors when light falls on natural elements, such as an iris, or cluster of irises, or a magnolia tree in the full bloom of spring. Such arrangements of color, whether close up or from a distance, lift up the human spirit, bringing aesthetic personal reward." A few moments later, in a ceremonial flourish, one of the dignitaries stepped to the side, lifted the black cloth covering the easel, and unveiled the Tiffany stamp. A collective murmur of appreciation emanated from the crowd.

To me, this Tiffany window honors life in all its vibrant and muted colors, its joy and pain, and the sorrow of saying goodbye. *This* great-grandfather died before I was born, but through his depiction of nature in stained glass, he bequeathed to the public many images that breathe beauty back into life. When the visceral experience of place connects me to the voice, smell, or movement of someone I love, it stirs my emotions and becomes personal in the places of natural beauty that I identify with.

Three such places of beauty represent three people who reverberate from my center out past my fingertips. I will never let them go. Why would I want to? Old Black Point, on the Long Island Sound in Connecticut, was the summer retreat of "Bompa," my great-grandfather Charles Culp Burlingham; Walberswick, Suffolk, England was my father's; and Sørenhus, in Kristiansand, Norway, my mother's. To pay tribute to Bompa, my father, and my mother, to re-experience connection to them, I return to revisit these places of remembrance.

Sweet Saltwater

Bompa—who at the age of ninety-four was completely blind and very deaf when I was seven—owned several properties in Old Black Point, a private, carefully groomed green summer haven for the prosperous. Most summers, we stayed in one of them. Old Black Point is the first miracle of my childhood. As soon as school let out, we piled into the family car and headed up the Henry Hudson Parkway toward Connecticut. By the time we arrived at the salt marshes leading out to the bay, I was jumping out of my seat. To live for two full months on this private peninsula made me wild with joy. Within minutes of arriving, I was sitting on top of the stone wall with my feet dangled over the edge, gazing out at the sparkling blue water.

When I visited Bompa, I would sometimes find him sitting stationary on his back porch, smelling the sea air. More likely, he'd be somewhere in his house, usually in a chair in the living room. He wore three-piece seersucker suits in summertime, though his shirt collars were often awry. His wiry eyebrows jutted out like old brushes, and white hairs grew out of his ears. He spoke in a refined voice, but loud. He was good at touch. He greeted me by smoothing my hair, his fingertips brushing my brow, nose, and mouth, his hands grasping my shoulders. He not seeing me but I seeing him, I waited for his victorious broad smile—like an anticipated move in a chess game when he boomed out "Lynnie!" Then I could relax into my visit, run to fetch the Braille backgammon set from the shelf, and set it up so that we could begin. I didn't mind his splotched papery hands, or his "old" smell. I knew he liked my spunky personality, and though he probably let me win the games, I did enough work on the board to feel smart.

It was okay to drop by Bompa's almost anytime. I loved to coast into his circular driveway, kick my bike stand down, pay my visit, then sit on a stool in the kitchen and chat with his cook, Nora. I loved walking across the clipped lawn in back of his house to the overgrown grassy knoll at the far side of his property.

I would sit down in the eelgrass, completely hidden from view, and take in the breakwater, watching the sun play on top of the waves. With each crashing wave, the sun shimmied forward, brightening the light spots in the seaweed and pebbles. Every time the waves went out, the sun shimmied back again. The view, the sweet saltwater smells, and the water's gentle rhythm soothed me.

Only one family member remains at Old Black Point: my great-uncle's son Charlie. I never knew him well.

Some summers ago, I took a hotel room in nearby Niantic and drove to Black Point. I called Charlie to get permission to use the beach. I changed into my bathing suit in a wooden bathhouse marked "Burlingham" over the doorway. Because of Bompa, there used to be ten of them. I stepped onto the pier, supported over the water by stilts, then walked down to its end and dipped my toe. Then, splash. I flipped over onto my back and let out a "Whooo" sound, just like Mom always did when we were kids in the icy waters in Norway. I breast-stroked out to the first raft and back, memories floating to the surface of my mind.

Later, I tapped tentatively at the door of what was once my Bompa's house. An old white-haired woman answered. After a few minutes, she recognized me as the childhood summer friend of her daughter. I sat stiffly on my chair recalling the days when I ran in and out because I belonged.

Squinting Through Carnelians

My father wore soft blue cotton shirts from America—flags waving in the wind, signaling a certain careless freedom. He had a salty smell, slightly pungent but clean. He often had a faraway look in his eye. I would follow his gaze, to see what he was looking at. He squinted at things. After a while, the wrinkles around his glasses relaxed, but I could tell that he was not done with whatever he saw. It was Dad who introduced me to Walberswick, the second miracle of my childhood. All day long during vacations, I was on my bicycle exploring the village, the beach, the heaths of the surrounding countryside. I loved the expanse and the complementary colors of purple heather and yellow gorse on the downs, the windswept beach, the canal ridged with billowy reeds, the old broken-down windmill, the private bridle paths for horses, the narrow country lanes, the thatched cottages, the fragrant, colorful English country gardens. Dad could usually be found ambling along the beach, painting the countryside on his easel, or playing his guitar in the garden.

After thirty-four years' separation, I traveled to Walberswick alone. Wistfully, I peered through the windows of Thorpe View, our old cottage. I unlatched the gate and meandered through the garden. Walking down the bare blistery beach, I found a gray stone with a gray heart rimmed with white at its center. I thought about the carnelians from this pebble beach that were Dad's sacred possessions. How his greatest finds happened on sunny days when light shone through the wet stones, revealing their yellow-orange to reddish-brown to rich red tones. How he laid these treasures out carefully on the chipped whitewashed windowsill at Thorpe View and took extraordinary pleasure in his collection as if he were looking at the variety of beauty in nature, past, present, and future. Later, I sauntered along the reedy canal path out to the old windmill. Later still, an old village friend I met in the pub said, "Your father, he was so handsome."

The day I left, rain came down in shifting sheets. I parked my car on the side of the road and pushed the button on my umbrella. Carried along by the wind, I swept across the bombed-out graveyard into the four-hundred-year-old church. A cleaning woman saw me, grabbed her pail, and left. Alone, I sat on the smooth wooden pew in the cavernous silence, my eyes closed.

Here lies . . .

I tiptoed out.

A Seagull's Freedom

I have a picture of my mother in my mind drawn from a vacation during her older years in Norway. We've made our way down the steep pathway in front of her cabin, and over the rocks to the icy water below. She's brought her "washing soap" and has dipped herself quickly in the Skagerrak, treading water while she soaped up. Now she's back on the rocks, one knee up, one leg out, chin pointing toward the sun, eyes closed, taking in the rays, the fresh pine scents, and the gentle breeze. I am thrilled to see her so full of peaceful joy. Norway brings her out. Never in America.

Norway is the most beautiful country. Sørenhus, overlooking the Skaggerak in Kristiansand, offers a small piece of a God-given world. When we visited, we children took the rowboat and fished in the icy waters of the strait. We picnicked with the family on little islands, foraged for blueberries, sunbathed, and swam off the rocks. During the long day, the soft summer light sent millions of rhythmic sparks dancing on top of the water, turning me sentient. The voice of nature whispered, "I'm here for all of you, always. Look at me, breathe me: delight."

The summer after Mom died, I flew to Norway. Sørenhus—my grandparents' summerhouse and its surrounding property—is still owned by family, divided up now among grandchildren. My sister Randi owns the section that was our mother's.

After I collected Mom's ashes from the Andås Funeral Home in Kristiansand, with a gentle rain drizzling my hair, I carefully carried the heavy box through the damp woods to her cabin, trying to avoid tripping on the tenacious tree roots or falling on the slippery path. I sat on the terrace as the sun came out and took in the panoramic view.

I looked through tree trunks of cracked bark, and over a large rock layered with dry pine needles, some cedar bushes, heather, grass, and thin, gently spiky tan reeds at the vast blue sea with caries dusted with pine trees in the distance. To the south lay the lighthouse, which appeared lit up by the shower of natural light. Gazing to the left and right, my eyes caught boats moving along down below. Two masts walked over the rock. I waited until I saw them in the opening between the pines. Then I knew it was a schooner.

These days, small yachts project proud noses at terrific speed over the surface of the water, little red flags with blue and white crosses whipping in the air off the stern. The old natural wooden boats, the white motorboats, the rubber Zodiacs, the yellow trawlers, the thirty-foot sailboats, the tourist boats, the fast and slow ferries, the tankers, even the kayaks all move proudly in and over the Skaggerak, claiming this sea territory for their own.

A seagull swept from sky to water and back up again in a graceful rhythm. I took in a deep breath. Let it out. My mother's country. My mother's land. My mother.

ဢ ဢ ဢ

Holding the Tiffany stamp close to my eye at this moment, I squint at the miniature themed view of the winding river of life in "Magnolias and Irises." My vision blurs from Louis's framed picture to my imagination, where these other places of beauty in nature provide peaceful joy and solace. And once again I am with my dear Bompa, my father, and my mother.

Lynn at 16

PART V

Treasures

I t was a typical winter day in Kansas. The howling wind and the driving snow were common for January, but they made me feel worse. The flu had left me feeling that a great battle had taken place with a demon, and I had lost. It left me weak and unable to meet the challenges of fighting the drive in deep snow and the rigors of a day at work. I was awake at 5:30 a.m., my usual time, but most of the morning was spent dozing, trying to make up for the sleep I had lost.

At two o'clock that afternoon the phone rang. It was Hazel, my mother-in-law. She lives in Wetmore, 9 miles from Dad. Her voice was quite calm but strained, that left me unexplainably anxious about what news she had called to share. "Your father's house is on fire."

I was silent. She repeated it again. My heart and mind both acknowledged the data, but I could not utter a word. Finally I asked, "Is Dad okay?" I was saying the right words, but the reality was unbelievable. The people I love should always be safe.

"No one knows—we just heard the news on the scanner," she replied.

How the conversation ended I do not recall, but I will always remember Roy walking up behind me and putting his hands on my shoulder without speaking a word—my husband's loving presence and reassurance that Dad was all right.

Random thoughts and prayers were flying through my mind. *God, please, make sure Dad is okay. Thank goodness we have four-wheel drive. The roads have been graded. What should I wear? Should I take time to dress or just wear my pajamas? Do we have enough gas?*

Tears streamed down my cheeks and fear clutched my heart so tightly I could feel it pounding in my throat. Normally I would be making lists and preparing for such traveling, especially in blizzard weather and with dangerous roads, but not today. Roy and I threw on some clothes, pulled on our boots and coats and headed out the door. Pictures of Dad kept popping into my mind. I could see him smiling with a gentle glow in his eyes, lovingly picking up our daughters Desiree and Wende when they were little. I could see him petting his horses and quietly talking to Bobby, his shepherd dog.

As my thoughts drifted through these memories, I mentally surveyed his home. I saw the family heirlooms and hoped they had been saved. They were not just furniture or heirlooms—they represented and documented my family's history. The hundred-year-old walnut desk with a fold-out writing area, drawers, and glass doors that protected shelves of books and memories. The desk was so old that it did not have hinges, rather, pegs were pulled out and used to support the desk lid, which was gently lowered onto them. Grandpa had told me that this desk was in my great-great-grandfather Jeptha Vawter's house in Wakarusa, Kansas. It was handed down to his father and later to him.

Books were as dear to my grandfather as that desk. Most of his collection of books was written by his maternal cousin Zane Grey. He was so proud of him, and he enjoyed reading the books. He also read these books to my little sister Susie and me when we were 2 and 6 years old. He would tell us the stories by inserting family names like this: "Uncle Bill drove the buggy" or "Uncle Bill whipped the bandits with his bare hands." We would sit spellbound at his feet, cross-legged on the floor, while he embellished each story to us. Mom warned that "not all the stories Grandpa tells are true." We didn't care—we cherished every word.

Grandpa was a character in his own right. He was 5 feet, 6 inches tall, with broad chest and shoulders like a little bull. He had black hair until the day he died at 71. He had the blackest eyes I had ever seen, and when he told you something you believed it! He would tell us about the Vawters who came from France and how brave they were. Now that Grandpa is gone, how would I remember all the stories without being able to touch the book covers and smell that musky smell of old paper and ink?

Mom had died in 1990, so the beautiful handmade afghans, the antique wool bedspread that covered their bed, the dishes she handpicked, her quilts, all the "things" that made that house their home and comforted us with her presence though she was no longer there. Suddenly I remembered the tomahawk artifact that was found in a field on the Wakarusa Vawter home. Would these things be saved, or would we all lose these connections to our family roots?

Roy was driving as fast as he dared on the one-lane snow- and ice-packed road. Fortunately, the weather and roads were bad enough that folks were tucked safely in their cozy, warm homes, so traffic was scarce.

When I looked up, we were passing Emmett, Kansas, about six miles from home. The snow was falling heavily now, driven by pounding wind, but all we could see was white. The windows were icing over. How Roy was able to see where he was going I will never know. Suddenly he slowed as if to examine something beside the road.

As we drew closer, we could barely make out someone walking on the side of the road. It was a large man, covered in snow, dressed in heavy coveralls with a sweatshirt hoodie on his head. He forced his body against the wind as he walked, while he grasped the hand of a small child. The child was also bundled in warm clothes, head held down to shield his face from the driving snow.

As Roy stopped the truck, the man approached. We could see that the child's face already had ice hanging on his long eyelashes and brows. His eyes were dark and dull, and his cheeks were bright red. There was no doubt in our minds that no matter what ransom the fire demanded, these folks needed our help first. In rural northeastern Kansas, you can travel 15 to 60 miles and not see another person, so if someone needs help, we are accustomed to stopping to help—especially a child in disastrously cold weather.

Roy opened the pickup doors, climbed out, and helped the child into the warm haven where he could begin to thaw. The man politely kicked the snow and ice off his boots, climbed in, and reached to place the child in his lap to warm him. He buckled the seat belt around them both and gave Roy directions to his house.

He explained how they had been feeding his cattle when the pickup got stuck in a snowdrift. They had walked over a mile before we had caught up with them on the road. He had given up all hope of a passing car because the weather was so bad. He had carried the child most of the way because the snow was so deep the child could not walk until they got to the road. He was breathing heavily while he continued the story of how the child had insisted on helping Grandpa feed the cows. Grandma had been against the idea but had relented when the child was so insistent. The child smiled shyly from the comfort of his grandfather's arms.

As we turned down the long drive to his two-story farm house, we could see a woman peeking out the window. We knew the relief she felt as she saw her family safely delivered to her door—we had felt the worry of a missing daughter after a car wreck. After the man got out and shut the door, he thanked us and shook Roy's hand. The woman opened the door and welcomed them both home with a big hug.

The sweet tightness in my throat disappeared quickly and was replaced by calm fear and then by panic. The truth was that no matter how fast we dove or how badly we wanted to help, it would not change the outcome we would find at the farm. We sat silently for the next fifty miles, each of us trapped in our own thoughts.

As we finally crested the hill to Dad's farm, the sky was orange and small flecks of yellow splashed upward, even as the snow draped over the fire. The house was completely gone except for the stone fireplace that stood defiantly. The fire was concentrated in the basement and its giant tongues feverishly lapped up the last remains of our home.

Roy looked at his watch and said "It has only been two hours since we got the call and the house is gone."

The trees that once stood protecting and shielding the home from danger were now ablaze. No longer did they have a home to protect.

The driveway was a blur of neighbors, cars, trucks, fire trucks, hoses, and equipment. The huge yard was so densely packed with equipment and people that we had no place to park. While Roy looked for a place, I jumped out and ran toward the house. Everyone stood motionless. It was as quiet as a funeral except for the interment popping and crashing as the wood burned. Why wasn't anyone fighting the fire?

My memories of the fire scene are muddled except for my overwhelming drive to find my dad. I only remember a slow-motion, white, foggy scene of equipment, people, and chaos. I was detached, as if I was watching a movie, walking through the faceless crowd of people. But no Dad. I rushed into the crowd. Everyone was bundled in heavy, duck tan coveralls, gloves, and hoodies, as well as, fire gear—protection from the fire and the cold. What irony. Time after time, I clutched the arms of neighbors and friends that I hoped were my dad. Again and again, none of them were! These people were the ones who had fought the fire and, I later learned, almost won. They now looked dejected and disappointed because they thought they failed their task. Each tried to comfort me, and many tried to explain, but all I wanted was to find my dad.

The weather continued to show no mercy. The wind was furiously fanning the fire and the snow continued to fall. Even the firemen stood by helplessly as the fire viciously devoured the place where my family had built our hopes, dreams, loves, and lives.

You can argue that the hopes, dreams, loves, and lives exist in the people that built them, but I tell you that when I look at myself in the mirror I do not see those contained in that home. That home housed a wedding. It sheltered two parents, one grandmother, three children, eleven grandchildren. It heard daughters and granddaughters playing the piano. It sponsored numerous huge Vawter Family Thanksgivings. It heard the giggles of many slumber parties and hay rack rides, Bible readings, and more prayers than the heart can imagine.

I helplessly continued to search the circle of people. Finally, I caught a familiar sight. At the far end I found my dad, standing near my sister Susie. Dad is a proud 5 foot, 8 inch tall man, but at that moment he looked much smaller. His head was lowered and his shoulders were limp. Although he is a simple man that values few material things except those needed to meet the necessities of life, but this was home. It was heartbreaking to watch his lifeless vigil, watching his home disappear. I ran to him and clutched him close, reassuring myself that he was safe.

He quietly spoke, not in anger or fear. He said, "I don't have anything to remember your mother!"

I remember feeling so grateful for the real treasure—my dad—safe in my arms.

Later Dad told me that the firefighters had nearly had the fire out but they ran out of water. He went to the pond about 300 feet from the house to break ice, but the snow was too deep to take the water tank truck into the pasture to pump the water. Dad had stood alone on the dam of the pond and watched the roof of his home fall in, and he had realized then that the fight was over.

Although I shared his pain of losing all of the "things" that had been important to us, I remember thankfully the friends and family that generously donated clothing, blankets, and housewares to rebuild his home. Dad moved in with Susie, who lived 6 miles away. He continued to care for his cattle and horses, and life changed.

In the spring, the real cleanup began. The charred remains of the home were hauled away, debriding the site for a new home and a new beginning. The excavation brought surprises. Jessica, my niece, found the ruby-red Fenton glass vase I had given Mom for Mother's Day unbroken in the basement. The Wakarusa tomahawk that was always on the fireplace mantel in the living room emerged intact, to be kept once more for the next generation. The skeleton of the wrought-iron stand of Mom's favorite treadle sewing machine, the one she used to sew her quilts, stood sadly waiting to be useful once more.

The excavation was the painful part of letting go of the comfortable and familiar, but it renewed our family's strength to build new memories. Dad replaced the house with a modern rancher, but it has never felt the same. Susie helped with all the details and womanly touches to make the house a home. Susie and I replaced pictures of Mom and Dad for his bedroom; a purple and white Navajo afghan that was one of Mom's favorite patterns hung over a chair; and some of her refinished oak table and chairs were brought from storage for the dining room.

Looking back, I believe the incident with the man and little boy on the road was God reminding me to appreciate the true gifts of life and love and not the "things" of a happy home. I knew when I saw the house that all the family heirlooms were gone. They did not matter. What drove my search through the crowd was my need to find Dad. He was irreplaceable, the true treasure. He was the heirloom that could never be duplicated.

Many times since that day we have reminded Dad that he will always have something to remember Mom by—he has us.

Char and her dad.

Heirlooms

Whatever we treasure for ourselves
separates us from others;
our possessions are our limitations.
—Rabindranath Tagore

My Grandma Carver and her six sisters spent the better part of their later years 'sorting.' This activity seemed to involve rummaging through all of their possessions, reorganizing everything into containers, and, on rare occasions, throwing something away. All of the Hiller sisters were packrats. Like most Americans of their generation, they had survived a meager childhood, the Great Depression, and two World Wars. They believed that to discard something was to waste it, even if it was no longer needed. They all lived well into their 80s and, over their lifetimes, they accumulated mounds of things. In the sorting days of their golden years, they catalogued and boxed their collections and marked each item, recording its significance for posterity. Among my Aunt Grace's effects, we found a bottle labeled "Kansas River Sand."

Grandma Carver knew that prosperity was elusive. Amassing things was her hedge against a future that she had come to regard as uncertain. She wasn't greedy and she wasn't particularly fearful—she just wanted to stay prepared. Unlike the people populating today's reality television shows who hoard things to dispel vague, deep-seated anxieties, her fears were real, with foundations in her own experience. Grandma stocked up to be equipped for the worst. She and her six children had once lived in two railroad boxcars pushed together—their own prototype of the double-wide mobile home—and she wanted to ensure her survival in the event that similar circumstances prevailed again. She kept at hand the tools and supplies necessary to procure food, clothing, and shelter.

The amount of stuff in her personal cache was remarkable. For example, when she died, she left an entire cabinet of little plastic drawers, each one filled with buttons, sorted by color and size. She never would have dreamed of discarding any of them for fear that she would throw away the very one that she might need some day. We inherited dishes, pans, umbrellas, books, fabric, quilt scraps, bobbins, thread, back scratchers, piggy banks, and vases. She left empty jars, trinkets, puzzles, paste jewelry, and coins. After she retired, she discovered garage sales and spent her new-found time accumulating even more stuff, reveling in the fact that she was getting things at below bargain prices. She left us a collage of relics, gleaned from the castoff objects of people we didn't even know.

I have recently begun the process of helping my mother sort her own belongings. My stepfather passed away from a stroke last winter at the age of 84 after several years of Alzheimer's disease. My parents have lived in a two-level ranch house that sits on several acres of land, containing a gazebo, various garden beds, three ponds, and a swimming pool. During their more than 36 years in this house, they have accumulated a little bit of everything, adding to the horde of belongings left behind by my grandmother. My mother is ready to downsize but has trouble knowing where to begin.

We actually began the process more than a year ago. Mom had already been considering a move for several years, as it had become increasingly clear that they could no longer keep up with even basic house maintenance. She had the idea that after an enormous garage sale in the spring, she would begin to get the house presentable enough to put on the market last summer. She modified those plans in mid-summer to thinking that a reasonably successful garage sale at the end of August would position her to have the house ready for sale sometime this year. When my father died in early March, she increased her resolve to clear things out, and she and I have spent the better part of most weekends tackling closets, drawers, storage areas, and spare bedrooms.

After several months of this, we have made an almost imperceptible dent in the mass of possessions. Whenever I feel good about making progress, we open a new closet or chest of drawers, and any sense of achievement dissipates immediately. I'm beginning to appreciate the patience that archaeologists must have when unearthing ancient artifacts buried under eons of newer civilizations. Occasionally, like a geologist who chips away a layer of rock and unearths a rare gemstone, we discover something priceless. We were pulling papers and notebooks out of a closet when Mom handed me an old blue three-ring binder, devoid of any distinguishing characteristics. I opened it, expecting to pull out and discard the contents, but then sat down when I saw what it held. Every Boy Scout membership card, achievement certificate, and badge from my father's lifetime scouting career had been carefully placed in this book, from his Cub Scout days in the 1930s to his Eagle Scout years as an adult. A few weeks later, among folders of wooden toy patterns and magazine clippings in a filing cabinet in the basement, we unearthed my grandmother's master's thesis about teaching art to special education students.

We've uncovered traces of my own childhood. In a bedroom that was mine for only one summer, there remain only a few artifacts. My long-suffering teddy bear rests on the bed alongside the newer, decorative ones Mom made one year. A sock doll and a couple of old children's books sit on the vanity next to a stack of remote control cars. Like stones from a ruined castle, as the landscape around them has shifted, they look out of place where they have come to rest.

Like our ancestral Hiller sisters, Mom and I have found that sorting is the best way to deal with the mounds of relics we unearth. Before we can establish what to do with all of it, we find it necessary to identify and quantify each item. We use plastic zip-lock bags to put items in, much the way a police forensics unit would do while gathering evidence. We have zip-lock bags full of toenail clippers, keys, lapel pins, and tie tacks, for example. There is a shoe box so full of pencils that the lid won't close. Once it is clear that we have way more than we need of anything, it becomes easier to discard things.

When we began this excavation a year ago in January, we started in the farthest reaches of Mom's basement, where she stores things with no immediate use. It seemed a natural place to start, since she was putting the Christmas decorations away down there anyway. I arrived with a stack of large plastic bins and a resolve to be ruthless and unsentimental. I envisioned making a broad sweep through their house, clearing out anything unwanted or unused, with decisions about what to discard and what to keep as clearly defined as black and white. The strategy included plans for cataloging items for later perusal by the multitude of relatives who will want keepsakes when the time comes to sell the house. We've all been secretly scouting the house for items we want, anyway. Mom has invited us to be more open about it and has encouraged us to actually mark things with tape. We have promised not to fight.

I have never thought of my mother as a sentimental person, so I've been surprised at her unwillingness to part with some things simply because of their attachment to a particular person. I was prepared to toss out an old plastic candle wreath when she took it from my hands. "Kay gave me that the Christmas we were in Springfield," she said and placed it lovingly back in its box. Discarding things that once belonged to one of the Hiller sisters, or given to her by an old friend, no matter how useless or ugly, is not even up for discussion. Then there are the things she wants me to have or, at least, wants me to want to have. I leave with at least one or two boxes full of things I don't have the heart to refuse. I suppose in 20 years I will be forcing these items on my niece. I am saving a Christmas ornament, made from a real chicken's foot, for just that time.

In the past 15 years, I have moved three times and, with each move, I am forced to confront my own possessions and, along with those, my obsessions. I am a souvenir keeper. My belongings have less to do with survival or sentimentality and more to do with my own strange gestures to posterity. I tend to form odd attachments to events, or people, or objects. I want to capture the things I like, preserve them, and keep them forever. When I travel, I have this urge to take entire places home with me. I want the *Book of Kells* on my coffee table, cobblestones from Prague streets in my back yard, the fog horn from the Split Rock lighthouse north of Duluth, Minnesota, for a doorbell, maybe. I pick up rocks and shells and pieces of rubble to bring back home, hoping that the mementos will somehow evoke the spirit of the places I have visited. I tend to be a kind of outsider, looking in on scenes I want to be in, but always on the edges, taking the photographs, recording the moments in my journal, and appropriating the relics to put in my museum. I rarely participate. If I had actually been fully present at the time I collected these things, I might be content with memories instead of souvenirs. But I'm the traveler who goes it alone, sitting on the sidelines at an outdoor café, watching the parade of other people pass by. I'm the one taking photographs with nobody in them. My souvenirs, years later, are often as empty as my photographs.

I have a box containing every name tag I've ever worn as a nurse. This collection provides a chronology of my professional life, including two name changes, the series of titles (from GN to RN to RNC to CPNP), my degrees (BSN and MSN), and the institutions where I have worked (LMH, SVRMC, CMH) and taught (WU, NCCC, BU). Photo IDs appear in the mid 1990s and I start to age. I've sorted through ticket stubs, magazines, cartoons, concert programs, photographs, drawings, political buttons, foreign coins, rocks, and seashells, somehow thinking that by keeping these things I could hold onto an experience forever. There are James Galway and Yo Yo Ma concert tickets, papers on Hopkins and Browning's poetry, *Time* and *Newsweek* issues about Mount St. Helens and the assassination attempts on the Pope and Ronald Reagan, and a collection of Far Side cartoons. I hang on to items the way nuns seize the relics of saints—those various body parts and bits of bone so coveted by the Roman Catholic Church—my own self reliquary.

Even when I'm not in the process of moving, I occasionally sort through my own hoardings and wonder why I keep the things I do. Five shoe boxes full of photographs, cross-stitch projects so old I can't find the patterns, children's books for the children I never had. Mostly

I find pottery and pictures and fine things that I had accumulated in anticipation of a future in which, unlike my grandmother, I expected everything to be right and happy. I cling to the past while I await the future and always manage to miss the trip along the way. I had somehow envisioned a perfect future with a perfect house, perfect children, and a perfect mate.

Grandma Carver enjoyed the things she had, either using them as they were intended, or repurposing them into other works. We have a couple of turtle-shaped pincushions made from fabric she harvested from old Santa Fe Railroad car seat covers. Her stash of bakelite and wooden back scratchers still make an attractive arrangement in a pottery vase near the downstairs kitchen sink. Hiller's Dairy milk bottles are a great way to display dried flowers. She once made a mosaic Christmas tree using costume jewelry on a bed of red velveteen fabric. She marked an outline around the tree with a strand of pearls and, to complete the work, added blinking lights. An old picture frame refinished with gold paint enhanced the gaudy effect. It has my name taped to the back.

Grandma Carver's effects have a little bit of her in each piece. She spent hours crafting gifts and, thirty-eight years after her death, her creations sit in relatives' homes, in places of honor on top of a mantelpiece or on a desk. I once wrote to all our relatives, asking each one to send a memory of my grandmother. My mother's cousin, Fred Carver, who lived alone in a house on his junkyard in Black Forest, Colorado, sent this:

> *I have on my table that I am writing from some artificial flowers that she made and they are in a little cream jar. They are faded and dusty but in the center there is still a little color. I suppose that I will keep them. Maybe someday someone will clean out my effects and wonder why, but you will know.*

Her last project and her last gift to each of us were small bouquets of dried yarrow. She spray painted the flowers burnt orange and blue and arranged them in small ceramic vases. Although Grandma Carver used industrial strength enamel paint to preserve the bouquets, the plants eventually disintegrated and had to be thrown away. Yarrow, or *Achillea millifolium,* has many ostensible medicinal properties, making it useful in antiseptic, antispasmodic, antibiotic, and anti-inflammatory concoctions. Milfoil tea, made from the plant, is purported to ward off melancholy. I love its feathery leaves and the tiny bunches of flower heads that form what is called a flat-topped panicle.

I still grow yarrow in my garden. If I remember to cut back the plants after their first flowering in May, I get another growth that lasts to September. On those rare days, when I have time to enjoy the outdoors, I think of her when I see the stalks of yarrow bobbing in a gentle breeze. I remember her joy in living and her generous spirit and any melancholy I might be harboring drifts away.

Uncle George

T he most revered man in my life was the husband of my mother's sister Annelise. To me, he was Uncle George. To the world, he was George F. Kennan, a famed diplomat. George met Annelise when he was training as a linguist in Russian during graduate study at Berlin University in 1930. Annelise was an *au pair* for a German family in Berlin at that time. My mother told the story of how skeptical her parents were about this match. After all, Annelise—a fetching beauty—already had a wonderful boyfriend in Kristiansand, Norway, from a very good family, who wanted to marry her. Who was this unknown American who had swept her off her feet?

Well, when Uncle George was invited to Kristiansand to meet his future in-laws, he came, he saw, and he conquered; even my taciturn grandfather was captivated. George was young, long, lean, good-looking, a gentleman, intelligent, ambitious, and utterly charming. The Sørensen women—my mother included—all swooned. George and Annelise were married in Kristiansand in 1931. George was twenty-seven, Annelise twenty-one.

The *New York Times* would later call George "a phenomenon in international affairs" who had an "extraordinary influence on American policy during the cold war." Two of his books won the Pulitzer Prize, and in 2012 a biography by John Lewis Gaddis titled *George F. Kennan: An American Life* won a Pulitzer of its own. During my childhood, adolescence, and young adulthood, however, I didn't pay that much attention to his reputation in the outside world. I knew George as the man in our family who thought things through, who got things done—

my intellectual uncle who, by example, wove a sturdy and lovely pattern through my life.

My mother turned to George for intellectual stimulation, practical ideas, and hospitality. When she used the words "Uncle George said," I would stand still and listen. Even better were the times I had direct access to him.

The most fun times of all were all the Christmases we Burlinghams spent with the Kennans at their farm in East Berlin, Pennsylvania. Our own homes—first in Hopewell, New Jersey, then in Riverdale, New York—were nothing but houses. The farm—the gigantic main manor with its sloping lawns, the farmer's dwelling, the barn holding cows, the chicken coop, the fields, and the creek—was a complete living, breathing rural world ready to educate us.

Our Kennan cousins showed us the ropes—which was the best haystack in the barn from which to jump, which were the cows whose behinds we could pat, what it meant when farmer wife Annie came into the chicken yard with her ax. Did we want to learn how to pluck the chicken and take out the innards?

Cousin Joanie took us under her wing and coached us in plays and musicals. When a scene drew forth Uncle George's guttural laugh, we knew we had hit the mark. In the evening, Dad would play the piano or his guitar while we all sang. Uncle George would also play the guitar in solo performance—and laugh at himself when he made mistakes.

A week with the Kennans at the farm meant plenty of room for everyone, adventures and roaming time, lively spirits, good food, cooperation, fires crackling in the fireplace, reading, listening, laughing. Uncle George was the lord of his manor, and Annelise was most definitely his lady.

I learned from both Annelise and Uncle George. My aunt was my role model in my first and continued efforts at entertaining. As the wife of a U.S. State Department official, she was a master at looking glamorous while effortlessly hosting social occasions with a fine table, gracious manners, and liveliness. With Uncle George, it was his silent power, the culmination of the life he had created being patient by consistently studying, thinking, writing, mastering, and taking decisive action.

After living in England for six years, my parents divorced, and I came back to the States with Mom and my brothers. We took up residence in the apartment over the garage—a quaint carriage house— of Uncle George and Aunt Annelise's house in Princeton, New Jersey. I will never forget how, as a somewhat lost eighteen-year-old, I heard Uncle George say words that esteemed me. That occurred at a time when, frankly, I was furious at the world for my low status. For all practical purposes I was now fatherless, and grandmotherless—both my father, who had become mentally ill and was living in London receiving psychoanalytic treatment from Anna Freud, and my grandmother, who had become a work-absorbed psychoanalyst, remained on the other side of the Atlantic. I was about to negotiate the American system of higher education, which at this time in history seemed to know little or nothing of what my English education had entailed. (Passing both my "O" levels and my "A" levels in England was an achievement that did not resonate in America.)

Mom walked across the gravel driveway from our garage apartment to the main house to seek out Uncle George for advice. She returned saying, "He wants you to write a letter recommending yourself, along with your official credentials."

I did what he asked, with Mom once again the emissary. This time she returned with bright eyes and a big smile. "He is impressed with your letter. He says you are most intelligent and articulate; he is proud of you."

How do I explain how much those simple words of praise from Uncle George meant to me? It was like the happy little girl somewhere inside me who tried so hard had just been told "You and your efforts are worth something."

Having been born in Milwaukee, it was Uncle George who thought Beloit College in Wisconsin would be the right choice of college for me. It was at Beloit that I began my foray back into American life, and it was where I met Paul, the man I am married to now.

♏ ♏ ♏

In my thirties, during a dinner party at my sister Randi's house one evening, I was alone with Uncle George for a moment and dared to ask my secret question.

"Uncle George, why do you think Dad was never able to take hold of life properly and ended up such a mess?"

His answer was simple, straight to the point: "He never bit the bullet." Having lived with Dad, I wasn't convinced George had the whole answer. Yet his reply gave me a clear perspective from which I could view it.

It was Uncle George who advised my mother not to go to England to rejoin my father when Mom was trying to make that decision in 1957. "It will only bring you more grief," he told her. He was certainly right about that.

Dad's will earmarked one item for me: a Russian icon that George and Annelise had given my parents when George was ambassador to Russia. Dad had always favored it, taking photos of each frame, researching each part of its religious story. When our family was intact, the icon had a place of prominence on our mantelpiece. When Mom and Dad divorced, Dad kept it. Now this Kennan-Burlingham family heirloom is mine. With its chain of legacies, it sits on my piano.

When Uncle George entered a room and I was there, he would greet me with genuine affection. From such a reserved man, this kind of greeting meant something. That was true of the very last time I saw him, when at our Christmas cocktail hour at the Kennans, I was told that he wished a visit.

One hundred years old, sitting upright in a chair in his bedroom, he brightened at my entry. He reached out for me, grasping my hands in his, smiling, and saying in a high-pitched, trembling voice, "Lynnie, it is so good to see you!"

When I descended the Kennan stairs a few minutes later, I was glowing inside.

George and Annelise

Aunt Stella

Why, O Absence, when the cry is most intense
is the silence most stunning?
—A Cry of Absence, Martin E. Marty

I wasn't there. But Aunt Stella, my godmother, was buried in a blue peignoir (not the green she requested, which color the funeral home didn't have) and a robe. Also at her request, the organist played Elvis Presley's "Are You Lonesome Tonight?" In the middle of the song, Aunt Lucille leaned over to whisper in my mother's ear, "Well, she ain't gonna be lonely tonight."

The joke was predictable—she'd be with The Man Upstairs, singing with the angels. The flowers I'd ordered contained a reference to this joke: I had written on my card, "To Aunt Stella, who will not be lonesome tonight." For me, the words were meant to commemorate a restless, giddy woman, my favorite aunt, who was, as my brother put it, about a half bubble off plumb.

Stella was my favorite because her delight in me was so transparent. While other aunts could be severe or distant, Aunt Stella seemed to take real pleasure in my off-the-wall energy, as if, when she was around it, she was able to sense something in herself that needed to get out. She laughed quickly at things I did and said. She let me iron handkerchiefs sometimes. She knew how hard I took defeat so that when we played games of rummy on Sunday nights with other family members, she sometimes orchestrated things so I could win a hand now and again.

Aunt Stella's death was welcome; she had gone into a hard-to-watch fade from 140 pounds to 80 by the time I made my last visit. There was no apparent cause. Suspicions of pancreatic cancer proved

319

groundless. Pneumonia invaded, but her lungs were aspirated. None of a series of small strokes paralyzed her speech or her movements. She just stopped eating is all. Finally, they stuck a tube in her belly. But when the bleeding from the rectum started, they cut her back to dextrose and the next day she was dead.

My final visit with her lasted about three hours. She'd just been moved that day into the nursing home. At her former weight and at a height of about 5'7", she'd always been pleasantly round. She had big bones and a big nose, like everybody on both sides of my family. My oldest memory of her was of a prominent and fascinating mole, a small and perfect bud of flesh at the juncture of the left side of her nose and face. Because it was so smooth, round and prominent and matched the color of her face perfectly, I couldn't, as a child, take my eyes off it. Her hair, as far back as I can remember, was an unchanging dome of tight, shiny silver curls.

But in the end she was just sticks and knobs, her hair dull, matted and disheveled from months of lying abed. Her roommate, June, smiled broadly and said daffy, senseless things. Stella herself seemed a bit daffy—too quick to startle and stare at anything passing in the hallway. It was as if she were seeing Fellini characters out there, and that may have been; her mother, Ella, had hallucinated at the end, young girls stepping out of the bedroom mirror.

Dying in a way she never expected—not at home but shuttled among institutions—bred an intolerant rage in Stella. Or maybe it was just a shift in brain chemistry that produced fear that surfaced as anger. Stella would raise her eyebrows in disgust when June said crazy things. She complained about the hospital where she'd been for weeks before her entry into the nursing home, how she had to ring and ring and ring at night to rouse a nurse. As her flesh had melted away, her laughter had left her, and her softness and sweetness dissolved. All the self-mocking and deference that had made her so dear to me disappeared. She turned into her opposite.

With bitterness came Bartleby-like refusals. She wouldn't eat or leave the bed. That exasperated my mother who, then in her upper 70s, had made a mantra of "staying active." I asked Mother to support Aunt Stella's obvious choice for death. Wasn't she just rehearsing for the Ultimate Inactivity? Why bristle about a torpor that Stella would not herself fight? But for Mom, it was hard. She treated Stella's naysaying as if it were a crime against God.

I sensed that Aunt Stella was in an existential crisis, even a collapse of faith, and maybe Mom did too, and that's why she was so upset. Like many women of her generation, Stella had not lived in a way that indicated deep caring for herself. Perhaps, at the end, the truth of that forced itself on her.

I took a tape-recorder to the nursing home because reminiscing seemed to please Stella. Better to try to connect that way than nudge her to eat a dollop of vanilla pudding. But her gauntness, anger, and pain spoke against any tape-recording. The day before Aunt Stella died, Aunt Lucille and Mother saw the pain crest. Standing by Stella's bed, they listened as she gasped, over and over, "Help! Help! Help!"

I spent most of my three hours with her just patting an arm, telling her I loved her. Rather than elicit new stories, I recounted a few she'd told me, verifying certain details, as if to assure her they would be preserved.

The room was mostly silent. Stella did take grateful note when a breeze stirred. We found momentary common ground in complaining about a jackhammer rattling nearby, the noise relieving us of the duty to talk. We asked the nurses when the work might be done. Nobody knew.

I had interviewed Stella four years before. At that point she'd been living alone several years, her husband, George, dead. This man, whom she had married so early, had been her Sunday school teacher. He was, all his life, willful, bull-headed, energetic, talkative. But then, five years before he died, a stroke had left him with a child's bad temper and an inability to say anything other than a frequent, emphatic "NO!" (His physical helplessness heightened an already capacious urge to control.)

Stella's caretaking for George was a crowning touch in a life she gave to others without thinking twice (or maybe even at all): For Stella, duty was not a choice. And she was proud of the results; she said, *They thought George was only going to live six months, but he lived five years.* One effect of her having lived so totally for others was that when those others died, so did her vocation and, with it, her identity.

When I visited Aunt Stella to interview her after George's death but before her health failed, my mother had come along. Stella was living in a trailer court. The shades were drawn, darkening the trailer's interior. Stella left enough space to peek out and check on the other residents' comings and goings. The tidiness of her apartment seemed confining, claustrophobic, as if Stella didn't want anything new in her world. When Aunt Lucille, who lived in the trailer next door, found a beau after Uncle Elmer died of stomach cancer, Stella didn't approve.

Stella's small living room was carpeted in orange and brown shag. On the wall was a reproduction of Warner Sallman's "Head of Christ," a 1940 portrait of Jesus as a swarthy spiritual hunk. A two-shelf bookcase was stocked exclusively with Reader's Digest condensed books. A large-print version of the *Upper Room*, a magazine of Christian devotionals, sat on a table. A 21-inch TV, manufactured in an era when TVs were supposed to be furniture, bullied the room with its size, but Stella said she didn't watch it much. I had given her a silly looking stuffed frog, which she perched on the back of her couch. She joked, "I polished the eyes before you came." When I went back to the bathroom, I peeked into her bedroom and saw more stuffed animals on her bed.

At my mother's previous visit, Aunt Stella had seemed more at loose ends than usual. ("The doctor says I've got a case of the nerves," she'd say, explaining why she sometimes scratched her shins until they bled.) On our way over to Stella's trailer, I had bought her a notebook and some pens. Maybe she could write her life story as a way of grounding her energy. But the spirit of refusal so evident at the end of her life had already begun to move in. When I asked, she refused. That accorded with my mother's descriptions of Aunt Stella's passivity—how Stella could not be cajoled into doing volunteer work or much of anything else.

In those days, every time I visited she would try to palm something off on me. This time, I carried away one of my bronzed baby shoes. She wanted me to take away the condensed books, too, but I was as uninterested in them as she was in writing what happened to her when she was 14.

She couldn't sit still during the visit. One leg kicked idly. One hand caressed the other arm absently. It was as if that hand were trying, in a world without her mother or husband, to comfort her. Her patter was the same as always. Her sentences sometimes stopped before all the words had been uttered—the listener was left in charge of completing them. Perhaps someone important to Aunt Stella had, at some time in life, made it apparent that he or she wasn't listening. Maybe Stella kept surrendering in mid-sentence because she'd been crushed by the inattention of that important listener. At the end, maybe she thought God had stopped listening, too.

I wonder whether those to whom she gave her life so instinctively, as many working class women did then, deserved her love. Both her mother and her husband possessed a sense of entitlement that found a match in her willingness to become a cipher. I remember a recurring scene: My uncle's face would break out in a broad grin, his eyes narrow to slits, as he described something Aunt Stella had said that he thought foolish. Still smiling, he would belittle her, then look at me, as if the two of us were in on a joke. Young as I was, I felt embarrassed. I sensed the pain of the taunting and wondered whether his mocking shamed Aunt Stella.

Her other master was her mother. Stella had no girlfriends in grade school, in part because Ella ordered her to be home by 3:30 every day, a half hour after school let out. The mother's call upon her daughter's dutifulness never stopped. During our 1991 visit, Stella said, "On my wedding day, Mama said, 'I went to visit my mother every day, after I married. I expect you to come visit me every day.' So after I married, I went to her house every day. When George and me went on vacation, I had to call her every night. We'd go to Denver and cross a time zone, and then I'd get bawled out for calling so late.

"Your Aunt Lucille says, 'My goodness, but your mother dominated your life.' I never would have thought about that if Lucille hadn't started talking about it."

Stella did not simply idle and chat with her mother. During her visits, she would wash and iron her parents' clothes, cook for them, clean. "And then I'd have to come home at night and do my own housework. Sometimes I was washing clothes 'til 11."

George and Ella wound up competing for Stella's services.

"Lucille says, 'I don't understand how George put up with that.' Well, after daddy died, Mama wanted to come to live with us. We had two bedrooms then. And George said, 'If you have her here, I'm walking out.' Her and George hated each other's guts."

Instead, Ella wound up living with my father and mother for the last five years of her life.

It wasn't that Stella never had a capacity to dream. As a teenager, she wanted to be a nurse and begged Ella to send her to Chicago to study nursing. But that wasn't part of Ella's game plan.

Stella would speak with deep affection for the family's youngest, Walter, whose death at 25 after a three-day illness elevated him to sainthood, making him more revered and loved than any of the surviving children. He was a year younger than Stella, and timid. "Walter, you could shove him and push him and he'd never fight back. So one day this boy was bullying him, and it got me mad. Pretty soon, we were rolling around in the garbage, in a dumpster. I was beatin' him up, and he went home crying, 'I'm gonna tell my sisters. They're gonna get you.' "

The dreams of becoming a nurse and the assertiveness that helped her stand up for timid Walter disappeared, though, as she moved into her life's work: giving away everything, killing off whatever instinct for dreaming she may have, as a teenager, possessed.

At one point during the visit at her trailer court, she said, "I cried all last night. I don't know why. And I'm not one to cry. Not at funerals, even."

She opened the Bible and took out a yellowed newspaper clipping, a piece of doggerel, which she read. In each verse, the poet described someone with a disability—blindness, deafness and so on—and then paused to reflect. The reflection took the form of a refrain that barely changed from verse to verse. The first refrain read, "God forgive me when I whine/I have two legs and the world is mine." In the next refrain, the poet said, "I have two eyes and the world is mine," and so on.

Talk turned to the Gospels. Stella said she liked Matthew, my mother that she liked John. The room quieted for a minute.

Stella said, "I don't know why I'm here."

I asked, "You mean why you, personally, are still alive? Or why God created humans and then left them to ponder about the meaning of it all?"

She said, "All of that."

At one point, Stella said, "Lucille says I ask too many questions. My fifth-grade teacher said, 'I never saw anybody ask as many questions as you.' But how are you going to learn if you don't ask questions?" I wonder why she never questioned her self-annihilating duty to husband and mother.

The trouble with questions is that the answers may elude you or, worse, not be what you want to hear. I imagine Aunt Stella living in her trailer alone at the end of her life, doubt stealing in. If she did not know why she was still alive, it surely wasn't for want of asking God. And what did God's silence, then, mean? Was God not communicating in a way she understood? Or at all? "I am forgotten, like a dead man out of mind," a Psalmist once cried out. "I have come to be like something lost." Is that what Stella felt?

If the same thing happened today as back then, I would ask her about her idea of God and how that fit with what was happening. I didn't know then about the ebb and flow of faith, about those times of "spiritual dryness" described by monks and others on spiritual journeys, times when God seems to go on holiday. The idea among Christians that God sometimes makes his presence felt through withdrawal never made sense to me, but it's dogma among some believers. Maybe it would have comforted Aunt Stella.

Something in her story brings to mind the elder son in the biblical tale of the Prodigal Son, the one who stayed at home, helping to manage the farm, while his brother busied himself squandering his inheritance. When the Prodigal Son returns home to a jubilant welcome by his father, the elder son gets mad. For Stella, there were no runaway siblings—only Saint Walter, the dead brother, who left home early, and for good. But wouldn't this thought have crossed her mind: I helped my mother and husband. Who's helping me? Where's mine? If it didn't, she would have been a saint, and her anger at life's end suggests that she wasn't.

I wasn't wise as a young man, so I failed to ask important questions of family members, ones that might have produced the answers I'd like to have now that I'm grown. I did not ask Aunt Stella the whys of her downturn and doubt she could have diagnosed it anyway.

So I am left to ponder the facts: She stopped eating, stopped leaving her bed, even to defecate, and died for no discernible medical cause.

And with this question: Is she lonesome tonight?

Letting Go

A s I sit in a downtown Lawrence coffee shop, trying unsuccessfully not to cry, I think to myself "Okay, I get it. I need to write about my Mom, or more specifically, her dying." It seems strange to write of her demise when I have written very little about her life, but the tears were an obvious sign. I had just returned from a work-related visit to Babcock Place, the senior living apartment complex that occupies the 1700 block of Massachusetts Street. I hadn't given much thought to the trip beforehand. It had been seven years since I was last in the building, cleaning out Mom's apartment. Surely I could go there after all this time without coming undone. Apparently not.

Constance Virginia Washburn Van Welden lived most of her life in Michigan. She was a proud 1945 graduate of the Kalamazoo Bronson School of Nursing, having eloped with my Army father two years earlier, and keeping her marriage a secret in order to graduate. She and my father lived in Big Rapids for a brief time while Dad went to pharmacy school, then returned to Kalamazoo (their home town) where Dad went to work with his father as a pharmacist in the drugstore business. My sister, brother, and I grew up there, too, never venturing away, except for two brief family vacations to Florida.

I never imagined Mom living anywhere else. I was, actually, the only one in my family who moved away, marrying in 1972 and ending up in Kansas. They didn't even come to visit. It was assumed that I would return to Michigan to visit them. We stayed in touch by letter and by phone. After Dad died, things began to shift and Mom started coming to Kansas for visits. We tried to arrange a trip for her at least every year, and she got to spend time with her grandsons. But Michigan was always home.

Through a complicated and stressful series of events, motivated in part by my mom's gradual declining financial situation, she ended up living, over a period of several years, with my brother (at the lake house in Michigan), my sister (in Portage, Michigan), and me. Not surprisingly, this caused further stress. Ultimately, she chose, surprisingly to everyone, to live permanently in Kansas, where she happily discovered she qualified for residency in Babcock Place.

She embraced this change to living independently with gusto, happily furnishing her small efficiency apartment with bits of white wicker furniture, bird houses galore (she was an avid collector), plants of various kinds, family photos, a few books, and her sewing/crocheting accoutrements. She quickly made friends, and she became especially close to several residents in the building, even providing nursing services on occasion. She took advantage of the shuttle service to get to doctor's appointments, and she went grocery shopping next door at Dillon's. Never having used a computer before, she took advantage of their shared computer and student tutors to set up an e-mail account, which she used regularly to keep in touch with everyone. She joined a church, came to our house regularly for visits and special occasions, and got to know her three grandsons for several years. She was happy, though I know she missed everyone in Michigan. She blossomed.

The summer of 2003 things began to shift. My oldest son, Jeff, married, and he and my daughter-in law, Kat, moved to Los Angeles so she could begin her graduate program at UCLA. My husband endured two major abdominal surgeries, almost back-to-back, and for awhile it seemed he might not even be present for the wedding. He made it. But he continued to have difficulties breathing, and tests revealed heart and lung problems. Then, on an early Saturday in November, shortly after Mom's 80th birthday, pain in her arm took her to the emergency room at Lawrence Memorial Hospital, where the doctors suspected a mild heart attack. They admitted her, planning to do a heart catheterization the following Monday.

My husband was already scheduled to have the same procedure performed at St. Luke's, in Kansas City, the same Monday. His cardiologist was certain that he would require follow-up procedures of an unspecified nature, and we were all already understandably worried. Now we added Mom's situation to the mix.

Mom's test was delayed a day due to broken equipment, and my husband's catheterization revealed, thankfully, no arterial blockage. However, he was kept overnight as he was not well, and it was discovered that he had pneumonia. Mom's catheterization revealed serious problems. She needed heart surgery, a five-way bypass, and we were cautioned by her doctor to think seriously about whether or not to pursue this, given her age and the likely impact that surgery could have on her quality of life. Without surgery she would die, we just wouldn't know when. With it, she might not be able to live or function on her own.

Before we could even talk about options with her, a new heart attack necessitated an ambulance trip to St. Luke's, where she was admitted. At least my mom and my husband were now in the same hospital. My sons and I hastily joined them there. I called my son in Los Angeles and my brother and sister in Michigan to fill them in. My brother and niece left right away to drive to Kansas.

Mom put on a brave front. She wanted to live, and though no one was really asking her, she decided that surgery was the right thing to do. She asked me once, "If you were me, would you do it?"

I said, "Yes." I was sure I would.

Mom survived her surgery. They took veins from her arms to repair her heart, and the wounds on her arms were left open to heal, as well as the substantial wound in her chest. She was taken off the ventilator, and was able to see that my brother and niece had arrived, smiling at them and saying their names. But shortly after this she was put back on a ventilator, unable to breathe well on her own. They sent the chaplain out to tell us.

Startled, I asked, "Is this a problem?"

He didn't know. We chose to be optimistic.

Over the days and weeks that followed, Mom progressed from the ICU to a surgical ward and back again, experiencing one set back after another, still unable to breathe on her own. My brother and niece returned home, unable to stay longer. I never knew where I would find Mom. Her things, few though they were, often did not make the transition. More than once I had to track down her glasses or teeth. She was alert in those early days, and though unable to talk, she and I communicated by writing on a dry-erase board that I brought in. She would write things like, "My butt hurts," or "Pay my rent?"

I would open her mail and read her cards and letters, bring her flowers (when she could have them). I stayed upbeat and positive. We would get through this. I worked hard to make sense of her confusing progression through the days, trying to understand the medical hierarchies in place and different teams working with her. She was attended to by cardiologists, pulmonologists, internists, nurses, respiratory therapists, physical therapists, dermatologists, wound-care specialists, and an infectious disease team. I quickly realized that the charts that everyone filled out meticulously were often not read carefully before a consult, and that the physical therapists may not communicate with the respiratory therapists, whose notes may not have connected with the doctors in charge that day. Often I did not understand which caregiving group I was talking to.

In addition to the confusing array of medical staff working with her, there was always the challenge of new lingo to comprehend. I'll never forget the first day I arrived to talk with a respiratory therapist who told me proudly, "Your Mom dangled for three minutes today!"

"She did what?" I asked in exasperation. I learned this was a term they used to describe the phenomena of having my mother sit on the edge of her bed and dangle her feet over the edge. There was a whole protocol to learn, not to mention a distinct vocabulary to memorize. I felt like I was in a moving crap game, never understanding all the rules, and desperately trying to keep up.

Mom, however, being a nurse, was in her element or, at least, was applying her nursing knowledge to her situation. Though she couldn't talk, eat or drink, or change into her own clothes, she understood the hospital, and was interested, when alert, in the goings on around her. She made sure I knew what she was thinking, writing once on her board, "This floor better. They pay more attention."

I tried to visit every other day. The long drive from Lawrence to the Plaza area of Kansas City, something I would normally find challenging (I hate highway driving) became routine. I continued to work full time. My boss was very flexible about the time off I needed, and I was grateful. I approached every day with hope and determination. We would bring Mom home. She would recover.

Time marched on. My youngest son graduated from high school. My husband continued to struggle with his own medical issues. Mom endured seizures, the insertion of a pacemaker, tubes in her ears when she lost her hearing, feeding tubes, a confusing array of medicines, a wound vacuum for her arms, and constant work to wean her off the ventilator. There was so much going on that it was hard to know what was really bad and what was "normal." When her tongue swelled up with what they thought was thrush, I said (outside her room to one of her nurses), "I imagine that you see a lot of things like this but to me that looks pretty disgusting."

Her nurse replied, "Honey, I've been a nurse for 30 years and that looks pretty disgusting to me."

As the days wore on and we came to understand that she was not going home anytime soon, we tried to make her room a little cozier with flowers and photos and a few items from home. Sometimes her room had a window, but often she ended up in one without a view, despite my constant lobbying.

One evening my son, Andrew woke me up from sleep to ask me, "Don't you think Grandma would like one of my drawings to put on her wall in her room?"

"Yes," I said, incredibly touched that he had thought of this, and, realizing that he, an artist, was as bothered by the sterile, impersonal, institutional aspect of her surroundings as I was.

We looked through his portfolio right away and found a nice landscape drawing that would please her. He took it to her the next day and she loved having it there to look at. I couldn't help but think of the movie "Terms of Endearment." My son Peter selected movies for her to watch, and we arranged for her to have a VCR in her room. She could not concentrate on them for long, though.

Mom loved flowers, and I created a wall of flowers for her, cutting out images of different orchids, roses, gardenias, carnations, violets, daffodils— anything, really, that was pretty and would be nice to look at—and mounted them in collage fashion with cards and photos sent to her. I didn't know if I was allowed to do this. I didn't care. The flower wall grew over time, and we moved it carefully, along with Andrew's drawing, every time she was placed in a new room.

We celebrated Thanksgiving and Christmas with her, decorating her room modestly for the holidays, and always wondering how many more of them would pass before she could come home. I would watch longingly as other patients, further along than Mom, would walk the halls with their families.

Our Christmas Day visit was cut short when her chest wound began bleeding profusely. I had sent the boys out of the room when I first spotted the staining on her gown, and called for help. The intern on duty came in and was quite flustered, opening her dressing and applying pressure, all the while trying frantically to figure out what was wrong. It turned out to be a minor issue, but I was right there and saw into my Mom's chest, an uncomfortable and incredible sight. What, exactly, was I looking at? It didn't seem appropriate to ask.

I tried to be my Mom's advocate. My way of dealing with the overwhelming amount of confusing information I received everyday was to record it all in notebooks. In rereading them I realize that I wrote very disjointedly, not even progressing in a linear fashion through the notebooks, a testament to my exhausted and overwhelmed state of mind. As Mom deteriorated, my writing, oddly, became clearer—as though I could make her well through more easily read notes and prose. My notebooks were my lifeline. Writing was my lifeline. But it didn't help. No doubt about it we were in a battle for my mom's life. We were losing, but I steadfastly refused to acknowledge this.

By the New Year we were told she would be moved to Overland Park Specialty Hospital where, I was assured, she would get more help in weaning her off the ventilator. I was sure they were warehousing her and was frantic, despite everyone's assurances to the contrary. Before she could move, she developed an infection and was whisked off to surgery to have a portion of her breastbone removed.

But move she did, accompanied by ten bags of medical supplies that the new hospital assured us they would never use and that we needed to dispose of. She was retaining so much water that she was literally weeping fluid through her skin. I found out later that they did not expect her to live through the first weekend there. Mom was tough. She endured.

Mom didn't like the new hospital and became very anxious every time they tried new ways to help her breathe on her own. I would be met by nurses who would say to me very anxiously, "Your Mother was very anxious today," and then hasten to add, "but that is normal."

Yet, there was always something conveyed to me in these conversations that all was not well; it made me anxious too. I took off more time to stay with her throughout the day. Sometimes one of my sons would be on one side and I on the other, holding her hands.

Throughout all this, my brother and sister and their families kept up to date with Mom through phone calls and letters and cards that I read to her. My son and daughter-in-law in California did the same, and friends from church and Babcock Place sent cards and letters that I shared with her.

I felt like I was connected to my mom by an invisible lifeline. I was holding on tightly, and if I let go for a minute I would lose her. But I would hold on. I wouldn't let go.

Mom gradually became more and more detached, seeming almost angry and unwilling to engage with us. They did not think she had a stroke. They thought she might be depressed. No kidding? I knew I would be. She could no longer communicate with the dry-erase board, but sometimes she would seem like herself. One day when my husband and I were visiting, she was allowed to suck on a small swab dipped in water. She desperately wanted the water and was not allowed to drink anything because of the tube going down her throat. We kept dipping the swab in water for her, and she kept asking for more. When it was time to go she managed to write, almost illegibly, on her board, "One more for the road?"

One day in late February, a nurse took me aside to say, "You don't really expect her to make it do you?"

I was angry. Of course I expected her to make it. I had hope and I wanted to instill that in Mom, too. The nurse talked gently to me about making sure that I was doing what my mom would want me to do for her, considering what she needed, not what I wanted. Would Mom want me to accept that she would die? I talked to her doctor, a gentle man, Dr. Pratip Patel, who said to me kindly, "Of course we have hope. It's important. It's the right approach. But your Mother's situation is very complicated and all we can do is take it one day at a time."

The nurses were surprised that Mom was not "DNR." I was told that most nurses, knowing what is involved in resuscitating a patient, cracking ribs, etc., would not want that. I asked the doctor about this. He said Mom would very likely not survive the efforts to resuscitate her given her current condition. Actually, he said if she did live she would probably be a vegetable. After talking to my siblings, we changed her status to " DNR." It seemed like the right decision. I'm pretty sure it was.

By early March, Mom was seldom with us. We visited, we pasted flowers on the wall, we cheerily read cards and letters to her, we prayed, we conferred, we cried. Gradually, I too, turned inward. Not knowing what to do, I started writing letters to my mom in my journal. I had come to accept that things were not looking good, and the invisible lifeline I thought I held was really slipping.

She had endured so much, and worked so hard to stay with us. But her body was shutting down. On March 10, 2004, I wrote "Dear Mom, ... Now, I think, that you've been through so much, that your mind has shut down to stimulus around you. Maybe, Mom, it's time to go. It's all right if you need to." My sister, visiting eight days later to say goodbye, told her the same thing.

On March 20 at 2:30 a.m., my Mom did just that.

Natural Strangers

I went to meet my biological mother, even though, or maybe because she was dead.

It seemed a long drive to the funeral home in northeast Kansas, although it was only a few hours west of my own home. The town had a Scottish name, and it felt as if I were driving to a foreign place with an ocean. My friend sat beside me because I didn't want to go alone and because she was the type of person that I wouldn't have to say anything to if I didn't want to, although I was the type of person who would anyway; we must have talked about books, or our children, or something, but what I remember was the bleak winter landscape, the few trees along the highway that looked like umbrellas, torn and blown inside out.

The news of my birth mother's death had come two weeks prior via a phone call from a friendly woman I'd met in the genealogy room at the library. She'd guided me to the city directories, and as we visited, it turned out that she had an adopted daughter around my age, and for a few days, she thought we might be sisters. Her husband had read the obituary in the paper and had told her about it as he was shaving. When she called early that morning to tell me that she was sorry but my bio mother had died suddenly, it didn't seem real, but it hadn't seemed real when she was alive either. As I'd followed the paper trail of her existence, it was as if I were watching a movie starring a woman named Marjorie who had led a sort of double life. First, married with four children, then not married with three more children, whom she gave up for adoption, then married with no children at all. I thought of the chains of cutout paper dolls I made for my own girls and of paper-cuts, and I thought of my own dad shaving every morning in the small bathroom of my parents' bedroom in the house where I grew up. The radio was always tuned to AM news and pop music. I loved looking at him looking at himself in the mirror, lathered with a white beard like Santa, but my dad was both jolly and good-looking. When he'd nick himself with the razor, he dabbed some powder on the cut from a tube, and the bleeding would magically stop.

I had never seen a corpse before. When attending other funerals with an open casket I had never looked, preferring to remember people as I'd known them when they were alive. But I had no recollection of this woman.

Naturally, I was curious; my concern was that I might look like someone at the funeral, a sibling or a cousin, or remind someone of Marjorie when she herself was thirty. As the funeral parlor in the small town promised to be the size of my own modest living room, I opted for the more open-ended viewing and seriously considered wearing a disguise; I didn't want to shock anyone, inadvertently divulge any secrets. It was only after experiencing the biological process of the birth of my own children that I actually recognized her as my birth mother and suddenly wondered on a hormonal level alone, if she'd ever wondered about me. I'd just found out where she was living and was still processing what to do with that information when she abruptly died at age sixty. Apparently, she'd had a fatal asthma attack. The caller said that she'd heard that Marjorie had been eating ice cream when she choked, which precipitated the attack.

I was glad I couldn't imagine her face at that moment—the panicked look—it recalled two chronic nightmares in which I couldn't get my own breath. In one, my child self is walking through a tunnel late at night and sees the headlights of a car turn in, then remain stationary. I turn around to go back, only to see another car blocking the way out. A man, a stranger, moves quickly toward me. He grabs my arm and as he pushes me into the car, I notice that he has beautiful gray eyes. He takes me to the airport and onto the tarmac where my parents and brother are standing with gas masks on their faces; the man puts a similar mask over my nose and mouth, and headphones on my ears. "You're going to die," his eyes say. All I can hear is breathing, shallow and fast, then gasping as he decreases the oxygen to my father, my brother, and my mother. The straining of my own breath wakes me.

Even though we were close and I could have, I had never told my parents about that childhood nightmare. It was one of those things that they wouldn't have been able to do anything about, and it would have made them feel bad. In my child mind, by not telling I had saved them from having to imagine their violent deaths. I thought I owed them that much, especially since it had seemed to be my fault; it was, at least, my dream, and I'd been no help to them in it.

In the other recurring nightmare, I'm awake and feel a strange presence in the room, someone very close and breathing on me, sometimes a laughing, staccato breath, sometimes a whistling breath against my skin. I try to bolt up but am paralyzed—unable to respond in any way—until an interminable amount of time passes and I can finally open my eyes and sit up, by which time I am always alone.

Growing up, I'd never even fantasized about hosting a body inside my own. I had always thought I would adopt, like my mother who had adopted me. I wanted to tell my mother everything—about the nightmares and the feelings of loss. To hear about hers. I wanted to have a conversation with her about love and biology, but we had always treated the other as if she might break. She had said that the day she adopted me and throughout the first year, she was afraid someone would come to the house and take her baby girl away. When I was old enough to talk, my mother instructed me never to speak to strangers. Although this was the typical advice given to all of my friends by their parents, I took it in a personal, special way.

For my part, I had treated my mother as if she were one of my favorite dolls. I looked at her every day, studying her features and the way her hair was combed. I might finger the material of her dress occasionally, touch her hand, or very carefully kiss her on the cheek. She was not like my Barbie that eventually ended up with a butch haircut, or like the doll that talked every time her string was pulled, who had had her teeth pulled out and replaced multiple times when I pretended to be a dentist. My mother had always been like a porcelain doll that I kept on the highest shelf where she would stay safe.

My parents had always told both my brother and me that we were adopted, from different places, but nothing more. I remember my mother reading us a book when I was two or three years old about parents going to visit a room full of smiling babies and choosing their very favorite. It always made me feel special to be adopted, that my parents chose me instead of being stuck with whatever baby was born to them.

As we mounted the steps to the building where Marjorie lay in state, there was a lone man descending. Despite my fear of appearing familiar to someone, I couldn't help looking directly at him: a tall, darkish-haired man, around 60, dressed for a funeral, with glasses, a slight mustache, and a distraught look on his face, as if he were sobbing without any sound, entirely oblivious to us. He was struggling against the wind with an umbrella as if he'd confused the elements, mistaking air for rain.

We entered a small anteroom where a funeral director nodded and gestured toward the guestbook. I was relieved that no one else was there and picked up the quill pen, hesitated, and signed an alias, to protect Marjorie's reputation and to protect my own children from an unknown and potentially dangerous family of strangers, which was the reason I had also dabbed mud on my license tag. It was as much a relief that others had already visited and signed the book before me, though I didn't read the names.

I tiptoed into the viewing room as if my mother were merely napping. The room was still, and I glanced at the casket, a large cradle or a train car without wheels, I thought, but I remained where I was, unable to move any closer. After some time, I took a deep, cleansing breath, walked the few steps to the center of the small room, and finally stood, eyes closed, before the casket where she lay. I waited in a sort of blind limbo until I began to feel dizzy, then opened my eyes and looked directly at my mother's closed eyes. I had somehow forgotten that her eyes would be shut. Instead of a flutter of tenderness or loss, it made me feel emotionally blank. Empty. The closure that promised that my natural mother was and would always be a stranger.

Peering closer, I tried to recognize something about the body where I once had lived. The delicate skin of her face was as pale and textured as gauze, with tiny crosshatches rather than wrinkles. Her eyebrows were slightly arched and auburn like her dyed hair that seemed to be long and gathered behind her head. She wore glasses with a tiny heart etched in the corner of one lens and was dressed in a white western-style ensemble, and I thought how different my life might have been. I didn't even like country western music.

Ever so carefully, I touched her folded hands, which felt like a candle that had taken on the chill of the room. I bent down close to her face and felt a presence, a tickle of breath along my neck. A tingling traveled down my spine and raised the fine hair on my arms. I closed my eyes, afraid to breathe. It was impossible to distinguish if the irregular breaths were coming from within or from without my own body. It took all my effort to open my eyes again. I straightened back up and stared at my mother's dead face.

When I was younger, I'd imagined that she had once been in love—with my father, an intelligent, kind poet who had died before my birth. She couldn't bear to see a child every day who would remind her of her loss—they had been so in love and so young. Later, I'd wondered if her own father had forced himself on her in her bedroom late at night, which had resulted in a pregnancy, or if I had been conceived in rape by a stranger. "Sexual experience depends on how you meet it the first time," she might have warned, her voice tense and low as if we were having a belated mother-daughter talk. But there was a father's name on my birth certificate and further research had revealed that he was a soldier from Ohio and that I had a full brother who lived in Kansas, but any curiosity to find them, to see if they wanted to know me, also suddenly ceased to exist, as if Marjorie had taken them with her.

Eventually, I leaned down and whispered goodbye to my once-upon-a-time mother; it was an end to our story. I was glad that I had gone to see her, even though and maybe because she wouldn't know, and I was glad that I had seen the man with the umbrella, obviously no stranger to her.

November

I have fallen into the habit, without thinking much about it, of coming back home just once a year. Usually this is for the Christmas holiday, when my brothers and their families arrive at our parents' house for a day of eating and catching up. Nothing of substance is ever discussed, but there is a little talk. And I get my annual update on the goings-on in the little place where I grew up, a refresher course on what is happening in the oil fields and down at the electric cooperative. One Christmas a brother will tell about playing poker at one of the casinos up over the Red River and winning $20,000. The next Christmas he will tell about hitting a patch of hard luck as big as Arkansas and losing everything but his ride home. Another brother has a new young wife and is starting his second family, and a few sisters-in-law joke that he might need to start dying his hair. People laugh at fading memories that seem as old as parchment now. There is a bit of bewilderment that it has all come and gone so quickly, and I am reminded of part of the 103rd Psalm, "as for man, his days are as grass, as a flower of the field for the wind passeth over it and it is gone."

Time has a way of etching itself into people, changing their faces and bodies in ways you don't notice when you see them day-by-day. But when you see them year-by-year you can see the changes. I look at my brothers and see them again in pajamas around the dining room table, wearing cutoff jeans and baseball caps, shooting BB guns and kicking footballs. Now they are called Daddy and Grandpa.

This year, I have come home in advance of Christmas, for Thanksgiving, but I don't know why, exactly. A few brothers and their families have come, too, and they don't have to drive very far. It's not exactly a requirement to come home for Thanksgiving, like it is for

Christmas. People show up, or they don't. This year, I have shown up—a sort of bonus trip. I find I have become nostalgically fond of the starkness here, the big sky, the earth colors, the voices of the people. Something about this place seeped into me, melted into my skin when I was young. I can feel it.

It's the time of year here when farmers spend long hours stripping their fields of cotton, white gold in this part of Texas; the time of year when cotton gins like my father's run night and day making bales and piling up seeds and burs. My father thinks he can work day and night, and he is trying to do just that. It is getting harder for him all the time.

Though none of us knows it, and my father doesn't know it either, a few of his cells are in the process of abandoning the cause—maybe they don't like the long hours, the stress, the lack of easy times, the many years of toil. No one knows. Way down deep in the darkness, chemical switches are going wild. Cells that should be dying off don't die; genes are mutating, switching themselves on to do bad. My father is carrying around with him the seeds of something that will try its damned very best to kill him, and it eventually will succeed.

For as long as I can remember, my father has seemed impervious to hardship. He works through the many discomforts with a single-minded focus on finishing whatever it is he is doing, which is usually something involving hard labor performed in bad weather. Now he is reaching an age where the accumulated hard knocks of the years are calling in their loan. He hasn't admitted it, yet, but I can see it: in the splotches on his face, in the rough broken skin on the backs of his hands. I can hear some tiredness in his voice, a little—but not much—resignation. He just keeps trying to do what he has always done.

My father has always taken pride in working harder than the next man, in getting a job done. Around here, as in many places, a man is judged by what he does, is defined by his work. My father hauled himself, and his family along with him, up onto the slippery lower rungs of the middle-class ladder—through ceaseless labor alone. Even now, with his children grown and out on their own, he toils away.

On this Thanksgiving trip home, a brother and I drive out to our father's cotton gin on the edge of a desperate, windblown little town not far from where we grew up. My father has given his hired hands the day off for the holiday. He sent them home to their families, warning them not to drink so much as to be late in the morning. He expects them to earn what he pays them. So the gin is deserted, or at least we think. We see my father's pickup and my brother toots our car horn a few times.

After a few moments, a door in the side of the main building opens and my father steps out into the sunshine. The day is clear but bitterly cold. He is wearing insulated coveralls and, surprisingly, a wool ski hat—not his usual choice in headwear. Cotton lint sticks to this hat and his coveralls, which I see he has patched in places with wrinkled strips of duct tape, some of it peeling away and fluttering against him. Like his clothing, the stubble on his face and neck has attracted the lint, which swirls through the building's machinery like softly falling snow. He looks toward the car and recognizes us. He shows us a tired smile, one in which I tell myself I see a hint of what he has never said to us—that he loves us. I have not seen him since the previous Christmas, and I am a little shocked at how much he has changed in the eleven months since. Has anyone else noticed this? He looks old and completely worn out.

Boyhood memories come rushing toward me in a flood of sepia and gray, waves of disjointed, grainy images of long ago, in which my father is young and strong, his face smooth and hard. I think for a hopeless moment of the inescapable futility of life, in that it ends no matter what we do.

I have been taking some time off in recent years to see some of the world. I went to Europe several times, and to Africa and Asia. Maybe those faraway places have made me a little homesick and led me home now, I don't know. My father has not seen much of the world, and I had thought I would tell him about the things I had seen – things majestic and beautiful, that inspired in me a childlike sense of awe and renewal. I could tell him that I watched the setting sun turn the Matterhorn purple and pink. I could tell him that I looked down on a thousand miles of savannah from the top of Kilimanjaro, or that I heard the tinkle of yak bells from a tent in a high Nepalese valley on the way to Everest.

But seeing him here now, in the full light of this place where he has lived his entire life, and where he will someday die, I know I will not tell him these things. I can't tell him, because now, at this moment, these things seem unimportant and even shameful.

I wish there was more of my life that I could share with him. I wish he would tell me about all the things he has done, and that he wants to do—before it is too late. But we are from different worlds, now. When I left here, I took along with me the things my father taught me: to work hard, to ignore setbacks, to find a way to get the job done—and when I finally got around to applying them to my life, they worked marvelously, as I suspect he knew they might.

There he is, with lint sticking to him like cobwebs. I realize that there is love, though we never express it. Like the cells and genes that conspire to kill us in the end, love is happy to hide deep inside. I want to make sure that my father knows that I appreciate his sacrifices and that I love him, but I don't know how, exactly. Mainly, though, I just don't have the courage. It is not in us to speak of such things, and my father would be embarrassed and irritated.

He talks with my brother and me for a minute, promising he will come home by dark. We put hands into pockets and shuffle our feet against the cold, looking down at the ground and all around, mostly. We don't look at one another, except for the odd quick glance. It's the intimacy of a direct look that we feel compelled to avoid, I think, though I don't understand why. It is not in us to show intimacy, in even the slightest way.

Our father doesn't want us to come into the gin because it's dirty and the machinery is dangerous. He tells us we better go on and see about our mother.

I stand awkwardly next to my father as I prepare to get back in the car. Finally, I pull a hand from a pocket and clap him on the shoulder and blurt, "Be careful, Daddy," in a husky soft voice. It's the best I can do. Even this clap on the shoulder, stiff and at arms-length, seems like going too far, like a confirmation of the great gulf that exists between us. This brings sadness, but also clarity. He looks at me oddly for a moment. I think he is about to say something to me. But then the moment passes, like they all do. In my family, we are experts at letting them pass. We go on to the next one, and the next.

ABOUT
THE
AUTHORS

Deronda "DD" Ashley joined
GPWG in 2012. She is enjoying her
retirement by trying her hand at many
things of interest to her, including
writing. She grew up in Kansas and had
five children before moving out of state.
DD has two surviving children, Dawn
Stewart and Nate Liska, both of
Lawrence. DD was widowed in 2009,
and after 35 years away from Kansas,
decided to return to be closer to her family, which includes 12
grandchildren and 10 great grandchildren (with another on the way).
She held many interesting jobs, including grocery checker, accountant,
and roofer, before deciding to get her doctorate in Chiropractic. She
says, "Life is a joyous adventure."

K.L. Barron lives and writes in the
Flint Hills. She suspects this landscape
may be what the creative mind would
look like: rolling hills and subtle
contours, a wide-open sky matched end
for end with the land, with four seasons
in no particular order. Her work in
poetry, fiction, and creative non-fiction
memoir has appeared in: *New Letters, Bennington Review, Little Balkans
Review* and *Voices of the Great Plains,* among others. She is on the
faculty of the English Department at Washburn University in Topeka,
Kansas.

Lynn Burlingham lives in Lawrence, Kansas, with her husband Paul. Between them they have four children. Lynn developed writing programs for public and private schools for 25 years. An excerpt from her memoir "The Freuds, the Tiffanys & Me" was published in *New Letters* and is nominated for the 2014 Pushcart Prize. She writes, "What is a pale noun? A word without vibrancy? A word that is shocked? A word pasted with makeup? Pale nouns camouflage a writer's intentions. Words like bed, dresser, rug, blinds, suggest an interior but that is all. We do not know what is lurking in the room that contains these objects . . . not unless the writer decides to tell you."

Nancy Lynne Payne Ellis lived in Kansas for most of her life. She graduated from the University of Kansas and now lives in Texas. She says, "Things in Texas are good, and I like the warm temperatures, except in the summer!" She is looking forward to writing more in the future—now she's adjusting to a new life. She writes, "I am now 50 years old and I cannot wait to experience the next 50 years."

Mary Kathleen Felton taught English, speech, and theatre from the junior high to university levels over more than 20 years. She directed musicals, dinner theatre, and summer community theatre. Her play, *Wild Horses*, was performed at Missouri Repertory's Black Box Theatre. Kathi worked in a second career as a substance abuse and family counselor for the following 15 years. Currently, she is recovering from health  problems that have left her partially disabled. She loves to play with words and to experiment with language to express her personal experiences. She comes from a long line of keen observers with big imaginations—Irish storytellers. "It is important to write and share for pleasure, upliftment, reminiscence, and to record history," she says.

Maureen "Mo" Godman teaches Shakespeare and composition at Washburn University in Topeka, Kansas. After a career in academic writing of one sort or another, she enjoys a new-found interest in memoir, especially in imagining contexts for people who have gone before and seeing ways that the past reemerges in the present. She grew up in Birmingham, England, and came to the  U.S. in 1986 when she married. Although she loves her native country and returns every year to see family and friends, she considers herself happily Kansan.

Bert Haverkate-Ens and his wife Dawn have lived in Lawrence, Kansas, for more than 20 years. He says much of his writing begins during his nearly daily walks to the Kansas River. "I process some of my experiences as I walk, and on benches and with pen and paper or in front of a computer screen at home. Walking and writing are ways I find and recall what matters to me," he says. Bert's essay in this collection reflects his growing up years in central Kansas. In addition to writing, Bert enjoys cooking, gardening, and working on his house.

Charles Higginson was born in 1950 in Manhattan, Kansas, to two teachers of English. He came to the University of Kansas as a student in 1969 and never left Lawrence. He has been a Linotype operator, a daycare cook, an auto parts counter-man, a letter carrier, a vaudeville/melodrama actor, a teacher, and an office support person, and is now a publications manager. He is a husband and father. For the past couple of years, he's been presenting bits of personal memoir orally at the monthly Story Slam events at the Lawrence Arts Center. He notes that these originally oral stories required some revision for this venue, and he is interested in exploring the contrast between oral and written personal history.

Linda Johnson has a
background in teaching. She spent
her first 12 years on a small farm in
southern Missouri. An avid reader
as a child, she developed an interest
in writing early in life. Classes and
other resources on writing
suggested daily journaling as a good
practice for writers. She now has 20
years of journals and has found

journaling to be both helpful in the writing process and therapeutic.
Now retired, she lives with her husband, Steve, and her son, Chris, on a
small farm near Meriden, Kansas. Her passions are gardening, art, and
friendship.

Margaret Kramar recently
completed a Ph.D. in English at the
University of Kansas, where she teaches
composition, literature, and drama
courses. "Star Wars" is from her
creative dissertation, *My Son the Actor*,
a memoir about a disabled child who
died. "The Soap Opera," a chapter
from the same memoir, captured the

first place award in the Kansas Authors Club District Contest. Her
creative nonfiction has appeared in *Reading Lips and Other Ways to
Overcome a Disability, Contemporary American Women: Our Defining
Passages*, and various magazines. Margaret and her family live at Hidden
Hollow Farm where they produce organically grown fruits, vegetables,
and free-range eggs.

Louise Krug is the author of *Louise: Amended*, a memoir about her experience with brain surgery and disability. She is a Ph.D. candidate in Creative Writing at the University of Kansas, where she teaches English courses in composition, literature and creative writing. She lives in North Lawrence with her husband, Nick, and daughter, Olive. For her, writing memoir is a way to understand her life, and reading it is a way to understand others.

Roger Martin edited *Explore*, a University of Kansas research magazine, and wrote commentaries about research that aired on Kansas Public Radio. He is one of three editors of *Cows Are Freaky When They Look at You: An Oral History of the Kaw Valley Hemp Pickers.* When asked about writing, Roger recalls being accused of monstrous behavior during a workshop taught by Phillip Lopate, for an essay he wrote about two women and his divided heart. He asked Lopate how to make his shortcomings more palatable. Lopate said a memoirist who wants a larger audience than his family and loved ones "has to shine a light into his own shadows. Help us see the monster in you more clearly. Think against yourself."

Mary "Bugs" McCoy was raised in the country near Kansas City, and her early contact with the natural world led her to study nature's creatures at the University of Kansas (Ph.D., Entomology). A subsequent 33-year career in biology at  Washburn University fostered a great passion for tropical rainforests and other wild places, and this infuses her memoirs in *The Animal Diaries* series. She finds her writings to be revelatory, engrossing, and sometimes emotional, but when reconstructing life's events, her mind and heart soar.

Nicole Muchmore edits scientific and academic publications. This is her second memoir group project. "Telling our own stories is a divine right of passage that enables us to sort out our pasts and to map our places in the historic landscape—personal, family, and otherwise. I have found that communicating my story in writing yields the only thing of true value that  I can pass to future generations. It's the DNA of history." Nicole enjoys the development that the Great Plains Writers Group supports. "Over time, I am amazed at the progress our writers make on many levels—including myself." Nicole lives in Jefferson County, Kansas, with her husband, two dogs, and a cockatoo.

Jennifer Nigro's love of writing began at the hands of her third-grade creative writing teacher. Jen's professional career has included writing scripts as a television news producer, and she is a regular contributor to the Kansas City Veterinary Medical Association's *News and Notes* newsletter. Jen enjoys the art of storytelling, and she gets her best material from her small-town Iowa upbringing as well as her family, which includes her husband, Dave, two young sons, a dog, cat, and an unknown number of fish.

Tony R. Pierce grew up in rural West Texas. "Memoir writing helps me make at least some sense of the past, and allows me to hold on to it. I was lucky to have grown up where and how I did. I want to remember that place, that time, and those people."

Nancy Pistorius was getting into trouble for writing "novels" in class when she was still in first grade. As a teenager, she penned a weekly travel column for her local Illinois newspaper and won the *Chicago Tribune* Voice of Youth essay award and two national poetry contests. Since then, her work has been published in more than 75 different publications, including *Woman's Day* and *Cosmopolitan*. She was a former editor of *the Spoon River Literary Review*. She has an MA in Literature from the University of

Illinois. Nancy's most recent honors are the 2009 Langston Hughes Creative Writing Award and the 2012 Bronze Award in the North American Travel Journalists Association Competition. Regarding memoirs, Nancy says: "What doesn't kill you, makes a good story!"

Lucy Price is a philologist in the original sense of the word—a lover of words, and thus of language and literature. Her career as a professor at Baker University has been devoted to studying and teaching the ways in which language produces meaning. Lucy has always been interested in the potential of  language to convey multiple layers of meaning within a variety of formal textual structures. As a writer of memoir and creative non-fiction, she is still a novice. Her experiences thus far have led her to consider especially the issues of selecting and shaping memories and finding her own narrative voice.

Charlotte Richards, better known as *Char*, was born and began her life on a farm in Ozawkie, Kansas, on land owned by her family for 100 years. Her love of family history started early thanks to stories told by her grandfather and documentation left by her grandmothers, great-grandmothers, and great aunt in journals, on scraps of paper, and in hand-  written notes. She has retired from nursing and spends her time with her husband Roy, father, daughters, grandchildren, and friends. Her favorite ambitions include traveling, reading (especially to her dad), photography, genealogy, gardening, and long walks with her buddies Gabie and Rascal.

Kathryn Schartz, in the 30 years she worked with children, has always been struck by how children need to tell and hear stories. Children often recount stories repeatedly, and she learned a while back that this is how they make sense of a world that is often confusing and frightening. Kathryn believes adults need to tell stories for the same reasons, that it is important to revisit the past though the lens of memory, with a perspective gained through experience and over time. For her, the connections that we have with friends and family are strengthened by this process. Writing memoir is a reminder that we are not isolated beings, but are connected to family, community, and others across time.

Haskell Springer was born and raised in New York City and earned a Ph.D. in Indiana, but he has lived most of his life in Kansas. His first essay was published in 1965 and the most recent in 2011. In between, he wrote and edited many books and articles. Happily retired, he and his wife, Anne, live in Lawrence, Kansas, with their two dogs. "Everything I write these days comes as if it benefited from nothing else I ever wrote. It seems no easier because of past experience; it seems no wiser. I probably revise about as much as I always did. Although looking back at my essays of 30 or 40 years ago I can see that I am today a better writer, it doesn't feel that way. If I only could, I'd turn my perfectionism switch to OFF."

Sue Suhler isn't sure when she decided to write about her family history, or how long she's been writing memoirs. She recalls, "I have cooked my mother's favorite recipe for two husbands. I have borne and reared two fine sons fathered by one husband. I have followed a husband across the United States because he had 'important work' to do. Where will I find my own recipes for life,  finding my own self in my timeline of truths?" Sue, a grandmother of five, has lived in Iowa, New York, and Kansas. Her career as artist, writer, editor, and publisher has taken her across the United States.

Sherry Williams resides, writes, reads, works, and plays in Lawrence, Kansas, her home for the last 34 years. But her heart and mind often wander back to Kalamazoo, Michigan, where she grew up. She loves working out at the gym, quilting, knitting with friends, playing with her grandchildren, and writing. She believes that everyone has a story to tell, and she is intent on telling her own.

Printed in the USA
CPSIA information can be obtained
at www.ICGtesting.com
LVHW010149170823
755489LV00024B/223